D0880089

ESSENTIALS

of Trademarks and Unfair Competition

Essentials Series

To keep up with rapid business changes today, professionals today need to get up to speed quickly with reliable and clear information. Wiley's Essentials series introduces the first concise guidelines to key topics in finance, accounting, performance improvement, operations, technology, and information management. These books provide in-depth coverage, tips, techniques, and illustrative real-world examples, exhibits, and best practices. The Wiley Essentials Series—because the business world is always changing…and so should you.

Other books in the series include:

Essentials of Accounts Payable

Essentials of Capacity Management

Essentials of Cash Flow

Essentials of Corporate Performance Management

Essentials of Credit, Collection, and Accounts Receivable

Essentials of CRM: A Guide to Customer Relationship Management

Essentials of Intellectual Property

Essentials of Trademarks and Unfair Competition

Essentials of XBRL

For more information and to receive periodic e-mail notices regarding forthcoming publications, please visit us at www.wiley.com

ESSENTIALS

of Trademarks and Unfair Competition

Dana Shilling

WILEY

This publication is designed to provide accurate and authoritative information in regard to the subject matter covered. It is sold with the understanding that the publisher is not engaged in rendering legal, accounting, or other professional services. If legal advice or other expert assistance is required, the services of a competent professional person should be sought.

ISBN 0-471-20941-4

Printed in the United States of America.

10 9 8 7 6 5 4 3 2 1

About the Author

D ANA SHILLING, ESQ., is the author of more than 20 books, including *Lawyer's Desk Book,* 11th ed. (Prentice Hall, 1988), *The 60-Minute Financial Planner* (Prentice Hall, 1997), *The Complete Guide to Human Resources and the Law* (Prentice Hall, 1998), and *Financial Planning for the Older Client,* 5th ed. (National Underwriter, 2001). She has written many articles dealing with legal and financial issues that have appeared in such magazines as *Vogue, CFO, Working Woman, Cosmopolitan, Aging Today, Estate Planning Studies, Brown University Long-Term Care Letter, Elder Law Advisory, Journal of American Society, CLU/ChFC, Senior Market Advisor,* and others.

In addition, she has been a featured speaker at many conferences and seminars, for the following organizations: the New York County Lawyers' Association; MANULIFE Insurance, United Methodist Church; NEFE/CFP; NAHU (two programs), Health Underwriters, Conference of Financial Trust Officers; American Society of CLU/ChFC, Estate Planning Council of NJ, Prudential (two programs), Estate Planning Councils of Pennsylvania and Ohio, Brokers' Choice, and the Society of Financial Services Professionals.

Shilling has also produced *The Elements of Elder Law* (3-1/2 hour instructional tape on basic elder law issues (1993); *Carry Me Back* (screenplay, 1993; unproduced); and *Financial Planning for the Older Client* (Bisk/Totaltape video 1999). She is a National Merit Scholar; and graduated *magna cum laude,* Phi Beta Kappa from Goucher College (AB). She received her law degree from Harvard Law School. She was admitted to the New York Bar in 1976.

Contents

CHAPTER 1

Trademark Basics— Overview

After reading this chapter you will be able to

- Understand why the legal system protects trademarks
- Identify trademarks
- Understand the scope of state and federal trademark laws
- Know how to use trademarks in commerce
- Compare trademarks to utility patents, design patents, and copyrights

Trademarks have been used for centuries—probably as long as there has been more than one person carrying out a particular trade, or selling merchandise of a particular type, at the same market, or in the same town. An important part of business is developing a reputation for selling unusual merchandise, or for quality or variety of products, or for high value.

A business can succeed only if customers buy its products or use its services. One of the most important functions of marketing and advertising is to create demand, not just for a particular type of product, but for the advertiser's or marketer's own goods. Trademarks (words, pictures, combinations of words and images, even sounds or fragrances) are important tools in identifying the business that provides the goods or services. A good trademark makes the product stand out.

Because trademarks are such a key part of doing business, federal and state law protect a business's right to identify its own merchandise and to keep other people from counterfeiting merchandise or using confusingly similar trademarks. However, the legal rules for trademarks (and the related concept of trade dress—the appearance and packaging of merchandise) are complicated and sometimes *counterintuitive:* they are not necessarily what a person in business would assume, based on experience in selling products. This book is designed to make confusing rules easier to understand.

Focus of the Book

This book covers a spectrum of related topics. Following the introduction of trademarks and trademark law in Chapters 1 and 2, the main concentration is on trademarks themselves. In addition, Chapter 2 touches on a large and growing group of issues: the difficult relationship between trademarks and the Internet, including but not limited to when trademarks can be used as URLs and when a *cybersquatter* can be punished for misuse of domain name registration. **Note:** Trademarks will be referred to in capital letter, such as COCA-COLA or NIKE.

In many ways, the concepts of *brand* and *trademark* are closely related, although *brand* is a more modern and *trademark* a more traditional idea. But even though they are similar, they are not identical. Both of them involve product image and goodwill, but the concept of trademark focuses on the *source* of the goods.

A consumer might have very high awareness of *brand*—might, for instance, have a shopping list that contains JIF peanut butter, ARRID EXTRA-DRY deodorant, DEL MONTE canned vegetables, CAMPBELL's canned soups, CREST toothpaste, and so on. This consumer might have a strong preference for these brands, based on a belief in their superior quality and attractiveness, and might take a rain check rather than purchase a competing brand, yet have no knowledge or interest in who manufactured the preferred brands. In fact, in today's business climate, where mergers and product divestitures are common, a brand might have been owned by several companies. Thus, the brand does not provide proof of source. In this book, we focus on the concepts of trademark.

Chapter 3 covers how to search to see if a desired trademark is available, and how to register a trademark. Chapter 4 discusses what to do in case of an allegation of trademark infringement or if the trademark owner believes that the trademark has been infringed. The subjects of service marks and trade dress are addressed in Chapter 5.

Chapter 6 covers threats to trademarks. However, a trademark is only one form of intellectual property. In the current business climate, businesses are becoming more and more aware of the importance of trademarks, trade secrets, patents and design patents, copyrights, and digital media assets to business success. The rules affecting these forms of intellectual property can be complex and overlapping. Inventing, manufacturing, and marketing a product can involve multiple forms of intellectual property, each with its own legal consequences. These issues are addressed in Chapter 7.

In addition to trademarks and related subjects, this book also covers the law of unfair competition in business, because other forms of unfair business practice can overlap with trademark infringement. Chapter 8 tackles this subject.

For your convenience, the book closes with several appendices and legal forms. When used in conjuction with the information presented in this text, the end material should equip you with the essential concepts you need in handling trademark issues.

TIPS & TECHNIQUES

Research Sources

There are Registers listing state and federally registered trademarks, but no counterparts for common-law trademarks. Nevertheless, there is a legal obligation to at least try to research common-law trademarks as part of the trademark search (see page 49)—for instance, by consulting telephone listings and business directories and examining the trademarks used on products available in stores.

Sources of Trademark Law

Trademark law was already in existence in England when the American Revolution occurred, and many of those concepts were adopted as U.S. law evolved. Merely using a trademark in commerce creates some protectable rights against unfair competition and imitation of the trademark. This is known as a *common law trademark;* the rights that arise are limited to the geographic area in which the mark is being used.

However, as described in detail in this book, registering a trademark (with the state, the federal Patent and Trademark Office, or both) is often worthwhile because it increases the rights of the registrant against a trademark infringer. Remedies for trademark infringement can include injunctions, seizure of infringing or counterfeit merchandise, and money damages: see Chapter 4.

Once a trademark is registered, it will become part of a large standard database that is open to the public. The practical effect is that businesses that are contemplating the use of a new trademark can search the database (see page 53) and discover if it is already in use, or if it might be considered confusingly similar to a trademark already in existence. The legal effect is that once a trademark is registered, or even published for objections (see page 70), everyone is deemed to have knowledge of it, and can be held responsible for the knowledge.

Once a trademark is registered with the federal Patent and Trademark Office (PTO), the symbol ® can be used in connection with the trademark. Any registered trademark, on either the Principal or the Supplemental Register, can use this symbol.

Any trademark, registered or not, can be identified with the symbol ™. This symbol just indicates that trademark rights have been asserted in the mark, not that any government agency has approved or registered the mark.

Another advantage of registering a trademark is that, five years after a trademark has been registered, the general rule is that it will become *incontestable*—that is, no one will be allowed to bring a legal challenge to the validity of the trademark.

However, the law contains a list of exceptions. A trademark can be challenged even after five years if it was obtained fraudulently, if the trademark owner has abandoned it (has stopped using it in commerce), and if the trademark has become *generic*—that is, if it is used to identify a whole class of products rather than the products of a specific company.

State Trademark Law

All of the states have some trademark and unfair competition laws of their own. In other words, even though patent law is considered so purely federal that states are not allowed to operate in this area, trademark law is shared by both the state and federal systems.

State trademark laws tend to come into play when a trademark is used purely locally, not nationwide or in a multistate area, or if a trademark is of a type that is not eligible for listing on the federal Principal Register (see page 82).

In general, state trademark law doesn't create a presumption that the trademark is valid, and doesn't make trademarks incontestable after a five-year period, the way federal law does.

Model State Trademark Bill

Forty-six states have adopted the Model State Trademark Bill (MSTB), which specifies how trademarks and service marks can be registered. Under the MSTB, radio and TV program titles and character names can be registered as service marks.

The MSTB provides that a mark is "in use" when it is used in ordinary business; token transactions to reserve a mark don't count. Like federal law, the MSTB calls for marks to be placed on the goods, their containers, their displays, or tags or labels attached to the goods. The mark is supposed to be used on sales documentation for bulk goods or other items to which marks cannot be affixed. Service marks are to be displayed in sale or advertising or services.

The MSTB, like the Lanham Act, discussed later, denies registration to marks that are immoral, deceptive, scandalous, or disapraging to individuals, that are just descriptive or misdescriptive (geographically or otherwise), or that are primarily merely a last name—unless the last name has become distinctive through use in commerce.

To preserve the right of publicity (see page 203), the MSTB does not permit registration of a mark that consists of or includes a living person's name, signature, or portrait, unless the person has given consent.

The term of protection under the MSTB is five years from the date of registration; it can be renewed an indefinite number of times, for five

TIPS & TECHNIQUES

Evidence

Under the MSTB, using a last name as a trademark for a five-year period before the attempt to register it counts as evidence that it has become distinctive.

years at a time, by filing a renewal request within six months before the expiration of the term.

If a second trademark is used that is confusingly similar to an existing trademark, the holder of the first trademark is entitled to get an injunction on the basis of unfair competition that will require the second trademark to be taken out of use. The confusingly similar trademark is subject to cancellation, and holders of the original trademark can get damages for trademark infringement and dilution. *Dilution* is imitating a trademark in a way that makes it less valuable by making potential customers associate inferior merchandise with the trademark.

Under the MSTB, trademarks are considered abandoned either when there has been a two-year period without use of the trademark or the registrant of the mark stops using it and intends never using it again. Abandonment also occurs when the mark becomes generic or otherwise is no longer used as a trademark.

Trademarks can be canceled for the following reasons:

- The trademark holder voluntarily requests its cancellation.
- A court holds that the mark has been abandoned.
- A court holds that the registrant doesn't really own the mark.
- There was fraud or other impropriety in the securing of the registration.
- The mark is confusingly similar to another mark.
- The mark has become generic.

Federal Trademark Laws

However, the most significant laws governing trademarks (and most other forms of intellectual property) are federal. The central statute covering trademarks is a federal law called the *Lanham Act*. The Lanham Act is a federal law, passed (and occasionally amended) by Congress. The federal agency responsible for administering federal trademark law is the Patent and Trademark Office (PTO). The PTO's regulations can be found in the Code of Federal Regulations (CFR).

Amendments to the Lanham Act include the Trademark Revision Act of 1988 and more recent laws banning *cybersquatting* (improper practices involving registration of Internet domain names) and counterfeiting of trademarked merchandise—for example, imitations of Louis Vuitton handbags.

The Lanham Act protects trademarks (as well as related types of marks such as service, collective, and certification marks) that are "used in commerce." At first, the Lanham Act protected only trademarks that had already been put into use. However, under current law, a trademark can be registered and protected on the basis of intent to use it in the future. For instance, it can be used in connection with a product that is under development and will be released in the future. This is known as an *intent to use* (ITU) application.

The final registration will not be granted until the intention to use matures and turns into actual use. The applicant has to update the application by submitting a verified statement and specimens proving that the mark has been placed in actual use in interstate or foreign commerce. Depending on the time when it is filed, the appropriate form is either an Amendment to Allege Use (AAU) or a Statement of Use (SOU).

Lanham Act §32(1)

A person who has registered a trademark has the right to bring a civil suit against anyone who does one of two things without the consent of the registrant:

1. The infringer uses in commerce any "reproduction, counterfeit, copy or colorable imitation" of a registered mark in business, if such use is "likely to cause confusion, or to cause mistake, or to deceive." (The provision about "colorable imitations" is there to

make sure that infringers can't make tiny changes in the mark and then use that as a defense against a §32(1) lawsuit.)

2. The infringer reproduces, counterfeits, copies, or "colorably imitates" a registered mark, and then applies the nonlegitimate mark to "labels, signs, prints, packages, wrappers, receptacles or advertisements" used in trade, once again if the likely result is confusion, mistake, or deception.

The difference between these two very similar-sounding provisions is that the trademark holder can only get an award of damages or lost profits in a case of the second type if the infringer committed its acts with knowledge that the imitation is intended to be confusing or deceptive. It is not necessary to prove that the infringer's intentions were wrongful to win a case of the first type.

Lanham Act §43(a)

The Lanham Act also forbids a very broad range of unfair or inappropriate conduct that could cause consumer confusion—even if there are no registered trademarks involved.

Section 43(a), which is often used in trade dress and false advertising cases, allows a civil suit to be brought by "any person who believes that he or she is or is likely to be damaged by such act." The forbidden acts are

- Use of words, symbols, devices, etc. (including combinations)
- False designation of origin
- False or misleading description of fact
- False or misleading representation of fact, either "on or in connection with any goods or services" or any "container," if the wrongful act occurs in "commerce."

Section 43(a) bans all activities that are likely to cause confusion or mistake "as to the affiliation, connection, or association of such person with another person, or as to the origin, sponsorship, or approval of his or her goods, services, or commercial activities by another person."

This is broad enough to cover, for example, an advertisement that describes rhinestone jewelry as diamond jewelry. It also covers trademark and trade dress infringement, because that misleads or could mislead consumers about who has produced the merchandise in question.

Use in Commerce

For legal purposes, trademarks do not exist in the abstract. They identify the goods or services of a particular provider and are related to the goodwill associated with the product. Therefore, federal trademark law does not allow a trademark to be registered until it is already in use, or unless the party that seeks to register the trademark is willing to go on record that it intends to use the trademark in commerce in the future.

Once the registrant stops using the trademark in commerce, it is *abandoned*. A defendant accused of trademark infringement can get the case dismissed by showing that the owner abandoned the trademark that allegedly was infringed.

Furthermore, even if a trademark has been registered and in use for five years (which would otherwise probably make it incontestable), someone else who wants to use the same or a very similar trademark

TIPS & TECHNIQUES

Abandonment

Under earlier law, failing to use a trademark for two years constituted strong evidence that the trademark had been abandoned. However, effective January 1, 1996, the Lanham Act has been amended. Now, abandonment is not presumed until *three* years have passed without use of the trademark.

can advance the legal argument that the trademark has been abandoned by its original owner.

Under §45 of the Lanham Act, "use in commerce" means bona fide use in the ordinary course of trade. Token usages that are merely intended to preserve the mark are not sufficient, because unless the trademark is used in connection with marketing and at least attempted sale of goods, there's no goodwill to protect. A service mark is "used" when two conditions are met: the mark appears in ads and promotional materials, and the service is actually being provided to the public.

Furthermore, §45 refers to trademarks being used *on* the goods. Therefore, as long as the trademark can physically be attached to the goods, it should be placed there and not just on the documents associated with the goods or in advertisements. Of course, some merchandise simply can't have trademarks attached—things sold in bulk like fuel oil, for instance—so in that case the trademark must be used on displays associated with the merchandise, or on the sales documents.

IN THE REAL WORLD

Some Uses Get a More Favorable Eye

Some literal-minded PTO examiners will reject applications for a mark that will only be used as a design on the front of a T-shirt (e.g., a T-shirt using the photograph and logo of a band; a HARLEY-DAVID-SON or BUDWEISER T-shirt). Their argument is that this is purely ornamental, and therefore doesn't use the trademark to indicate the source of the shirt. To avoid this problem, the trademark can be used on the shirt's label and the garment tag attached to the shirt. Examiners have less trouble with smaller logos—for example, the POLO horseman embroidered on a shirt.

The Risk of Confusion

One of the most basic trademark concepts is the *risk of confusion*. The PTO Examining Attorney will refuse to register a trademark if it is close enough to an existing trademark to create such a risk. The potential for confusion is a key issue in infringement suits.

Legal analysts identify several kinds of confusion that can be harmful to competition. Therefore, trademark law tries to eliminate these types of confusion:

- *Source confusion* (the source of the goods is the business that controls the production, including quality, of the goods)—that is, consumers think a Company A product is actually made by Company B.

- *Confusion about sponsorship, approval, or certification*—for example, potential buyers think that mint cookies from a nonapproved bakery are GIRL SCOUT COOKIES, or are induced to believe that a fabric bears the WOOLMARK when this is not the case.

- *Reverse confusion*—the public thinks that a newcomer to the market makes goods that actually come from an established source.

- *Subliminal or associational confusion*—consumers think that they have seen the trademark, or something like it, somewhere before; this weakens consumers' association between the goods and the actual holder of the trademark.

Although usually the test is consumer confusion, other parties' confusion may also be relevant: people who influence purchasing decisions, or distributors and wholesalers; lenders and investors; employees; and people who receive the goods as gifts or buy them second hand.

According to the *Restatement (3rd) of Unfair Competition* (a Restatement is a volume of legal trends in a particular subject, compiled by lawyers who are experts in that subject), likelihood of confusion is hard to prove, because it is unlike most other questions of evidence. Those other questions involve past events, but likelihood of confusion involves a future state of mind. It may be necessary to draw conclusions by projecting existing consumer attitudes and behavior (in the relevant market) into the future.

For trademarks that are word marks, or include both words and designs and therefore can be pronounced, confusion might be found on the basis of similarity of pronunciation, even if the marks are spelled differently. This is especially true if the merchandise is sold by telephone or advertised on radio or television. It is less likely to become an issue if the product is sold in stores where customers see it on the shelf.

Common prefixes and suffixes used in a particular industry, such as *Ultra-* or *-col* or *-icin* for medicine, are likely to be disregarded in deciding whether confusion is likely.

Many court decisions consider nearly all items of clothing to be closely related, so they are considered together in terms of likelihood of confusion. For example, a defendant would not have a very strong argument that the plaintiff's trademark was used on sweaters and the defendant's was used on blouses. In fact, because some items of clothing are unisex, and manufacturers often make both men's and women's clothing, clothing for both is often treated as a single market.

The legal system assumes that trademark owners have an interest in expanding their product lines. So another issue is whether the trademark owner would be likely to "bridge the gap" by manufacturing the product that the defendant claims is in a completely separate market where consumers would not be confused.

The basic legal rule is that using trademarks in comparisons is acceptable ("THRIFTY GAL moisture cream has the same percentage of Vitamin C and alpha-retinol as LUXURYPOSH moisturizer—but

IN THE REAL WORLD

When Are Two Names "Confusingly Similar"?

Because this is such a critical issue, there have been many court cases on the issue of confusing similarity. Courts have decided that these marks are confusingly similar:

ONLINE TODAY and ON-LINE TODAY

JOY and DERMAJOY

PLAY-DOH and FUNDOUGH

KANGA ROOS and KANGOL

OFF THE RAX and OFF THE RACK

On the other hand, various court cases have found that these marks are *not* confusingly similar to one another:

FRANKLIN and FRANKLIN CREDIT

TOPOL XL and PROCARDIA XL

BOY SCOUTS and PEEWEE SCOUTS

SUMMER BLONDE and SUMMER SUN (hair color products)

ALLIGATOR raincoats and ALLIGATOR cigarettes

AMICA insurance and AMICA perfume

BAILEY'S liqueur and cigarettes

BLUE SHIELD health insurance and mattresses

CHUCKLES candy and dolls

HOT SHOT insecticide and shaving cream

SUNBEAM electric appliances and fluorescent lamps

ours costs $10 an ounce and theirs is $100 an ounce!"). The theory is that comparison ads make it clear that two different brands are involved, so there is no risk of confusion, and the public is entitled to accurate information about different brands. (If the information is inaccurate, it becomes a false advertising or unfair competition question.)

Trademarks and Other Forms of Intellectual Property

Trademark law is part of the law of intellectual property. It is important to understand how trademark law interacts with other intellectual property topics, especially because the same product—and certainly the same marketing campaign—may include several different forms of intellectual property protection.

Patents exist to protect functional features of manufactured items (utility patents) and the way manufactured items look (design patents). Copyrights protect the way that ideas are expressed in written, musical, dramatic, and visual works—although not the ideas themselves. Trademarks protect the words, designs, and other indicators of the source, origin, and sponsorship of merchandise.

Patents

A *utility patent* is what most people think of when they hear the word *patent*. A utility patent protects the functional features of an item, a "composition of matter," or a novel method or process, for a period of 20 years (for patents issued on the basis of applications filed after June 8, 1995) or 17 years from the date of issue or 20 years after the filing date, whichever is longer (for filings before June 8, 1995; of course, many of those patents remain in effect). A utility patent can only be granted to a useful, novel, nonobvious invention that makes a meaningful step forward from the "prior art" (the state of technology existing before the new invention was created).

A *design patent,* on the other hand, protects the aesthetic appearance of an object. For instance, a utility patent might cover a new way for vacuum cleaners to collect dust and dirt, whereas the distinctive shape and appearance of the vacuum cleaner might be entitled to a design patent. A design patent can be granted only to the nonfunctional form of an object, and the patented design has to be novel and not obvious, considering the designs already on the market. The term of a design patent is only 14 years.

In 1993, the Seventh Circuit decided that the configurations of sink faucets and faucet handles could be registered as a trademark, as a "package" or "configuration of goods" (Lanham Act §23), so this can be another avenue if a design patent is not available or not desirable, or if there was a design patent but its term has expired.

In some ways, a patent is the most desirable type of intellectual property protection, because it is so absolute. A patent is a legal monopoly. During the term of the patent, no one except the patent holder and its licensees is allowed to "practice" the patent by using the process or manufacturing the invention that is covered by the patent. Even someone who independently discovers the same way to do the same thing (*reverse engineering*) won't be allowed to use it as long as the patent is

TIPS & TECHNIQUES

Design Patents Don't Determine Trade Dress

According to a 1996 case from the Southern District of New York, the existence of a design patent is neutral in its effect on whether trade dress (configuration and packaging of a product) is protectable —the design patent neither guarantees nor rules out protection of trade dress using trademark-related concepts (see page 123).

still in force, because all patents are registered and on display where the public can access detailed descriptions of the invention.

Disclosure is an essential part of the patent system. On one level, it serves to protect the patent holder, because everyone is expected to perform patent searches to avoid infringement. On another level, it benefits the concept of the progress of general knowledge, because inventors and technicians can keep current on what has been invented, and they might get new ideas for improving on the *prior art* (the database of existing and expired patents) and making new inventions that, in turn, can be patented. However, as soon as the patent expires, anyone is allowed to take advantage of the information contained in the patent application.

Most forms of intellectual property protection come into effect automatically, even without registration (although property owners' rights are greater in the case of registered intellectual property). In addition, the registration process is automatic in the case of copyrights and most trademark applications achieve approval. In contrast, review of patent applications is lengthy, painstaking, and expensive for the applicant.

Even once a patent has issued, the patent holder's life is not always smooth and easy. The owner may be embroiled in complex, expensive litigation against alleged infringers—or the validity of the patent may be challenged in court by others who claim that it infringes their patent, or that the patent should not have been issued in the first place.

Comparing Copyrights and Trademarks

Sometimes it is hard to decide where copyright protection ends and trademark protection begins. This is especially true for series properties (e.g., a series of mystery novels, a television show, or even movies that launch several sequels). The title of just one work can't be a trademark, but a series title can be, because, like all trademarks, it identifies the source. Furthermore, there may be protectable trademark rights in depiction of characters from fiction.

As mentioned, the purpose of a trademark is to serve as a distinctive identifier of the source of goods. Designs used in a trademark must be nonfunctional. On the other hand, copyright protects original creative works of expression (including three-dimensional designs, as long as the form is not purely functional).

One area of overlap comes from §102(a)(5) of the federal Copyright Act. This section allows copyright registration of pictorial, graphic, and sculptural works, including labels and cartons—items that might also be defined as, or include, trademarks.

The Copyright Office won't register labels or cartons unless they include copyrightable material (for instance, if the hangtag for ED'S LUMBERJACK JACKETS included a story about how a lonely lumberjack spent his evenings sewing warm, sturdy jackets). Copyright registration will be denied if the material submitted for registration only includes trademark material and nothing that is entitled to copyright protection.

A common-law trademark lasts as long as the mark is in use. A federally registered trademark lasts for 10 years, and can be renewed for an indefinite number of additional 10-year terms as long as the mark is still in use.

The term of copyright protection (for works copyrighted in or after 1978) is the author's lifetime plus 70 years. For a work for hire, the term is 95 years from the date of publication, or 120 years from the date of creation, whichever comes first.

Section 101 of the Copyright Act sets out two categories of works for hire. The first is work done by an employee, as part of his or her job. The other category covers work that is specially ordered or commissioned as part of a collective work (such as an anthology of essays, or a movie made up of several shorts), translations, and supplementary works such as tests and teachers' guides for textbooks.

A 1989 U.S. Supreme Court case says that the fee paid to an independent contractor (not an employee) who creates a work for hire only entitles the commissioning party to one-time use of the work. The creator would be entitled to extra compensation if the commissioning party wants to re-use the work—unless at the beginning of the transaction, the parties agreed to transfer all rights in the work in return for a one-time fee.

CHAPTER 2

Trademark Types

After reading this chapter, you will be able to

- Identify trademarks, service marks, collective marks, and certification marks
- Know the difference between fanciful, arbitrary, suggestive, and descriptive trademarks
- Understand why generic terms are not entitled to trademark protection
- Understand nontraditional trademarks
- See how trademarks and Internet domain names relate to each other

Types of Marks

The trademark, used to identify the source of products, is the most common type of mark recognized by U.S. law. There are also three other kinds of marks: service marks, collective marks, and certification marks.

The *service mark* acts the same way for services (e.g., dry cleaning; financial planning) as a trademark does for physical merchandise. Trademark protection can be granted to a wide variety of ways of communicating, including letters, words, names, abbreviations, acronyms, monograms, phrases, slogans, titles, symbols, numerals, logos, devices,

IN THE REAL WORLD

Service Marks

Service marks are available in many contexts. According to court cases, some of the services that will support the issuance of a service mark include

- Management and investment services

- Housing development services

- Advertising and promotional services

- Sponsorship, such as of sports events or beauty contests

- Speed-reading instruction

- Hotel and motel services

- Entertainment services, whether rendered by an individual or a band or theater group

character or personality images, pictures, labels, shapes, packages, and configurations of goods—even building designs.

A *collective mark* indicates that the user of the mark participates in an association, such as an association of orange growers or raisers of a particular kind of beef cattle. Associations try to create a unified image for the product—for example, via nationwide cooperative "image" advertisements.

A *certification mark* is used when a distributor or seller other than the manufacturer sells the merchandise. The purpose of the certification mark is to indicate that the merchandise meets standards, such as geographical origin (for instance, Florida grapefruit juice) or high quality.

TIPS & TECHNIQUES

Typography

The convention is to use ALL CAPS to indicate a trademark—XEROX or VERIFINE, for instance.

Ineligible Marks

The Lanham Act makes it clear that some kinds of marks are not eligible for registration:

- Generic marks that identify a whole type of merchandise, not one manufacturer's merchandise of that type. In other words, *hamburger* is a generic term for a particular kind of sandwich; MCDONALD'S is a trademark for a fast-food chain that sells hamburgers. *Shampoo* is the generic name for a hair care product; PANTENE is a trademark for one brand of shampoo.

- Marks that are immoral or scandalous.

- Marks that are deceptive (PLATINUM for rings made out of tin, for instance; CANCER CURE for quack nostrums).

- The flags or coats of arms of countries or governments.

- The name of any living person, unless that person gives consent (e.g., even though Tiger Woods is admired by many people, manufacturers need his consent to sell TIGER WOODS golf clubs, chewing gum, or soft drinks).

Two kinds of marks are not outright barred from registration, but they do require proof of secondary meaning (i.e., consumers' association of the mark and the merchandise).

- Marks that are geographically descriptive—or misdescriptive. In other words, EAST RIVER bottled water is a geographic mark (whether the water really comes from the East River or not). Sometimes geographic terms are considered fanciful and not descriptive—if they suggest an air of luxury rather than explaining where the merchandise comes from, for instance.

• Marks that are made up primarily of surnames. However, name marks are weak. If the defendant in an infringement suit actually has the same name, he or she might be allowed to keep using his or her own name in business, maybe with modifications (J.T. JONES instead of JONES to avoid confusion with RAYMOND V. JONES) or with an explanation to prevent consumer confusion ("LAURA SAUNDERS AUTO PARTS is not connected with SAMMY SAUNDERS AUTO PARTS in Elmfield").

Secondary meaning can be proved with surveys or testimony from consumers. The amount and type of advertising for the trademarked product, the volume of sales, and how long the trademark has been used (and how) are all important.

If a mark has been used for a long time, that tends to imply that it has developed secondary meaning, but this is not true in all cases. Thanks to better mass communications, it is also possible for a trademark to develop secondary meaning quickly—so even a fairly new trademark can have secondary meaning.

Trademark Strength

Trademarks and potential trademarks are often divided into either four or five categories: generic, descriptive, suggestive, arbitrary, or fanciful. The first category, *generic* marks, is not entitled to trademark protection at all; the other categories are either entitled to protection to a greater or lesser extent, or may be entitled to protection based on evidence provided by the holder of the mark, but not protected if the evidence isn't there.

A *generic* term, such as "furniture" or "chocolate," cannot be a trademark by itself, because a generic term does not distinguish products of one company from the products of its competitors. (A generic term can

IN THE REAL WORLD

How Generic Is That Product?

It is very hard to draw hard-and-fast lines between trademark categories, and different examining attorneys or Trademark Trial and Appeal Board (TTAB) panels, or different courts, may reach conflicting results. Furthermore, a word or phrase that is generic for one kind of merchandise could be protectable as an arbitrary trademark for another kind of merchandise: VELVET is generic when it comes to a particular kind of fabric, but arbitrary (or maybe descriptive) for cosmetics and arbitrary as the name of an automobile model.

All that can be done is to look at history and try to predict which category a particular trademark or would-be trademark will be assigned.

be part of a trademark if the trademark as a whole is protectable.) Terms such as Gold Card (for high-prestige credit cards), Lite (for beer), superglue, and surgicenter have been legally deemed to be generic terms that can't be trademarked.

Just translating a generic term into another language doesn't stop it from being generic. So, for instance, SHIRT is not a registrable trademark for shirts, and neither is CHEMISE (French) or CAMISA (Spanish).

A *descriptive* trademark describes something about the product, such as the intended purpose, use, size, or effect of the goods, or the ingredients of which the product is made. If a trademark would be descriptive if it were spelled correctly, a deliberate misspelling won't change its status.

A gel medication to treat arthritis called ARTHRITICARE has been held to be descriptive; CHAP STICK, FOOD FAIR (supermarkets), PERSONAL COFFEEMAKER, PUDDING TREATS, VISION CENTER (opticians), AUTO PAGE (automatic dialing

TIPS & TECHNIQUES

We're #1

Self-laudatory trademarks that the manufacturer uses to praise its own goods—for instance, IDEAL, BLUE RIBBON, DELUXE, or SPEEDY—are treated as descriptive trademarks.

for pagers) and HONEY-BAKED (for ham) are other examples of descriptive trademarks.

A descriptive mark that has secondary meaning is entitled to the same scope of legal protection as an arbitrary or fanciful trademark. A descriptive mark that doesn't have secondary meaning can't be registered on the federal Principal Register—but it can go on the Supplemental Register. (The difference between the two is that registrants have more legal remedies against infringers if their mark is on the Principal Register.) After a mark has been on the Supplemental Register for five years, the legal system presumes that secondary meaning has been established, so the mark can be transferred to the Principal Register.

A *suggestive* trademark provides a more subtle relation to the product and its features. It can be protected as a trademark as soon as it is put into use. HABITAT (home furnishing), AT-A-GLANCE (calendars), GOBBLE GOBBLE (turkey cold cuts), FRESHIE and ORANGE CRUSH (soft drinks), PLYBOO (bamboo plywood) and Q-TIPS (cotton swabs) have been held to be suggestive.

An *arbitrary* trademark is a word that can be found in the dictionary, but that is not normally considered related to the product. It can become a protected trademark immediately. CAMEL for cigarettes, and HORIZON for banking services, are arbitrary trademarks.

The strongest type of trademark is the *fanciful* trademark, a coined word such as EXXON, XEROX, or KODAK. KOTEX, CLOROX, and POLAROID have been held by courts to be fanciful trademarks. This is the strongest type of trademark (entitled to protection immediately upon use) because consumers cannot associate the trademark with anything except the particular provider's goods; it has no meaning otherwise. (However, if the holder is not careful, a fanciful trademark might become generic, if it becomes accepted as the name of an entire category of merchandise).

Suggestive, arbitrary, and fanciful trademarks are considered inherently distinctive. Inherent distinctiveness is sometimes referred to as "secondary meaning": i.e., consumers' association between the trademark and one—and only one—source of supply for the goods.

The strength of a mark has a lot to do with public perception, so that even a trademark that is too recent to have become incontestable, or even one that has never been registered, could create a strong public impression.

Trademark Use of Slogans

Trademark law does not limit trademark protection to single words, designs, or designs accompanied by single words. A slogan can act and be registered as a trademark if—but only if—it identifies the source of the goods. A descriptive slogan, like a descriptive trademark in general, can be protected on the basis of having acquired secondary meaning.

TIPS & TECHNIQUES

Registration Effects

If the mark has already been registered in connection with other products, the PTO will consider this excellent evidence that the mark is distinctive.

However, many slogans will not be entitled to trademark protection, on the following grounds:

- The slogan does not create a commercial impression that is separate from the other material on the label.

- The slogan is only a familiar expression that has an ordinary, nontrademark meaning that the would-be registrant should not be allowed to monopolize.

- The slogan is a mere explanatory or informational statement about the product ("Fresh from your microwave in only five minutes!").

- The slogan is part of a phrase that conveys an advertising message (rather than a trademark, which identifies the source).

- The slogan is only a minor feature of advertising copy for the goods.

IN THE REAL WORLD

"You've Got Mail"— and So Do I

In February 2001, the Fourth Circuit decided a case involving a conflict between America OnLine (AOL) and AT&T over the use of the phrase "You've got mail," in connection with e-mail accounts. The Fourth Circuit decided that if the phrase is simply used to inform e-mail users that they have messages, the phrase is generic and can't achieve trademark status.

According to the Fourth Circuit, AT&T should also be allowed to use the phrase, because AOL did not use it consistently to describe a service. And anyway, even if AOL could have proved that the phrase had secondary meaning (i.e., that consumers associated it with AOL and nobody else), AOL would not have the right to keep other businesses from using common English words in a functional manner.

Color and Design Use in Trademarks

Many trademarks consist of nonverbal designs, or combine verbal with design elements. (See Chapter 3 for procedures for registering design marks.) However, a design cannot serve as a trademark if it is purely ornamental; if it is background material that merges with a word trademark without creating a separate commercial impression; or if it consists of common geometric shapes (such as squares, circles, ovals, etc.) that have not achieved secondary meaning.

Similarly, although the Supreme Court and other courts have recognized the possibility of color trademarks, a color or combination of colors will probably not be eligible for trademark protection under these circumstances:

- The colors are pure decorative background or ornamentation.

- The color defines a common design such as a heart or triangle.

- The color is generic (e.g., safety gear must be bright yellow or orange so it will be easily visible).

- The color is functional because it identifies a kind of product rather than one product within a market.

Trademark law doesn't always treat "ornaments" in the same way that business does. The PTO publication, *Trademark Manual of Examining Procedure* (*TMEP*), says that "subject matter which is merely a decorative feature or part of the dress of the goods does not identify and distinguish the applicant's goods and, thus, does not function as a trademark."

In other words, the PTO won't register ornamentation. However, if the decoration or ornamentation is inherently distinctive, and if it is really a logo whose primary purpose is to identify the source of the goods, then it can be registered on the Principal Register.

The *TMEP* gives the example of ornament that identifies an endorser—for example, an authorized University of Pennsylvania T-shirt—as an arbitrary symbol that can go on the Principal Register. If the ornament isn't inherently distinctive and doesn't indicate a secondary source of this type, it can go on the Principal Register once the trademark owner can prove that the ornament has acquired distinctiveness. If the ornament could gain trademark significance in the future, it can start out on the Supplemental Register (and possibly be transferred later to the Principal Register). But pure ornamentation can never achieve trademark significance because it is just there to make the item look better, not to make consumers think of a particular source.

The *TMEP* goes on to say that whether an ornament acts as a trademark depends on the overall commercial impression it makes on potential buyers, including the size, location, and dominance of the mark as compared to the whole object. The larger the graphic, the more likely it is to be treated as an ornament and the less likely it is to be treated as a trademark.

What Is a "Good" Trademark?

Most of the new products put on the market quickly fail—and one reason is that the manufacturers and distributors of the products are unable to create a trademark program that reminds consumers of the availability of the product, and that makes them think of the product as useful, desirable, and better than competing products.

Some of those problems, in turn, are caused by selecting trademarks that are not strong and do not create corporate identity. In a crowded field, sometimes the best potential trademarks are already in use.

A good trademark

- Is distinctive and memorable. Sharp "c" and "k" sounds can be helpful for this.

- Suggests favorable qualities about the product. STINKWEED would be memorable, but most consumers would not be inclined to buy the associated product! Focus groups can help clarify consumer attitudes and preferences toward trademarks that are under consideration for adoption.

- Is attractive to the target audience. This is another matter where focus groups can be productive.

- Reinforces the product's image. For example, VELVETLEAF might be a trademark for an all-natural cold remedy that promises gentle relief, whereas GERMHAMMER would be more likely to suggest fast, powerful therapy.

- Is not obscene or distasteful in languages other than English, and does not convey the wrong ideas about the product. A classic example is the CHEVY NOVA, which suggested to speakers of Romance languages that the car *no va* (doesn't go).

Nontraditional Marks

In addition to trade dress (see Chapter 5), protection may be available for nontraditional marks such as colors, sounds, and fragrances.

For a while, some courts denied that a color could ever be a trademark. The judges were afraid of "color depletion"—that soon, manufacturers would not be able to find colors for their products and packaging that had not already been claimed.

However, for several years, it has been established that as long as stringent tests are satisfied, color trademarks can be valid. A 1995 Supreme Court case upheld the trademark registration of a color (greenish-gold) used to set the manufacturer's brand of pressing pads apart from other pressing pads used by dry cleaners. The decision suggested that secondary meaning is required to protect color marks, because the product's color doesn't automatically remind consumers of a particular brand.

In the right circumstances, a color can become a trademark. (This was true of the pink color of Owens-Corning home insulation, which gained tremendous consumer recognition, in large part through a very successful ad campaign featuring the Pink Panther cartoon character.)

To qualify as a "color mark," the color must have these characteristics:

- It acts as a symbol.

- It has secondary meaning.

- It is nonfunctional. For example, it would not be possible to trademark the bright fluorescent colors used in safety gear.

The *Trademark Manual of Examining Procedure* says that a color can be registered as a trademark only if it has become distinctive of the trademark applicant's merchandise in commerce—in other words, if it already has secondary meaning.

In 1990, the TTAB issued its only decision about fragrance as a trademark. It approved an application for a lemon scent in toner, probably because the fragrance was considered inherently distinctive for that product.

The TTAB's position, since 1978, is that unique or distinctive sounds can be registered as trademarks without supporting evidence. However, an ordinary sound, or a sound that consumers have heard in other contexts (like a bird song or doorbell) can be registered only if it has secondary meaning.

In 2000, the Second Circuit tackled some tough issues about musical trademarks. A TV commercial for golf clubs used swing music and the caption "Swing, swing, swing." Originally, the advertiser wanted to get the rights to use the Benny Goodman song "Sing, Sing, Sing (with a Swing)," but decided that the price charged by the music company EMI, which owned the rights, was too high.

The Second Circuit said that the Goodman song itself could not be treated as a trademark—that copyright, not trademark law, covers songs.

Copyright law doesn't allow titles to be copyrighted, but Lanham Act §43(a) does protect against unfair competition in the use of titles.

The defendant tried to get the case dismissed, but the unfair competition part of the case was allowed to proceed to settle the issue as to whether "swing, swing, swing" was fair use because it accurately describes the use of golf clubs even though it does suggest the Benny Goodman song; thus it should not have to pay a fee to the owner of rights in the song. However, the Second Circuit did not want to add a trademark claim in every copyright infringement case.

Trademarks and URLs

The Lanham Act itself dates back to 1946, and reflects trademark law concepts that were decades, or even centuries, old even then. Even if the members of Congress had been ardent science fiction fans, they would not have been able to predict the Internet!

So it is no surprise that the legal system has not yet been able to create a simple, harmonious relationship between trademarks and URLs (Web addresses). Nor is it surprising that the Internet, which creates many provocative business opportunities, also creates many problems for businesses, including businesses in their role as trademark owners.

Because domain names at least have the potential to be memorable, they serve some of the same functions that trademarks and service marks perform in traditional commerce. However, for legal purposes, trademarks and URLs must be analyzed separately.

According to a 1999 case from the District Court for the District of Massachusetts, trademark law doesn't provide legalized monopolies. So it is not automatically true that the holders of even a famous trademark (like the CLUE mystery story board game, for instance) will be entitled to use that mark as the domain name if they want to set up a Web site. Although CLUE was a famous trademark for board games, a

TIPS & TECHNIQUES

Policing Trademarks on the Web

The Web is a great tool for policing trademark infringement. At very low or no cost and with little effort, the holder of a trademark can find out exactly where its trademark appears on the Web, and can at least try to contact those who misuse the mark. (Those who engage in knowing misconduct often provide incomplete or inaccurate contact information.) Internet monitoring companies include http://www.corsearch.com, www.cyveillance.com, www.markwatch.com, and www.webclipping.com.

However, the downside is that this easy access may create a duty to police. If a trademark holder knows or should have known about online infringement, or should have been able to collect evidence online of infringement in brick-and-mortar stores, then not doing this could be evidence of abandonment of the trademark.

service company called Clue Computing was allowed to retain its domain name, www.clue.com.

Choosing a Domain Name Registrar

Before June 1999, there was only one central registrar for all domain names. Since then, free competition has been opened up. A company that launches a business Web site will want to make the best deal it can for reserving and using domain names.

Registering a domain name isn't as standardized as buying a five-pound sack of sugar. Prices vary, although most registrars charge less than $35 a year. Standard length of the registration term is either a year or two years.

Even though the Internet Corporation for Assigned Names and Numbers (ICANN) controls some of the terms in the agreement

Using Trademarks on Web Sites

Does a business that operates a Web site need consent from the trademark holder every time it uses a trademark? Not always. For instance, computer and software companies such as APPLE allow Web developers to use their trademarks and logos in contexts such as This Site Was Built With [name of software or hardware tools].

However, the marks should not be used in a way that implies that the site is affiliated with the trademark holder, or that the trademark holder sponsors the site (unless this is the case, of course). Site designers should be especially careful not to mingle trademarks used in this way with certification marks (such as TrustE for secure transactions, or Bobby for sites accessible by people with disabilities) or with logos indicating that the site has won awards.

between the registrar and party registering a domain name, many provisions of the agreement can be changed by the individual registrars. By now, there are more than 80 registrars located throughout the world. It probably makes sense to choose a registrar in the same country, and the same U.S. state if possible, so that it will be easier to press any legal claims that do arise.

Good registrars provide convenient customer service: e-mail reminders to renew domain names that are about to expire, for example. They make it reasonably easy to transfer ownership of a domain name—but not so easy that they make it easy to do this fraudulently! ICANN has rules for checking to make sure that cybersquatters do not submit false data to registrars (to prevent their being tracked down later), and conscientious registrars should follow these rules.

TIPS & TECHNIQUES

Choosing a Registrar

The International Trademark Association (INTA) offers some useful guidance on its Web site: see http://www.inta.org/basics/registrar.shtml. Also see http://domainnamebuyersguide.com (no www).

In 2001, several new domains became available to take registrations: .aero (for the aeronautics industry), .biz (for businesses, to relieve some of the pressure on the crowded .com domain), .coop for cooperatives, .info for informational sites, .museum for—well, museums, .name (for personal names), and .pro (for regulated professions such as law and accounting).

.Biz, .info, .coop, and .pro are open domains, but a registrant in one of the other domains has to prove that it really is a museum or airline or whatever. When this book went to press, registration had just been opened, but it was too soon to see how popular the new domains would be (or even if they would be supported by the common browsers and search engines).

For Internet users, domain names work pretty much the same way as trademarks do in ordinary bricks–and–mortar business: they identify the source.

However, that does not mean that every piece of identifying information used on the Web is a trademark. For example, a photographer named Leigh sued Warner Brothers for using a photograph he took of a famous Savannah landmark in promotion for the movie *Midnight in the Garden of Good and Evil*. But Warner Brothers got the photographer's trademark and copyright claims dismissed even before a full trial. The Eleventh Circuit (a federal Court of Appeals) said that Leigh could not prove that he had trademark rights in that photograph. He used it on his own Web site, but the court said that that was just a description of his work, not an identification of the source of goods or services. He also lost on his claim that a reduced image of the photograph was used as a link to an art gallery Web site. Leigh said that the photograph acted as a trademark for the gallery. But once again, the court said that this was not a trademark use, just a signal that works of art were available for sale.

In a case in the Southern District of New York decided in 2000, defendants located in Italy had already been found by a U.S. court to have infringed the plaintiff's trademark ENERGIE. The plaintiff wanted to have the defendant cited for contempt of court because of advertising and promotional activity in the United States that continued to infringe on the trademark.

The plaintiff was only partially successful. The defendants had three Web sites using servers in Italy and two sites registered in the United States. The Web site http://www.energie.it (registered and located in Italy) displayed the clothing items that infringed the ENERGIE trademark. All of the sites were listed on U.S. search engines, so it was not unlikely that Americans would be able to access them.

The Southern District of New York refused to find the defendant in contempt. It did require the U.S. sites to remove links to the www.energie.it site. However, because the defendant was allowed to advertise the ENERGIE trademark outside the United States, its sites did not have to be removed from search engines.

Metatags

Behind the words and images that are visible on the computer screen when someone accesses a Web site lie many lines of computer code. Some of this code is used to create internal identification of files within the site. *Metatags* are identifiers that are not usually available to Web

IN THE REAL WORLD

Moviebuff: Trademark or Domain Name?

One of the classic cases about trademarks and the Internet was decided by the Ninth Circuit in 1999. (Considering how short a time widespread Web access has been available, that *is* a classic.) A company called Brookfield Communications, which started up in 1987, used the trademark MOVIEBUFF for software about the entertainment industry. That software was available on the Internet starting in 1996, using the domain name brookfieldcomm.com. The plaintiff didn't apply for a federally registered trademark in MOVIEBUFF until 1997; the registration was issued in September 1998.

But the defendant, West Coast Entertainment Corporation (a video rental chain) registered the domain name moviebuff.com in Feburary 1996. The defendant had registered the trademark THE MOVIE BUFF'S MOVIE STORE in 1986, and had used it ever since.

In October 1998, the plaintiff learned that the defendant planned to put a searchable database about entertainment topics, like the plaintiff's MOVIEBUFF database, on the defendant's moviebuff.com Web site. The plaintiff sent a cease and desist letter to get the defendant to cancel its plans, but the defendant went ahead, and the case ended up in court.

The Ninth Circuit decided that the defendant's use of moviebuff.com as a Web address was likely to cause confusion. The plaintiff's MOVIEBUFF trademark was entitled to protection because it was an inherently distinctive suggestive mark. The trademark gave the plaintiff prior rights. The defendant's use of the slogan "The movie buff's movie store" didn't give the defendant any rights in the word *moviebuff* taken by itself.

The Ninth Circuit also said that acquiring a domain name doesn't create trademark rights. In other words, when this is compared with the "Clue" case mentioned earlier, the domain name and trademark

IN THE REAL WORLD (CONTINUED)

systems are separate. Having a domain name doesn't automatically convey trademark rights, and having a trademark doesn't automatically convey the right to use the trademark as a domain name.

The plaintiff in a Western District of New York case from 2000 owned a newspaper, which appeared in both print and online versions. The defendant owned an apartment listing guide, which also had both print and electronic versions. The defendant was angry at the plaintiff for copying the defendant's apartment listings, so it created a parody site making fun of the newspaper, with links to the defendant's Web site.

The plaintiff sued the defendant for trademark infringement and dilution. The court decided that the defendant's parody site constituted "use in commerce" and "in connection with goods and services," as defined by the Lanham Act. Because the Internet is international in nature, the court held that Web sites are always in interstate operation. Furthermore, because the parody site was linked to the defendant's commercial apartment listing site, the site was published "in connection with goods and services."

users (although they can be accessed by clicking on "View Sources" in the View menu when the site is displayed).

In addition to the intended use of making it easier to search the site, metatags can be misused by Web designers who want to subvert the search process and misdirect consumers who search for a particular trademark. For example, an obscure perfume manufacturer might code metatags into its site using CHANEL, CALVIN KLEIN, and other brands of perfume that have established an excellent reputation. Someone who entered CHANEL into a search engine might be given a link to the perfume manufacturer's site, even though it has no connection with Chanel and, in fact, is engaging in unfair competition with it.

Both the Ninth Circuit and the Southern District of Indiana have found that using someone else's trademark as a metatag can cause "initial interest confusion" and thereby use the other party's goodwill wrongfully.

There have been many cases involving use of PLAYBOY as a metatag on adult-oriented Web sites, because this is such a well-known trademark in this area. Playboy's publishers have won most of the cases, but lost one involving a Web site displaying pictures of a model who was accurately described as a one-time PLAYBOY Playmate of the Year. The court's take on the situation was that she was not using Playboy as a trademark; she was simply giving an accurate description of her own connection with the magazine.

ISP Liability

A federal law called the Communications Decency Act includes some provisions that protect Internet Service Providers (ISPs) against liability arising out of the ways in which subscribers use (or misuse) the Internet access that the ISP provides.

The Anticybersquatting Consumer Protection Act takes various court rulings and builds them into the statute. A domain name registrar can't be sued for contributory trademark infringement (i.e., acting in a way that makes it easier for someone else to commit trademark infringement) if it registers a domain name that infringes on someone else's trademark, or that dilutes a famous trademark. But if the plaintiff wins an in rem suit against a domain name (see page 96), and the registrar is ordered to transfer ownership of the domain name to the plaintiff, then an injunction can be issued to make the registrar comply with the court order.

In 2001, the federal District Court for the Southern District of New York refused to dismiss a case brought by Gucci America against

Mindspring, an ISP. A company called Hall & Associates had a site at http://www.goldhaus.com, selling jewelry that imitated Gucci trademarks. Gucci e-mailed Mindspring twice to inform it of the infringement, asking Mindspring to cancel Hall's account.

Mindspring didn't cancel the account, and Gucci sued both Hall and Mindspring for trademark infringement, false designation of origin, false description, misrepresentation, and unfair competition. Gucci asked for an injunction, damages, and costs. Mindspring could not get the case dismissed, because the Communications Decency Act does not affect existing intellectual property concepts—including contributing to infringement by allowing an infringer to do business.

Keywords

Many Web users either connect to the Internet through America Online (AOL) or use a Web *portal* as their entry point. Sometimes the user interface allows the user to enter a *"keyword"* to get a list of relevant Web sites. The portal may use the keywords as an advertising device, with more prominent display going to advertisers who pay the most. (Technically speaking, keywords are slightly different from metatags because they are used by portals in site administration, not designed into a Web site by the owners of the site.)

Perpetual plaintiff Playboy Enterprises sued Netscape Communications and Excite for trademark infringement and dilution because of Netscape's business practice of selling keywords—including PLAY-BOY—to competitors of the owners of the trademarks that were equivalent to the keywords. Playboy's case was dismissed. The Southern District of California said that Excite doesn't use the term *Playboy* in a trademark sense. The search engine only refers to Playboy in a comparative manner. Consumers aren't at risk of being confused, because the search engine doesn't identify the source of goods or services.

ESSENTIALS of Trademarks and Unfair Competition

Linking and Framing

The whole purpose of the Internet is to allow free connection from one site to another. It is probably true that someone who does not want other people to link to a site should either restrict access to the site (through encryption or password-protection) or simply refrain from putting the material on the Net at all. However, there can be some trademark and unfair competition problems on the Internet, especially if third parties put up material to which they do not have rights.

There's also a difference between simple linking and framing. If there's a link on Site #1 to files on Site #2, it will usually be clear that the Web surfer has left the first site. Furthermore, Site #2 will be displayed the way its designers intended. If there are advertisements, they will be visible in their original place.

Framing is somewhat different. In effect, framing makes Site #2 part of Site #1. So Site #2 may look like Site #1. Viewers will see the Site #1 ads—and reports of Web traffic will show that the viewers went to Site #1, even though they saw Site #2's content there.

Not only is this an economic issue (especially if advertisers pay for their Web ads wholly or partly on the basis of the amount of traffic on sites), it can be an issue of tarnishment if "respectable" content is framed in a "disreputable" site—or simply in a site representing a contrary ideology. For example, although it was not a framing case, an injunction was granted against an antiabortion activist using plannedparenthood.com as a domain name, because his intention was to provide a viewpoint opposite to the one that Web surfers would expect when they tried to contact the organization Planned Parenthood. So his registration was intended to be deceptive and to divert traffic away from Planned Parenthood. This was not a First Amendment issue, because he could have expressed his views through a site whose domain name indicated his antiabortion stance.

Deep linking—establishing a link to specific information within a site, rather than to the home page of the site—shares some features of linking and some of framing. In 2000, the Central District of California refused to dismiss Lanham Act claims of passing off, reverse passing off, and false advertising in connection with *deep linking* to an inside page of Ticketmaster's site from a rival ticket booking company's site. (The rival company's sales pitch was that if it couldn't sell the Web surfer the ticket he or she wanted, it would send the surfer over to Ticketmaster's site—but this was deep enough into the site that the advertisements on the home page would be skipped. Understandably, surfers liked this better than Ticketmaster and its advertisers did.)

Ticketmaster was entitled to get a full trial on the issues, but it could not get a preliminary injunction, because the court didn't think that deep linking was unfair competition unless it could be shown that Web surfers were confused about the true source of the information they viewed. In January, 2001 the Ninth Circuit agreed that a preliminary injunction should not have been granted. At press time, the basic issues still hadn't been settled.

In mid-2001, the Sixth Circuit, admitting that there aren't many legal precedents, suggested that maybe the Internet should be considered like national advertising. The Sixth Circuit was involved in a contest between two computer companies with the same initials. One did business nationwide, the other only in Ohio. The Sixth Circuit suggested that both should have some kind of rights to use the Internet. Otherwise, *concurrent users* (who are allowed to use the same trademark in geographic areas that do not overlap) would never be able to use the Internet.

So far, the major U. S. cases have been settled out of court, so the courts haven't given any hard-and-fast rules about trademark law in the context of framing. In 1999, the Southern District of New York did grant an injunction against framing, but that was because it violated the terms of a license between the trademark owner and the licensee who operated the site that did the framing.

Morton, the defendant in this case, had a license to use the mark HARD ROCK HOTEL in a limited geographic area, and only for management of the Hard Rock Hotel and Casino. The license allowed him to create a site, www.hardrockhotel.com, to promote the hotel.

The problem is that Morton made a contract with a third party, The Tunes Network, to sell CDs on Morton's site. Morton's site not only linked to but framed the Tunes Network site, using Hard Rock Hotel trademarks. To the court, this was objectionable and should be enjoined, because Morton was using the HARD ROCK trademark in a way that was broader than the license allowed. Music buyers outside Morton's geographic territory might buy CDs from The Tunes Network.

PTO Approach

In September 1999, the PTO published its position on the interface between trademarks and URLs, in USPTO Examination Guide No. 2-99. The Guide can be accessed at the PTO Web site, http://www.uspto.gov/web/offices/tac/notices/guide299.htm. It is

TIPS & TECHNIQUES

Avoid Implied Endorsements

Designers of sites that link to other sites, and especially sites that frame others, should be careful to avoid using layout or typography (especially typography and design of links) in a way that implies endorsement or sponsorship of the site that contains the links by the site to which the links lead. To avoid potential confusion, it might help to include an EXIT screen that indicates that the Web user is leaving Site #1 and going via link to unrelated Site #2.

well worth reading, because some of its conclusions are very surprising and do not really fit in with real-life Internet use and Web design.

Domain names actually consist of several parts, and the different parts have different legal consequences. The PTO ignores "http://," which is part of *all* Web addresses that use a particular program for connecting to the Internet, and also ignores "www," which is found in most but not all Web addresses. The PTO's position is that these obligatory elements of the address don't do anything to indicate the source of the Web site.

All URLs (Web site addresses) are assigned to a "top-level domain," or TLD. Some new TLDs are coming into usage, but right now most domains are registered in the domains .com (for commercial enterprises), .edu (for educational institutions), .net (for networks), .org (for non-profit organizations), and .gov (for government agencies).

Some domains, like .gov and .mil (for the military) are "closed" domains. That is, the registrant has to prove that it really is a government agency or military site to qualify for the domain name. But .com, .net, and .org are "open" domains, where no proof is required. Many business organizations apply for .com, .net, and .org registration for every domain name they try to register—in part, to keep competitors from creating confusion by using the same name with a .net or .org extension.

The PTO's position is that the same requirements apply for an application to use a domain name as a trademark as for any other trademark registration application.

A mark composed of a domain name is registrable as a trademark or service mark only if it functions as a source identifier. The mark depicted on the specimens must be presented in a manner that will be perceived by potential purchasers as indicating source and not as merely an informational indication of the domain name address used to access a Web site.

In other words, the PTO treats the business's Web address in pretty much the same way as its street address, and not necessarily in the same way as its trademarks. According to the PTO, a business's using the Internet to advertise its own goods and service online is not a service. So if a site created is created for that purpose and that purpose alone will not allow the business to get trademark registration for the URL of a site used in that way.

Furthermore, the PTO position is that a URL is a pure address, not a trademark, when it is used on a letterhead or business card, or used in an advertisement as part of the company's contact information. Therefore, it cannot be registered as a trademark. For example, "Visit us on the Web at BLURCH.COM," would not be considered a trademark use. Neither would a letterhead or business card that gives e-mail and Web addresses as well as street address and telephone and fax numbers.

This PTO position is the opposite of the position taken by many courts with respect to trade dress. In the trade dress context, for example, an ad that says, "For fast, soothing cough relief, look for BLURCH Cough Lozenges in the blue-and-yellow striped box," might very well be considered valuable evidence of the distinctiveness of the trade dress.

TIPS & TECHNIQUES

Drawings for Web-Based Applications

The drawing page for a URL trademark application can usually include only the top-level domain part of the URL, such as BLUR-CHOTCDRUGS.COM, even if the specimens submitted include www. or http://www. However, if the drawing shows something like XYZ.COM, a specimen that only shows XYZ is not adequate.

The PTO also says that the top-level domain has no significance in a mark that includes a surname (e.g., JONES.COM) or a mark that is purely descriptive (SOFT.COM for tissues; BOOKSTORE.COM). The PTO treats ".com" like (800) or (888) in a toll-free phone number: something without trademark significance. Therefore, if the mark would be refused registration as primarily a surname, or as purely descriptive, in the bricks-and-mortar world, turning it into a URL will not make it easier to register a trademark.

IN THE REAL WORLD

Addresses Are Not Trademarks

In a 1998 TTAB case, an attorney tried to register www.eilberg.com as a trademark for the legal services he provided to his clients. The specimen he submitted was his letterhead, including his e-mail address and the domain name. The examining attorney refused to register www.eilberg.com as a trademark, saying that it merely indicated where the site could be found but did not identify the site as a source of legal services to be provided by the attorney. The TTAB agreed with the examining attorney. The TTAB's suggestion was to rename the law firm Eilberg.com and establish that as a business name. (However, bar associations limit the names that law firms can use—this tactic might work better for other kinds of businesses.)

CHAPTER 3

Establishing, Registering, and Defending a Trademark

After reading this chapter you will be able to

- Decide how broad a sweep to use in trademark searching
- Avoid pitfalls in preparing the trademark registration application
- Use the PTO's Web site to get information, and even register trademarks online
- Prepare the all-important drawings and specimens to go with the application
- Protect yourself or take action against cybersquatters
- Register a trademark using the state system, or outside the United States

Trademark Searches

The basic assumption that lies behind trademark law is that anyone who wants to register a trademark first has to find out whether the same trademark has already been registered, or even applied for. This is definitely a situation in which ignorance of the law—or ignorance of the facts—is no defense at all. In fact, since trademark law also penalizes the use of a trademark that is confusingly similar to another trademark that is *not* identical—the search has to extend past the exact combination of letters and words.

Trademarks can be confusingly similar in many ways. If they sound alike (even if they do not begin with the same letter), if they mean the same thing or even suggest the same concepts, or if they mean the same thing but in different languages, consumer confusion is a possibility that the legal system will seek to avoid.

Therefore, the search report has to extend beyond the exact mark that the business wants to register. For example, if the proposed trademark is CEEZEE, the report should search for CZ, CZEE, possibly even DEEZEE, DZ, and DZEE and other letter combinations that sound similar.

Goods and services do not have to be competitive for there to be confusion, if the trademarks are closely related. However, sometimes even very similar marks can be used without confusion, even on similar merchandise, as long as the items are marketed through different channels (e.g., one sold at retail, one at wholesale) or if their purchasers are different (e.g., beauty shops versus consumers who buy beauty products in drugstores, department stores, or supermarkets).

Furthermore, for many trademarks, visual appearance is highly significant, so the more difficult task of looking for and analyzing visual elements must be performed.

An added complication is that, if a mark is considered *famous* (see page 145), additional remedies are available against anyone who *dilutes* the mark (i.e., makes it less valuable by reducing its good reputation). Therefore, special care must be taken to avoid conflict with famous marks that might be interpreted as dilution.

In today's commercial world, it is common for manufacturers and retailers to have Web sites (or even to have a separate Web site for each product line). So one consideration in choosing a trademark is whether the trademark will be available as a Web address. For example, James Murchison Music, Inc., might want http://www.jmm.com as a Web address—only to find out that the domain name belongs to someone else. (It belongs to Jupiter Media Metrix, a company that does market research about trends in Internet usage.)

When the person who staked out the Web address first is a legitimate business, or a person or organization making legitimate use of the address, then the latecomer is simply out of luck. However, see page 94 for a discussion of remedies against cybersquatters who hoard domain names that they hope to be able to sell back to legitimate businesses who need them. Also see page 111 for a discussion of the domain name dispute resolution process established by ICANN, the Internet regulatory organization.

Designing the Trademark Search

Developing and marketing a new product can be very expensive. It is tempting for a business to rush to market as soon as possible—but one of the risks in doing this is that, unless the name and image of the product have been carefully researched, the company might be infringing on other trademarks or even diluting famous trademarks.

Therefore, a trademark search should be one of the very earliest steps in researching the feasibility of a new product, and should occur long before the product itself has been produced or even prototyped. Otherwise, time and effort are committed to a particular name, and image might have to be scrapped if a trademark search performed at a later stage shows that the desired product name cannot be protected as a trademark, and might even lead to charges that the company has infringed someone else's trademark.

A trademark search could take forever and consume all of the company's resources—but at some point, a balance has to be struck. The point at which the search is terminated, and the proposed mark actually adopted for products or services, is a question of how much risk the company is willing to take.

TIPS & TECHNIQUES

Slogan Searches

It is also a good idea to search for slogans already in use. Some slogans can be protected as trademarks, and even slogans that are not trademarks might give rise to unfair competition claims.

And that, in turn, depends on how important the mark is to the company's business, and what happens if the mark becomes the subject of TTAB proceedings or litigation. A mark that is used on only one, obscure product is much easier to change than a mark that has been the center of an expensive ad campaign, or that is the name of a high-profile corporate division. Marks that are used by licensees or franchisees are especially hard to change, because of the impact on other businesses.

Trademark searches help predict whether the PTO is likely to reject the application based on risk of confusion with an existing mark. However, there are other potential grounds for rejection, such as "immoral" or "scandalous" matter, violation of a living person's privacy, or the excessively descriptive or generic. Advice from marketing consultants and experienced intellectual property counsel should stave off problems like this.

Scope of the Search

There are two basic kinds of trademark search (although each one has variations and subdivisions). A *preliminary, screening,* or *knockout* search is done to find out if the effort and money to do a full search would be justified, or if the desired trademark is too much like an existing mark even to be worth considering. The preliminary search can be enough to rule out a potential trademark—but a lot more work is needed before a trademark application for that can even be considered.

If time or budget is short, then a simple preliminary search can be done in-house using Internet search engines, telephone directories, business and industry directories, and the public records of the various state Secretaries of State (for trademarks registered with a state and not federally) and the U.S. Patent and Trademark Office (both online and in the depository libraries in Washington, D.C., and in each state). The PTO publishes CDs containing a trademark database called Cassis, which is distributed to the Patent Depository Libraries for free access by the public.

Today, business is highly internationalized, so it is also important to check to see if the mark is already used as a European, Asian, or South American trademark. Trademark search companies do regional and worldwide screening searches (Thomson & Thomson's WISS and RISS

IN THE REAL WORLD

Sources for Trademark Searches

Some ways to get access to searchable databases of trademarks:

- Search over the Internet (which can be cumbersome and time consuming).

- Subscribe to one of the CD-ROM services that provide a flat monthly or annual fee for unlimited use; subscribers can go to a Web site for updates.

- Subscribe to a fee-basis database from a publisher such as DIALOG, LEXIS, or Westlaw.

- Check the periodical *Trademark Alert,* which lists trademark applications, and the PTO's *Official Gazette,* which publishes the text of applications so that members of the public can "speak now or forever hold their peace."

systems; CCH Trademark Research Corporation's Exact International Search packages, for example).

Databases of trademark applications and registrations are available online, covering Canada and much of Europe. However, these tend to be less comprehensive than the corresponding U.S. databases. In some countries, the descriptions are in the native language, not English, and only verbal descriptions, not images, are included in the database. That is one more reason why registering a trademark in other countries, or at least making sure that a U.S.-registered trademark will not infringe on a local trademark when goods are exported from the United States, requires having a good local trademark attorney as well as a good U.S. trademark attorney.

Although it might be necessary to at least start the search process in-house in the interests of economy, usually trademark searching, especially for detailed searches, is done by trademark lawyers (and their paralegal staff) or by specialized professional firms that have significant experience and large databases of relevant records.

IN THE REAL WORLD

Search Companies

Trademark search firms include Thomson & Thomson, http://www.thomson-thomson.com, (800) 692-8833. It offers the SAEGIS electronic search service. Electronic search services are also offered by DIALOG (TRADEMARKSCAN), CORSEARCH (CCH), MicroPatent's Trademark.com, LEXIS, and MarksOnline. Mr. Trademark and Identity Research Corp. (Name Protect) perform clearance searches combining online and more traditional methods. The American Trademark Company, http://www.trademrk.com/ [sic]m (888) 723-3675, offers a variety of trademark search and registration services.

TIPS & TECHNIQUES

Finding Common-Law Trademarks

Common-law trademarks (those that are not even registered by the state) can be found through various news and information databases. It will probably be necessary to pay a fee for each query.

An ordinary trademark search usually takes between one and two weeks, although 48-hour, 24-hour, and even same-day service is possible at a higher cost. It is a good idea to search ad slogans, too.

These are some of the issues involved in doing a trademark search, evaluating the results, and integrating them with market research for the projected new product:

- What is the mark to be searched?

- Has it been used by anyone else?

- For what products/services?

- What country(ies) was the mark used in?

- Are there plans to use the intended new trademark outside the United States?

- Have applications been filed for use (trademark applications— not just issued registrations—are public documents)? Are they anticipated?

- Is it anticipated that the use of the trademark will be extended to additional types of goods or services? (For example, a garment manufacturer might expand to make household linens and decorating items; a manufacturer of paints or power tools for contractors might seek a market with homeowners.)

- Who is the target market for the items with which the intended trademark will be used?

- What wholesale and retail channels are expected for the new product?

- What is the derivation of the proposed mark? Does it contain material that could be offensive?

- Have words in languages other than English been translated and used in the search? For example, MANZANA might be considered confusingly similar to its English equivalent, APPLE. Technical terms should be explained.

- Does the order form for the search describe similar marks already in use by other companies?

- Does it include a copy of the logo or design that the company intends to use with its word mark?

- Has the search firm gotten copies of actual or proposed advertisements, brochures, and package designs?

- Is the mark intended to operate as a corporate or division name?

- Does the company plan to sell or advertise the new product on the Internet? If so, is the mark available as a URL? (Even if it is not available as a URL, this might not be a problem if the company already has registered another domain name that can be used to market the new product.)

- Is the mark intended to be part of a family of marks (e.g., LIVELY LIME, LIGHT-HEARTED LEMON, AGILE AVO-CADO and PERKY PEACH soaps)?

Search reports should also be prepared for variations of the mark that the company thinks it might use instead or in addition to the mark that is being developed.

Although the various online databases can give near-instant results, traditional search methods still have some utility. For example, defini-

TIPS & TECHNIQUES

Pattern Trademarks Not Recognized

Even though using a whole family of similar names to describe a group of products is a reasonable marketing technique, it is not accepted by the PTO. Trademarks must be registered individually; a registration will not be granted for a "pattern" mark such as SUN-RIPENED [name of fruit] Candies.

tions from general and technical dictionaries can help establish whether a proposed mark is generic or descriptive.

Atlases and geographic dictionaries show whether the mark is geographically descriptive or misdescriptive. Whether a mark will be considered primarily a surname can depend on evidence from telephone directories (as to whether it is a common surname). Telephone directories (this time the business listings) can also provide helpful evidence about locally used trademarks.

Reasons for Problem Searches

Even if a search is done carefully, it might fail to uncover everything that causes problems with the mark in the future. There are several possible reasons for this:

- Even if the search includes state registrations, unregistered marks will not turn up; yet their holders may have common-law rights that create future problems.

- An application might have been filed with the PTO too recently to appear in its public records.

- State databases are updated slowly and irregularly, so fairly recent information might fail to appear.

- Because of typographical errors, the preexisting mark could have been filed in the wrong place—or the typo could be in the new mark being searched. Either way, the result could be that relevant information is not found.

- A trademark might continue to be used (with common-law rights) even after registration has been allowed to lapse.

- It is much harder to search for design marks (e.g., logos) and nontraditional marks (such as trade dress) than plain word marks. However, searches can be done for design phrases— the descriptions of design trademarks that appear in the trademark application and registration.

- The person doing the search might make the wrong decision about what is relevant and should be reported.

TIPS & TECHNIQUES

Weak Marks

In addition to checking trademark registrations and pending applications (at the state as well as the PTO level), it is a good idea to look at trademark opposition and cancellation actions involving similar trademarks. They give an idea of whether the trademark and marks like it are strong or weak.

There are both pros and cons to weak marks. It is easy to adapt a mark enough to prevent it from conflicting with an existing, but weak, mark. However, the same process can be followed by others with respect to the second mark! So probably the best choice when developing a product is to choose a strong trademark and investigate carefully to make sure that it is not confusingly similar to existing marks.

Disclaimers should also be checked carefully. It is very difficult to register something that has already been disclaimed as unprotectable by many other applicants!

Under some circumstances, it might be possible to share a mark if the registered user of the mark is willing and the use of the mark is different enough to prevent confusion (e.g., a bakery in California and a manufacturer of fishing tackle sold in the Southeast). This is achieved by negotiating with the owner, and then having a concurrence proceeding before the TTAB. If the trademark is inactive, it might be simpler just to make an offer to pay for an assignment of all rights in the trademark.

Abandonment of a trademark by its owner is a defense to an infringement suit. Some ways to see if a trademark is abandoned, at least in connection with specific products are:

- Check the company's Dun & Bradstreet listing to see if the product appears.

- See if the product is listed in SEC filings of the corporate annual report.

- Call headquarters and ask where the product can be pur-chased—if no one has heard of the product, there's a good chance that the trademark has been abandoned.

Registration

Unlike patent rights—which exist only on the basis of a patent issued by the USPTO—a limited degree of protection of trademark rights is available whenever items are sold in commerce using the trademark. This is known as an unregistered, or common-law, trademark.

However, for most businesses, registering a trademark is a good idea, because it greatly expands the amount of protection available to the trademark. It also significantly increases the remedies that the trade-mark owner will have if it charges someone else with infringing the trademark.

Section 7(c) of the Lanham Act (15 U.S. Code §1057(c)) says that registering and using a mark proves that the registrant was using the trademark on the date the application was filed. That makes the registrant's rights superior to those of everyone except those who used the mark before the date of the application, or who filed an earlier registration application for the mark.

Therefore, registering a mark puts *junior users* (those who started using it later) on notice that the registrant has the exclusive right to use the mark commercially. However, a *senior user* that was already using the mark in a geographic area can continue to use the mark in that geographic area even after the federal registration—but will not be allowed to expand the geographic area of usage. Someone who registered the mark in a country outside the United States may also be entitled to an effective filing date based on that foreign registration that entitles that party to priority.

Using the PTO Web site

One of the best and most convenient resources about trademarks is the Web site maintained by the Patent and Trademark Office: http://www.uspto.gov/teas/index.html. And one of the best introductions to the site comes from the special pages set up for first-time users.

According to the PTO site, automation is needed to handle the huge volume of trademark applications. In fiscal 2000, the USPTO got close to 300,000 trademark applications—27.2% more than fiscal 1999, and the 1999 level was also 27% higher than the previous year's total.

TIPS & TECHNIQUES

Read the Manual

The PTO recommends reading the HELP instructions for each section before beginning the application process, even if the process seems to be simple and intuitive.

Site Features

The features of the PTO Web site relating to trademarks include:

Services

TESS (search for pending or registered trademarks)

Copies of documents and publications

Learn the fee schedules for various services; make payments

Addresses of the PTDL (depository libraries) where trademark files can be consulted in person. The main PTDL is in the PTO office, 2900 Crystal Drive, Arlington, Virginia, but there is at least one PTDL in each state.

Registration

TEAS (online filing of trademark applications)

TARR (check application and registration status for trademarks)

Form TMEP-700: responding to office actions

Form TMEP-1500 or TBMP-1200: appeals

Form TMEP-1504: amendments after publication of a trademark

Form TMEP-1700: petitions

Form TMEP-1503 or TBMP: opposition to registration

Publications and Guides to Trademarks

Intellectual property options

TMEP-100, explaining the various types of trademark

Guidance and manuals

How to correspond with the PTO about trademarks

Text of trademark laws and regulations

PTO policy and procedures

International Issues

Text of trademark law treaties

Information about the Madrid System for international registration of trademarks

Information about intellectual property regulation throughout the world

TIPS & TECHNIQUES

e-Sigs

As of June 21, 2001, the PTO will accept electronic signatures on applications and other official documents. Technical guidance about signatures, and other aspects of the online system, can be found at the Frequently Asked Questions About TEAS page, http://www.uspto.gov/teas/TEASFAQ.htm.

In fiscal 2000, the PTO issued 106,383 registrations, covering a total of 127,794 classes. (Many applications cover multiple classes, which explains why there were more classes than registrations.)

In its first year, 1999, there were 20,600 e-TEAS (electronic) filings. That number more than doubled, to 44,100 in FY 2000.

Applying On Line

TEAS—the Trademark Electronic Application System—is an important part of the PTO Web site. This program allows applicants to fill out the application form and check it for completeness over the Internet. Once the applicant is satisfied that the form is complete, there are two filing options. The official filing of the application can be made electronically (e-TEAS) or hard copy can be created using the PrinTEAS program to be mailed to the PTO.

On August 30, 2001, the PTO filed a Notice of Proposed Rulemaking in the Federal Register. The Federal Register is a daily newspaper in which federal agencies publish their newly adopted and proposed rules. This one is the PTO's proposal that using the TEAS system become mandatory instead of just strongly suggested. If this rule is adopted, using "snail mail" or hand delivery to file trademark documents with the PTO would no longer be allowed.

IN THE REAL WORLD

Filing On Line

In order to use e-TEAS, the trademark applicant must be able to satisfy a number of criteria:

- The browser used to access e-TEAS must be Netscape Navigator 3.0 or higher, or Internet Explorer 4.0 or higher. Earlier versions will not work because the site uses frames, JavaScript, and other sophisticated coding. Macintosh users must use IE 5.0 or Netscape, and users of IE behind Microsoft Proxy Server must use version 5.01 or higher.

- If an initial application is being made for a stylized or design mark, the applicant must be able to submit the drawing in the form of a black and white .gif or .jpeg file. Those are the only two acceptable file formats; other graphic formats, such as .tiff, are not acceptable.

- Specimens of actual use of the mark in commerce (see page 76) must be submitted as either scanned images (e.g., of packaging, tags, and advertisements) or digital photographs. These, too, must be in the .gif or .jpeg format.

- Applicants who do not have a deposit account with the PTO are required to use an approved credit card (MasterCard, Visa, American Express, or Discover) to pay fees. Furthermore, the system does not accept credit card payments from 12 a.m. to 4 a.m., EST, on Sundays.

- The FAQ says that credit cards will be charged only once, even if the applicant receives Error messages and has to use the Return button several times to transmit information.

- To correct errors in an electronic application, the applicant has two choices. The applicant can send e-mail to ecomL0102@uspto.gov (but *not* to other addresses, including TEAS@uspto.gov) explaining the correction in the body of the e-mail message itself (*not* as a file attachment).

IN THE REAL WORLD (CONTINUED)

The subject line of the e-mail should include the serial number and the mark (or a description of a design mark). A hard copy of the proposed correction, including the mark and the serial number, can also be mailed to the Commissioner for Trademarks, 3900 Crystal Drive, Arlington, VA 22202.

- Once an application is validated, the FAQ suggests that the applicant save the application as a portable form by clicking on Download Portable Form or bookmarking the Validation page of the USPTO site.

On the other hand, PrinTEAS users must either have a PTO deposit account or must pay fees by check or money order. Credit cards are not accepted. The PrinTEAS system is available every day, 24 hours a day. If there is a technical question or problem with PrinTEAS, the technical support e-mail address is PrinTEAS@uspto.gov. Questioners should include a telephone number at which they can be reached.

The PTO Web site includes both standard forms and electronic *wizards* for creating and printing out individualized forms. The PTO strongly recommends using the wizards to generate custom forms. However, the Forms section at the end of this book reproduces the standard forms, just to show what they look like and how to use them.

According to the PTO, electronic filing with e-TEAS helps trademark applicants by

- Cutting the time that the PTO needs to review applications

- Reducing the time that the PTO needs to issue a serial number and receipts (which, in turn, comes in very handy if there is a dispute about who is entitled to priority on the basis of earlier filing)

- Speeding up the work of the examining attorney

TIPS & TECHNIQUES

Status Information

Once a serial number has been assigned to an application, the applicant can get automated tracking information about the status of the application, either by calling (703) 305-8747 or accessing the Trademark status area on the PTO's Web site.

However, applicants have to be patient. The TEAS FAQ says that status information will not be available for at least 45 days after the application is submitted, because it takes at least that long for the PTO to update its databases.

- Eliminating errors that occur when forms are transcribed from paper to the PTO's databases
- Saving money on postage or express service

The Registration Process

The procedure for registering a trademark is fairly simple, although it can be beset by pitfalls for those who are not careful to learn and abide by the Trademark Office's rules.

One of the best places to learn about the rules in detail is the *Trademark Manual of Examining Procedure* (*TMEP*), published by the Patent and Trademark Office. The *TMEP*, available both in print and online, gives detailed guidance to trademark examiners when they determine whether a trademark application is acceptable, so it is good for applicants to consult it for insight into examiners' ideas.

Getting Ready for an Application

Before the registration process begins, the potential registrant has to determine if the desired trademark can be registered at all. For example,

TIPS & TECHNIQUES

Communications

A telephone number for general trademark assistance from the Trademark Assistance Center: (703) 308-9000. The "snail-mail" address for corresponding with the PTO's Trademark section is:

Assistant Commissioner for Trademarks
2900 Crystal Drive
Arlington VA 22202-3513

According to the PTO Web site, all papers filed with the PTO should include a stamped, self-addressed postcard that lists the following:

- The mark

- The serial number or registration number (if this has already been issued)

- What is contained in the correspondence—for instance, whether a filing fee, a drawing, or specimens are being submitted

When papers (including checks) are filed, they should have the serial or registration number written in. Before they are issued, other identifying information will be provided (such as the mark, the applicant's name, and/or filing date).

it might be ineligible for registration because it is vulgar or scandalous, or because it is just a last name. This is discussed more later in the chapter.

The next question is whether the trademark can be used as intended, or whether other parties will allege that the mark is improper because, for instance, it is confusingly similar to their existing registered mark. This is one of the purposes of doing a trademark search (see page 49).

Federal law includes several provisions tackling such questions. Lanham Act §§2(d), 32(1), 43(a) forbid registration or use of trademarks that are "likely to cause confusion." Lanham Act §43(c) forbids use of

EXHIBIT 3.1

Filing Fees

Filing Fees, as of October 1, 2001

(See http://www.uspto.gov/web/offices/ac/qs/ope/1999/fee20011001.htm)

Registration application	$325/class
Amendment to allege use, or statement of use	$100/class
Renewal application	$400/class
Publication of mark	$100/class
Notice of opposition or petition for cancellation	$300/class
Printed copy of registered mark (regular service)	$3 ($15, if certified)
" " (next-day hard copy or fax delivery)	$6 ($30, if certified)
Recording assignment of a trademark	$40 for the first mark per document, $25 for each other mark in the document
Session time on the X-SEARCH terminal	$40/hr

a trademark that "dilutes" an earlier trademark (reduces its commercial value; see page 145) even if it is not likely to confuse consumers.

When the application is filed, the first step in processing is that a clerk checks it to see that all the elements are included. Next, a PTO employee called the Attorney Examiner makes a legal analysis as to whether the trademark applied for is confusingly similar to an existing registration or the content of an earlier application.

A few months after a paper application is filed, the PTO will issue a filing receipt to the applicant, giving the serial number and filing date and an estimate of how long the examination process can be expected to take.

IN THE REAL WORLD

The Trademark Application

The trademark application is a fairly simple document. Under the Lanham Act (see 15 U.S.Code §1051), the essential elements of the application are:

- The applicant's name and address.

- (For an application to register an existing trademark that is already in use) The date the trademark was first used in commerce; the first date it was used in interstate commerce.

- (For an intent to use application) A verified statement of the registrant's bona fide intent to use the mark in the future.

- A drawing of the mark. The PTO has very detailed requirements for what constitutes a proper drawing for various types of marks (see below).

- How the mark is used.

- A list of the classes of goods and services for which registration is sought.

- The applicant's sworn statement that he, she, or it is not aware of any existing mark to which the mark applied for is confusingly similar. A 1997 case from the Sixth Circuit rules that the registrant's belief in its ownership of the mark is enough to rebut a claim that the registration was obtained fraudulently.

- Filing fee. The fee is $325 per trademark per class registered, and since there are 45 possible classes and multiple registration is common, this can get expensive!

Some documents can be filed by fax: for instance, renewal applications and statements that a trademark is actually in use after an application was filed on the basis of intent to use. However, applicants are not allowed to file the trademark application itself by fax. Nor can they fax any document that has to be certified or the drawings submitted to show what the mark looks like and how it is used. (TMEP §701.04).

Expedicted Handling

The PTO rules published in the Code of Federal Regulations allow a petition for expedited handling to accelerate the process. Such a petition would typically be granted on the basis of actual or threatened infringement, pending litigation, or need to register in the United States to get foreign registration.

Trademark applications are examined in the order of filing, but many applications are filed and it usually takes at least six months from the initial filing for the examination process to begin. (The time to start examination and processing is called *first action pendency*.)

Final disposition (*overall action pendency*) averages about 20 months, and can be much longer if the trademark is contested. One problem with the trademark system is that the pendency of the action might be longer than the entire useful life of a property (for instance, merchandise based on a movie or band that could sink back to obscurity after a few months). At least broader adoption of online filing may speed up the process.

Various factors could make the registration process longer than usual in a particular case. The Attorney Examiner has the right to ask for additional information or modifications. The Attorney Examiner also has the right to take what is called an Office Action. This means that the examiner rejects an application that is not in allowable form, and explains to the applicant why the rejection occurred.

Typically, the applicant has a six-month period to respond to these challenges and cure the defects. If the defects are deemed removed, the application is published as if it had succeeded on the first try. If they are not removed, the Attorney Examiner is allowed to finalize the rejection.

TIPS & TECHNIQUES

Relief for Descriptive Trademarks

If the trademark is rejected under Lanham Act §2(e) [because it is merely descriptive], the applicant has the right to amend the application and ask that the trademark be registered on the Supplemental Register instead of the Principal Register. However, the trademark must still be able to distinguish the applicant's goods and services from those that come from other providers—so not every descriptive trademark will qualify.

In most cases there is no trouble. The Attorney Examiner finds the application is acceptable, and therefore the proposed trademark that is intended to go on the Principal Register is published in the weekly PTO publication the *Official Gazette*. The purpose of publication is to allow other trademark owners and applicants review the application and bring any allegations that the trademark is inappropriate because it could be confused with theirs.

Trademarks that will go on the Supplemental Register are not published for opposition, which is one reason why protection is weaker for these trademarks; no one else has had a chance to comment on the registration.

The public gets 30 days to file an opposition to marks published in the *Official Gazette*. A party that plans to file an opposition can ask the PTO for an extra 30 days to prepare its case. This extension is routinely granted.

After the statutory period, if there have been no objections asserted, then the trademark is registered. The applicant receives a certificate of registration, and the trademark is added to the database of registered trademarks. That is not necessarily the last step.

IN THE REAL WORLD

Long Odds

Only about 3% of marks are opposed.

A federal administrative panel, the Trademark Trial and Appeal Board (TTAB) has the power to hear *"opposition"* proceedings brought by parties that claim that a particular registration was improper in some way.

The TTAB has another role. Examining Attorneys who are not satisfied by the changes made by the applicant can enter a second Office Action. They have discretion to make this second action final. Finality triggers the applicant's right to appeal to the TTAB.

The losing party in a TTAB case has the right to appeal the agency's decision to the appropriate U.S. District Court (the District Court is the lowest level in the federal court system). The District Court's decision (no matter where the court is located) goes to the Court of Appeals for the Federal Circuit, which is located in Washington, and not to the Court of Appeals that would otherwise handle cases from that District. This is true because of the special status of intellectual property cases within the federal court system.

Marks That Cannot Be Registered

Under §2(d) of the Lanham Act (15 U.S. Code §1052(d)), the PTO will not register a mark that has a close enough resemblance to another mark that is already on the Principal or Supplemental Register to cause confusion with that mark.

It doesn't matter if the goods are not identical, or even if they are not competitive at all, as long as they are related in some manner, or the circumstances of their marketing are such that they are likely to be

TIPS & TECHNIQUES

Status Checks

There are two easy ways to check on the status of a registration: telephoning (703) 305-8747 or going online to check the Trademark Applications and Registrations Retrieval (TARR) database, which is found at http://tarr.uspto.gov (no www).

encountered by the same person under circumstances that would create a mistaken impression they originate from or are associated with the same producer.

Another important point is that a generic term—one that covers a whole product category, not just a specific item within that category—can't be registered as a trademark. A term is generic if, for the particular class of goods or services at issue, the relevant public considers the term to cover the whole category. The relevant public means those who are likely to buy and use the product or service. For example, for a surgical tool, the question is whether health care personnel think of the word *hemostat* as generic or specific. If a term starts out as a protectable trademark, but later becomes generic, then Lanham Act §14 allows the trademark to be canceled at any time after it becomes generic.

If a mark is primarily a surname (last name), it can be registered on the Principal Register, but only if the applicant can show that it has acquired distinctiveness. Otherwise, it can be placed on the Supplemental Register. Not every name is considered primarily a surname—a name like King has other meanings too.

U.S. trademark law does not allow trademark protection for "functional" matter, which has to be protected (if at all) with a patent, design patent, or as a trade secret. Not only will examiners turn down registration applications on the basis of *functionality,* they won't even allow

TIPS & TECHNIQUES

Adding Prefixes or Initials

Adding prefixes (Mr., Mrs., Doctor, etc.) or initials (J.M. Wilson, D. Connors) doesn't take away the nature of the mark as primarily a surname—in fact, the PTO says that it strengthens it. A mark that consists of both a surname and a generic term (BOLLINGER'S ICE CREAM) is still considered primarily a surname.

registration of such a trademark on the basis that it has acquired distinctiveness by being used in commerce. Although the general rule is that trademarks become incontestable after five years of use, this is not true of functional trademarks, and anyone who is or will be damaged by use of the functional trademark can file a petition to cancel the trademark.

Registration: Details and What to Do

The information in this section comes from the *Trademark Manual of Examining Procedure*. The most recent edition appeared in August 1997. Section 102 of the *TMEP* allows titles, character names, and other distinctive features of radio or television programs to be registered as service marks, even though they (or the programs they represent) advertise the merchandise of the show's sponsors.

The application for registration of a trademark or service mark in a single class can include more than one item that falls within that class— for instance, a Class 14 (Jewelry) application could include necklaces, bracelets, and brooches using the image of a cartoon character. See *TMEP* §202.01(a). The applicant must identify in detail the goods and/ or services with which the mark will be used. *TMEP* §804.01 tells the applicant to use common names and generally understood terminology, not obscure technical terms. However, if there is no common name for the goods or services, "language which is as clear and succinct as possible should be used," and lengthy descriptions should be avoided.

Preparing the Drawing

Most marks are visual in nature. Therefore, a drawing showing what the mark looks like, and the samples that show how it is used, are crucial to the process of examining the application.

If an applicant only wants to register a word, letter, numeral, or any combination (for example, BLURCH, KXC, GLOOM22J), the application is called a "Typed Drawing" application. The drawing can consist of nothing but typed capital letters. A typed drawing application covers the mark in whatever typeface, printing style, form, or color it appears in.

A "Special Form Drawing" application, including a properly prepared drawing of the mark, is used to register a mark whose appearance is critically important.

The PTO scans drawings submitted as part of applications into an automated search system, reproduces them in the *Official Gazette* so potential opponents can state their claims, and also reproduces the drawing on the Certificate of Registration issued when a trademark application is successful.

Because of the requirements for scanning and reproduction, the drawing cannot be larger than 4 inches by 4 inches, and it is preferable to keep it less than 2.5 inches in both height and width (*TMEP* §807.01).

Although samples are generally in color or are color photographs, the PTO is only set up to accept black-and-white drawings. Of course, it is common for applicants to assert color as an important part of the trademark. The Code of Federal Regulations (CFR) includes an official color chart, showing how to use "lining" to represent colors. *TMEP* §807.06 says that stippling should *not* be used to represent shading or colors.

However, the CFR has only eight color lining patterns (representing brown, blue, green, orange, red or pink, gray or silver, violet or purple, plus black). Most people can recognize thousands of colors, and the difference between one shade and another can make the product more appealing—and can also determine whether a color mark is easily distinguished from, or confusingly similar to, another mark.

TMEP §1202.04(e)(ii) tells applicants to supplement the "lined" drawing of a color mark with a written description of the mark—for instance, an area lined for red should be described as "maroon" or "pale pink," or whatever is applicable. The application for a color mark should also provide specimens of the use of color.

TIPS & TECHNIQUES

Nonvisual Marks

For those rare marks that can't be represented visually at all—for instance, scents and sounds—*TMEP* §807.03 says that the applicant should submit a Drawing page with "NO DRAWING" typed where the drawing would otherwise go, plus a concise explanation of what the mark is. For example, a scent mark might be described as a fragrance combining vanilla, lemon, and cinnamon, used to identify a product for cleaning woodstoves.

If the mark has three-dimensional features, *TMEP* §807.03(a) calls for the drawing to be a single rendition showing the mark in perspective. If the way the mark is positioned on the goods is characteristic (for instance, a red band around the neck of a bottle), the application should describe the positioning (*TMEP* §808.05). The statement will be published in the *Official Gazette* and printed in the Certification of Registration.

Trademark Specimens

The very first section of the Lanham Act, §1 (15 U.S. Code §1501), requires trademark applications (including intent to use applications) to specify "the mode or manner in which the mark is used or intended to be used." Typical uses include on the goods themselves, or on labels, tags, containers, and/or displays.

The applicant must submit specimens—that is, samples of the packages and labels actually used in trade, or photographs of the goods in the form in which they are offered for sale. The Examining Attorney uses the samples to determine how the public sees the mark, and the commercial impression it makes. If color is a feature of the mark— which is true in most cases— *TMEP* §905.02 requires that the specimens be in color (so photographs will probably be acceptable specimens, but black-and-white photographs will not).

As a general rule, three copies of each specimen should be submitted, so that if an opposition is filed, the opposer can get a sample for use in preparing its case, and there will still be two specimens in the file.

The file wrapper for a trademark application is only 9 inches by 14 inches by 1 inch when expanded to its fullest extent, so all specimens must fold flat, and must either be or fold up to a size that does not exceed 8 1/2 inches by 11 inches.

If the goods, or the packaging where the trademark is used, are bulky, then §905.03 calls for submission of photographs that clearly

How Many Specimens Are Needed?

Usually, specimens of only one item will be required for a one-class trademark application, even if the application covers more than one item ("chocolate bars, boxed chocolates, and lollipops," for instance). However, if the range of items is broad, or the application extends to unrelated items, the Examining Attorney has the power to demand additional specimens. (*TMEP* §905.01(a)).

In a combined or multiclass application, specimens will probably be required for use of the mark in each of the classes for which registration is sought. But, to reduce the size of the file, it might be acceptable to submit fewer than three specimens per class.

and legibly show the mark as specimens. *TMEP* §905.02 says that "specimens of value" should not be submitted. Therefore, for example, a *photograph* of jewelry using a trademark, not a piece of jewelry, should be submitted.

If the mark appears on the goods or containers for the goods on a label, then the label will usually be an acceptable specimen (§905.04(a)). A catalog will provide an acceptable specimen of a display associated with the goods, if it meets these requirements:

- It includes a picture of the goods.

- The mark is close enough to the picture of the goods in the catalog to create an association between the two.

- The catalog includes all the information needed to order the goods (*TMEP* §705.06(a)).

TIPS & TECHNIQUES

Ads Aren't Specimens

Oddly enough, the TMEP says that advertisements are generally *not* acceptable specimens: §905.05.

Registration Problems: Prevention and Cure

The best way to solve problems with trademark registration is to learn enough about trademark law and PTO practice to make sure that problems do not arise! However, this is not always possible—especially because a particular Examining Attorney might take an unduly narrow view of what is, in fact, an acceptable application.

It has never been considered acceptable to hoard a lot of trademarks just so they can be available in case they are wanted in the future. (In fact, this disapproval is one reason why Congress passed a law against *cybersquatting*—see page 94.) Certain activities make the PTO suspicious about whether the registrant has the appropriate reasons for filing an Intent to Use (ITU) application:

- Multiple ITU applications are filed for the same mark (or for a grossly excessive number of different marks), covering far more new products than the PTO believes the applicant might actually intend to manufacture and sell.

- Multiple ITU applications are filed for a variety of marks that might be used on a single new product.

- Multiple ITU applications are filed containing elements that might be considered descriptive of an important characteristic of a new product.

- The applicant makes multiple refilings to replace past applications that lapsed because proof of use was not provided on a timely basis.

- The description of the goods given in the application is so vague that the examiner cannot determine precisely what the applicant intends to do if the mark is eventually granted.

Lanham Act §2(d), which forbids registration of a mark that is confusingly similar to an existing registered mark, is the most common reason that the PTO gives for denials. The application will certainly be denied if the PTO position is that the application covers a mark that is too similar to an already registered mark.

If the similarity is to another mark for which an earlier application was filed (but that application is not yet final), the applicant will be notified that if the earlier application results in a registration, that registration may be used as a bar to registration under this application.

The description of goods and services with which the mark will be used should be given in ordinary, not technical, language, and reflect the point of view of the end user—not the manufacturer or dealer. The description should use definite terms ("consisting of three green triangles in a horizontal line") not indefinite and possibly ambiguous words such as *including*.

The preliminary steps in preparing a one-class application include making sure that all the goods or services claimed fall into that class! The description of goods and services in a multiclass application should be broken down into the separate classes, starting with the lowest-numbered and moving upward.

TIPS & TECHNIQUES

Finding Good Descriptions

At this stage, it can be helpful to reread the trademark search report, this time looking for good examples of descriptive language from applications that have already been successful.

TIPS & TECHNIQUES

Avoiding Confusion

Watch out for terms like *accessories* or *equipment* or *parts* that could fall within several classes and therefore could confuse the Attorney Examiner about which class(es) the applicant wants to register.

The PTO rules allow applications to be amended to clarify or limit—but *not* to broaden—the identification of goods and services. An indefinite specification can also be amended to make it definite.

In most cases, the application can be amended to cope with the questions raised by the Examining Attorney. These are some of the most common problem areas:

- The Examining Attorney thinks that registration has been requested in the wrong class.

- He or she thinks the description of the mark is inaccurate.

- The drawings fail to correspond to the description of the mark.

- The application is incomplete.

- The application is not accompanied by payment of the necessary fees—or the amount submitted is wrong.

- The application has not been verified, or the verification is defective in some way.

In addition to problems with the trademark itself, or technical problems that might arise because of the way the application is drafted, the specimens submitted with the application can create problems that delay the processing of the application.

The Examining Attorney looks at specimens to see if

- The desired trademark can be registered at all.

- The applicant is actually using the mark in commerce.
- Other parties are also using the mark.
- The drawing is an accurate representation of the mark as it is actually used.
- The Examining Attorney thinks that the mark whose registration is requested does not correspond with the way the mark is used in the specimens.
- The application involves multiple classes, and not enough specimens have been submitted to show the full range of uses.
- The specimens seem to show ownership of the mark by someone else.

With this in mind, drawings and specimens can be tailored to the PTO requirements.

Characteristics of Registered Trademarks

Patents have a definite and fairly short term. Copyrights usually last for the lifetime of the author plus 70 years—a fairly long term, but one that will eventually come to an end. Trademarks, however, can last indefinitely.

When a trademark is federally registered, its initial term is 10 years. (It was twice as long before the 1988 amendments reduced the term.) The registration automatically expires six years after the registration

IN THE REAL WORLD

Be Thorough

Usually, the best strategy is to give the attorney handling the trademark application examples of all the ways in which the mark is used. A knowledgeable intellectual property attorney should be able to choose the best examples for a smooth application.

date—unless the registrant files an affidavit of continued use to rebut the potential for considering the trademark abandoned. At the end of the 10-year term, the registrant can apply for an additional 10-year term, and there is no limit to the number of extensions that can be obtained—hence the potential for indefinite duration.

The federal system includes two categories: strong trademarks that get the highest degree of protection, on the Principal Register, and weaker trademarks that get less protection on the Secondary Register.

Registering a trademark on the Principal Register offers many advantages. It notifies everyone (and makes them legally responsible for knowing) that the trademark is claimed by the person who registered it. It is strong legal evidence not only of the ownership of the trademark but that the trademark is valid. Trademarks on the Principal Register can be recorded with the U.S. Customs Service, whose duties include seizing merchandise at the borders if the merchandise is counterfeit or infringes on trademarks.

Last but not least, after five years on the Principal Register, a trademark becomes *incontestable*. That is, in most circumstances, the validity of the trademark cannot be challenged by anyone.

Intent-to-Use Applications

When the Lanham Act was first passed, registration was only permitted for existing trademarks that were already familiar to consumers because they had been used in commerce. Current law, however, allows trade-

IN THE REAL WORLD

Contacting Customs

The U.S. Customs Service toll-free number for trademark owners is (800)-ITS-FAKE.

mark applications based on intent to use. Once the registration has been approved, the trademark has not been opposed, and a Notice of Allowance has been issued, the applicant must file a statement of use with information supporting its good-faith intent to use the trademark within six months.

Intent-to-use applicants are required to follow up by "perfecting" the application with proof that the mark has been used commercially. This can be done in two ways:

- Filing an amendment to the application indicating that commercial use has commenced

- Filing a statement of use with examples of the use plus a $100 fee

The federal trademark regulations (see 37 CFR §2.89) provide the basic rule that the applicant will be required to start using the trademark within six months of filing the intent-to-use application. However, one six-month extension is automatically available even without showing a reason for the delay, and up to four more six-month extensions are available if good cause is shown. A $100 user fee is imposed for each extension of the time for use.

The basic rule is that a trademark can't be assigned before use has been shown (see *TMEP* §501.01(a)). The assignment of a trademark has to go along with the goodwill of a product. Trademark law disapproves of *trafficking,* which is defined as filing a trademark application without bona fide intent to use the mark commercially, for the sole purpose of selling or otherwise transferring the application and rights in the mark to someone else.

Concurrent Use

Although the basic rule is that registered trademarks not only must be unique but also must not be similar enough to other trademarks to cause confusion, 15 USC §1052(d) allows *concurrent use,* which means the use of the same trademark in different contexts.

To prevent confusion, the concurrent uses must be quite distinct, and limitations must be imposed to keep them apart. For example, the trademark can be used on goods that are so different (e.g., bicycles and cookies) that consumers would be able to differentiate.

Concurrent use might also be allowable if the trademarks are limited to local use in distinct geographic areas. However, given the prominence of mail, phone, and Internet orders for goods, it can be difficult to assert that the use of a trademark is purely local.

There are two ways that concurrent use can be approved. Either the PTO issues a registration permitting concurrent use, in order to comply with a court order, or a company that wants to share a trademark files a request for a "concurrent use proceeding" to be held by the Trademark Trial and Appeal Board (TTAB).

The trademark must appear on the Principal, not the Supplemental, Register. In the application, the applicant must state, as far as the information is available:

- The extent of the concurrent use by other parties

- What applications have already been made, and what registrations have already been received, relating to the concurrent use

- The various types of goods involved in concurrent use

- The geographic area, types of goods, and way in which the mark will be used if the applicant's concurrent use application is granted.

Categories for Indentifying Trademarks

From 1973 to January 1, 2002, the PTO used the 42 categories under the Nice Arrangement for the International Classification of Goods and Services for identifying trademarks in applications and registrations.

The categories were drafted by the Committee of Experts of the Nice Union and are published by the World Intellectual Property Organization (WIPO).

As of January 1, 2002, WIPO changed the system slightly, breaking down Class 42 into four new classes (42–45) because the old Class 42 was much too large and diverse. The PTO's announcement of the new classes appeared in the *Federal Register* for September 20, 2001. The categories are listed in Exhibit 3.2. The notes about what is included and excluded in certain classes come from the FAQ on the PTO Web site.

EXHIBIT 3.2

International Classification of Goods and Services

Goods

1. chemical products used in industry (includes compost; excludes chemicals used medically and pesticides)

2. paints, varnishes, lacquers (includes dyes for clothing; excludes cosmetic dyes)

3. cosmetics and bleaching preparations (includes deodorants for personal use; excludes other deodorants)

4. industrial oils and greases

5. pharmaceuticals

6. metals and alloys

7. machines and machine tools (excludes hand tools, which are in class 8)

8. hand tools (includes "cutlery of precious metals"; excludes surgical knives)

9. electrical and scientific instruments (includes electric tools but excludes certain motorized kitchen tools, clocks and watches, and electric razors and toothbrushes)

EXHIBIT 3.2 (CONTINUED)

10. medical and surgical instruments

11. heating, lighting, etc. equipment

12. vehicles (excludes motors, engines, and motor and engine parts)

13. firearms

14. precious metals and jewelry (excludes valuable art objects that are not made of precious metals)

15. musical instruments (excludes sound recording and play-back devices)

16. paper and printed matter

17. rubber and plastics

18. leather goods (excludes clothing, footwear, and headgear)

19. building materials

20. furniture

21. household utensils (includes kitchen utensils, pots and pans, and electric toothbrushes; excludes electric cooking utensils)

22. rope and fibers

23. yarn and thread

24. fabric (excludes special textiles listed in the PTO's publication *Alphabetical List of Goods* and electric blankets)

25. clothing and shoes

26. lace and embroidery

27. carpet and wall hangings

28. toys and sporting goods (includes fishing tackle; excludes fishnets and playing cards)

29. food

30. coffee, tea, bread, and cake

31. live animals, plants, and agricultural products

EXHIBIT 3.2 (CONTINUED)

32. beer and soft drinks (excludes beverages that are predominantly made up of milk, or that have a coffee, cocoa, or chocolate base)

33. wine and liquor

34. tobacco

Services

35. advertising and business

36. insurance and financial

37. construction and repair

38. communications

39. transportation and storage

40. material treatment

41. education and entertainment

42. scientific and technological services, including research and development; computer hardware and software design and development; legal services (but excludes business research; word-processing services; installing or repairing computer hardware)

43. providing food, drink, and lodging (excludes discotheques, boarding schools, and rest homes)

44. medical and veterinary services; agriculture; hygiene and beauty care services (excludes health clubs, boarding for animals, and retirement homes—a somewhat tactless juxtaposition)

45. personal and social services, including security services (excludes financial services, insurance, and legal services)

Disclaimers

Sometimes the trademark that a party wants to register contains certain elements that are common to many trademarks; that are generic; or that are otherwise not entitled to protection or are only entitled to limited protection. As long as the trademark as a whole is registrable, the potential problems can be solved by *disclaimers*.

That is, the registrant voluntarily concedes that some parts of the desired trademark cannot be protected, or are descriptive terms that are used by the whole industry and are not unique or special to the registrant. Another option is that the Examining Attorney may require the disclaimer.

For example, if the intended mark is KITTYUM CAT FOOD, the registrant could make a claim for the whole mark, while disclaiming having any special rights in the words *cat* or *food,* or the combination *cat food*.

As if this concept weren't complicated enough, *unitary* marks can be registered without disclaiming the generic material that they contain. A unitary mark creates just one, single commercial impression— people who see it do not separate it out into its various elements.

Some of the factors in deciding whether a mark is unitary:

- Whether the design features of the mark (such as lines) make a physical connection between the elements

- If the generic elements are side by side, or on the same line as the mark, or if they are placed somewhere else on the specimen

- How the elements relate together and to the goods.

Nonfederal Registration

In addition to federal registration on the Principal or Supplemental Register, businesses may register trademarks in two other settings: with a state, with a country outside the United States, or both.

Registration Under the MSTB

The procedure for registering a trademark under the Model State Trademark Bill (MSTB) is quite similar to the federal process.

The MSTB procedure is to file with the Secretary of State for the state (or agency designated by the Secretary). The application must be signed and verified by the applicant (if he or she is an individual) or by a partner or a corporate officer (for an application by a business). The application process calls for the following information:

- The applicant's name and business address

- (For a partnership) State in which the partnership is organized; names of its general partners

- (For a corporation) State where it was incorporated

- What goods or services the mark is used with; how it is used; the trademark class of the goods with which it is used

- The first date the mark was used; and, if it is different, the first date the applicant (or whoever transferred the mark to the applicant) first used the mark in the state where registration is sought

- Statement that the applicant owns and uses the mark

- Statement that the applicant is not aware of anyone else registering the mark (in the state or federally) or has rights to use either the same mark or a slightly different mark that is similar enough to create confusion, mistake, or deception.

Three specimens of the mark in use must be submitted with the MSTB trademark application. The application has to be signed and sworn to by the applicant or a partner or corporate officer.

In addition to these items required by the MSTB, the MSTB gives state Secretaries of State the power to demand statements about the status of any attempts to register the mark federally, and to require submission of a drawing of the mark. The MSTB gives Secretaries of State the option to require examination of trademark applications.

In case of concurrent processing of applications for the same mark or a confusingly similar mark for the same goods or services, or related goods or services, the first application to be filed is entitled to priority. This implies, of course, that if the marks are used on entirely unrelated goods or services, then the mark can be used by both applicants.

If the examiner intends to deny registration, the applicant is notified and can reply or amend the application in light of these expressed concerns, or can abandon the application.

Naturally, most applications will be accepted, and a registration certificate will be issued.

Trademark Registration in Other Countries

To an ever-increasing extent, business is being done globally, not just locally or even nationally—a trend that is only being accelerated by the option of instant communication via the Internet. It is possible that merchandise imported into the United States will carry trademarks from outside the United States—and exporters must consider the pros and cons of registering their trademarks outside the United State to provide protection when that merchandise is sold in other countries.

However, there is no question that trademark practice outside the United State involves learning new techniques, entering into alliances with new parties (such as trademark search firms and trademark counsel in other countries), and undertaking additional costs.

A 1998 survey published by the INTA shows that, in that year, the average cost of doing a trademark clearance search within the United State was $650, whereas the cost of a non-U.S. search averaged $1,200 per trademark per country, plus fees for search firms and attorneys in either case.

IN THE REAL WORLD

Should a Business Register Its Trademark outside the United States?

Some of the pros and cons a business should consider in deciding whether to seek registration of marks outside the United States:

- What is the value of the particular trademark or trade dress to the company (secondary brands don't always justify the trouble and expense)?

- Where will the goods or services will be advertised and sold? Advertisements printed or broadcast in U.S. media often reach Canada and Mexico, and may reach other countries as well. The Internet reaches the world.

- How likely is it that the product using the market will be counterfeited in countries outside the United States? Legal remedies in the country of manufacture may be contingent on having a local trademark registration.

- Does the product have a broad consumer market? If the product is sold only to professionals, they are likely to be more sophisticated and less likely to be deceived by trademark counterfeiting or dilution, so less effort outside the United States may be required to protect the genuine product.

- What is the extent of actual or potential competition? For instance, a producer of fruit juice might want to register its trademarks in fruit-growing countries.

In most of the countries of the world, trademark rights are almost completely dependent on registration (common-law trademarks are not recognized). Marks can be registered without proof of use—but probably can be canceled if the owner fails to use and continue using the trademark.

The European Union maintains a program for filing a single application in order to secure a Community Trademark (CTM), covering all 15 countries within the European Union. The application is filed at the Office for Harmonization in the Internal Market (OHIM), which is located in Alicante, Spain. A single enforcement action can be filed for the entire Community as well. However, care must be taken, because a CTM might be granted that infringes a valid prior registration in one of the countries within the European Union.

No single registrations system covers trademarks both inside and outside the European Union, although treaties such as the Madrid Protocol do provide some uniformity. Under the Madrid Protocol, an applicant for a trademark in one country can designate other countries in which the same application will be deemed to have been filed. So far, the United States has not joined the Madrid Protocol, although bills have been introduced in Congress to do this. Meanwhile, another treaty, called the Paris Convention, allows U.S. federal trademark registration to serve as the basis for registration in other countries.

Most countries take the position that, except for "famous" trademarks (i.e., trademarks that are famous in that country, whether or not they are famous in the United States) trademark rights are enforceable only for the class or classes in which the trademark has been registered. Therefore, the cost of registering a trademark in such countries will be multiplied by the number of classes in which it is sensible to seek protection.

Furthermore, many merchandising programs will involve multiple trademarks. For instance, licensed merchandise using the name of a

Relevant Web Sites

For trademark databases created in other countries, see

- www.patent.gov.uk (United Kingdom)
- www.dpma.de (Germany)
- www.aipo.gov/au/atmoss/falcon.frame (Australia)
- www.strategis.ic.gc.ca/cgi-bin/trademarks/search_e.pl (Canada)
- wwww.marksonline.com

television show might also cover the names and images of several characters from the show. Registering to preserve rights in the show, plus five characters, in all 29 of the classes most relevant to merchandising can be an expensive business!

In the United States and Canada, the items for which registration is sought not only have to be assigned to a class, they have to be described in detail within the class. In contrast, however, most countries allow a registration that simply says "All goods in Class...."

Choosing the wording for the description is a very important tactical decision. On the one hand, registrants often choose to describe the goods being registered in the broadest terms possible: *shirts* or even *clothing items* instead of narrowing down the category to *T-shirts* or *sweatshirts.*

On the other hand, if the registrant believes that the trademark can be registered, but there is some potential overlap that could lead to conflicts, the registrant might wish to narrow down the registration and limit its trademark claim to particular types of goods, trade channels, or classes of purchasers so that it can argue that there is no real risk of confusion because the mark is only used in a limited way.

Anticybersquatting Consumer Protection Act (ACPA)

Perhaps under the influence of traditional trademark concepts (that trafficking in unused trademarks is bad; that trademarks can only be assigned in connection with established goodwill), Congress took action in 1999 by passing the ACPA (Public Law 106-113, starting at 15 U.S. Code §1125(d)).

The ACPA only covers wrongful behavior; it doesn't offer any remedies for a situation where two companies acting in good faith dispute who should be allowed to use a particular name, or whether a legitimate business name is confusingly similar to another legitimate business name.

However, if two companies are legitimately making concurrent use of a trademark (if they are allowed to use the same trademark because the goods are different, or geographic territories don't overlap), they can probably make an arrangement where one sells the other the right to use the trademark as a domain name. This is not cybersquatting, because they both have legitimate rights in the name.

Cybersquatting is a lot like the securities law concept of *greenmail.* A greenmailer buys up a lot of a company's stock, not as part of an effort to acquire the company whose stock it is, but in the hope that the company will pay a high price to buy back the stock and get the greenmailer to go away.

Cybersquatters reserve a lot of URLs that are the same as someone else's trademarks, or that are easily confused with existing trademarks, either to exploit that confusion commercially or to get the trademark holder to pay off the cybersquatter for the domain name. The difference is that it costs millions of dollars to buy huge blocks of corporate stock, but only a few dollars to reserve a domain name!

There are three major elements in proving a case under the ACPA:

- Registering a domain name that is identical to, or confusingly similar to, a "distinctive" mark.

OR

- Registering a domain name that is identical, confusingly similar to, or dilutes a "famous" mark (the plaintiff can also claim both infringement and dilution if the mark is "famous").
- The registrant registered the domain name in bad faith, and intended to profit from it.

To win an ACPA case, the plaintiff only has to prove that the domain name was registered, not that it was ever used commercially, or even that a site was put up using that domain name. Just registering a domain name and not using it is not considered "use in commerce"—but intending to earn profits (e.g., from selling the name back to the trademark holder) *is* use in commerce.

However, the plaintiff does have to prove that the mark in question was not just distinctive, but was actually in use as a trademark when the domain name was registered. Only the registrant of the domain name or its authorized licensees can be liable under the ACPA. People who link to the site are not liable.

The ACPA lists the factors to be considered in determining whether the domain name was improperly registered:

- Does the registrant have trademark or other intellectual property rights in the name? In a famous case, for example, both DELTA airlines and DELTA faucets, both legitimate commercial enterprises, wanted to use delta.com for their Web site.
- Is the domain name the registrant's own name or nickname?
- Has the registrant used the domain name in good faith, to do business? (If so, the registrant is probably a legitimate business, not a cybersquatter.)
- Outside the commercial realm, did the registrant engage in fair use (commenting on current events or reviewing products, for example) or engage in good-faith noncommercial use?

- Was there intent to lure Web users to a site that could harm the goodwill of the mark?

- Did the registrant attempt to exact money from the trademark owner to use its own trademark as a domain name—or was there an attempt or threat to sell the domain name to a competitor of the trademark holder?

- When the registrant got the domain name, did it give the registrar false or misleading contact information, to make it harder to track the registrant down?

- Has the registrant made a practice of hoarding domain names?

- To what extent is the plaintiff's mark distinctive and/or famous?

In our legal system, nearly all lawsuits are filed against either one or more people or against an organization such as a partnership, corporation, or not-for-profit organization. These are called *in personam* suits—a Latin term that means that a person (natural or legal—corporations have the status of *artificial persons*) is involved.

In rare cases, however, an *in rem* action (against a thing rather than a person) can be brought. This is true under the ACPA if it is impossible to find the defendant (which often happens when cybersquatters give false contact information during the registration process), or if there is no court where the defendant can be served with a summons and complaint and then sued.

TIPS & TECHNIQUES

Contact Information

A database of domain name holders that can be searched for contact information about alleged cybersquatters can be found at http://www.networksolutions.com/cgi-bin/whois/whois.

In cases where the defendant cannot be located, or cannot be sued in federal court, the *in rem* action proceeds against the domain name itself, not against a person or corporation. If the plaintiff wins, it is entitled to seize the domain name.

The successful plaintiff in an ACPA case can get an injunction and/or actual damages and costs. The court can order *disgorgement:* that is, the defendant can be forced to surrender profits that it got through improper means. If the judge thinks it is appropriate, damages of $1,000 to $100,000 per infringing domain name (plus attorneys' fees) can be ordered. These damages are not linked to the actual damages that the plaintiff suffered because of the improper registration. However, if the domain name was registered before the November 29, 1999, effective date of the ACPA, the only available remedy is an injunction against further use of the domain name by the cybersquatter.

For First Amendment reasons, the ACPA probably doesn't apply to situations in which a person sets up a Web site to criticize the company, using a variant of the company name as a domain name. A classic example is the www.ballysucks.com domain name that was protected against a challenge from the Bally Corporation.

 IN THE REAL WORLD

Protecting Your Good Name by Owning the Bad Ones

Many companies now register domain names such as "ihate-blurch.com" or "blurchsucks.com" at the same time they register "blurch.com." That prevents these names from being used to criticize the company.

CHAPTER 4

Handling Trademark Disputes

After reading this chapter you will be able to

- Structure ads and other communications to protect, not weaken, the trademark
- File opposition and cancellation proceedings before the TTAB
- Bring infringement suits, or defend against charges of infringement
- Get remedies against counterfeiters
- Go to domain name arbitration

Protecting the Trademark

The process of maintaining a trademark and keeping it safe from infringers not only requires detecting infringement after it happens, it also requires a program of defending the trademark. Above all, the trademark's owner has to make sure that its own actions do not result in abandonment of the trademark or to the conclusion that the trademark has become merely the generic name for a type of product.

Trademark defense requires attention to the way the trademark is used and described on products and in advertising. The ™ symbol should be used with all unregistered trademarks, and the ® symbol on all registered trademarks. That puts everyone on notice that a trademark has

99

been asserted. Typography for trademarks should make them stand out, whether they are larger than other words, capitalized, in italics, or in a special type face.

If that would be too distracting in a long piece of copy, one possibility is to put an asterisk after each use, directing viewers to a note at the bottom of the advertisement, saying something like "WODJIT is a trademark of the Glutz Group."

To avoid any suggestion that the trademark is generic, the trademark should not be used by itself. It's better to use it with "brand" or a generic noun (WODJIT carburetor ruffles or WODJIT brand carburetor ruffles, instead of "Use a handy WODJIT to make your carburetor look really nifty.") Trademarks shouldn't be used as verbs, either ("Proud car owners WODJIT every week!") and they shouldn't be pluralized.

If the trademark is licensed (i.e., if other manufacturers are allowed to make and distribute goods that carry the trademark), the trademark holder must be sure that the licensees respect and protect the trademark. It is also crucial to make sure that they maintain the standards of quality set out in the licensing agreement, because poor quality weakens the trademark.

Inter Partes Proceedings Before the TTAB

In most situations, if two businesses have a dispute, one of them files a complaint with the appropriate state or federal court. (Sometimes one files a complaint, and the other files a counterclaim—for instance, Company A sues Company B for not paying for a machine it bought from Company A. Company B counterclaims that not only doesn't it have to pay for the machine, Company A should pay Company B for selling it a defective machine that ruined thousands of dollars' worth of merchandise.)

However, because of the special nature of intellectual property, and the special role that the federal government plays in managing and enforcing trademark rights, two very important kinds of disputes between companies are *not* decided by ordinary lawsuits. These disputes give rise to what are called *inter partes* proceedings, which are held by the Trademark Trial and Appeal Board (TTAB) rather than by regular courts. (*Inter partes* means between commercial parties—i.e., not a proceeding started by an enforcement agency.)

The proceedings are *Opposition* and *Cancellation* proceedings. The two types are quite similar, but an Opposition proceeding's objective is to prevent a trademark from being registered, whereas a Cancellation seeks to remove a trademark from the register. (*Concurrent use* proceedings, seeking the right to use the same trademark in different geographic areas or on different goods, are also heard by the TTAB instead of the courts.)

Both Oppositions and Cancellations are started when a party files a petition with the TTAB asking for relief. Both of them are supposed to contain "short, plain statements" of the facts supporting the petition: why registering the mark or allowing the registration to remain valid will harm the petitioner.

The grounds for opposing or canceling a mark include the following:

- It contains immoral, deceptive, or scandalous matter.
- It contains a government insignia that the registrant has no right to use.
- It uses the name or image of a living person without that person's consent.
- The mark is likely to cause confusion with other marks.
- The mark is purely descriptive or misdescriptive (geographically or otherwise).
- The mark is generic.
- The mark has been abandoned by its registrant, who no longer uses it in commerce.
- The registration was obtained by fraud.
- The mark dilutes the value of other marks.

- A contract or court order prohibits the registrant from using the mark.

When such allegations are made, the respondent (the one who wants to register the mark that is opposed, or who holds the trademark that the other party wants to cancel) is entitled to use various defenses:

- The other party has been neglectful about pursuing its claims, and has left them for so long that the claims should be dismissed. In legal terms, this is called *laches.*

- The same legal and factual issues have already been decided in another TTAB proceeding or court case, so this proceeding is not serving any useful purpose.

- The complainant doesn't have standing (legal authority) to bring the proceeding.

- The trademark has been registered for more than five years, so it is incontestable—and none of the exceptions to incontestability applies.

- The complainant has an improper motive (such as ruining the respondent's business) for bringing the proceeding.

- The allegations in the petition are not true.

- The petitioner's evidence is technically defective, so the TTAB should not consider it.

Trademark Infringement

A company that believes its trademarks are being infringed by confusingly similar marks can bring suit against the infringer—and can also bring suit for *contributory infringement* against anyone who makes it easier for infringement to occur (such as a flea market that allows the sale of goods that it knows to be counterfeit).

As discussed further on page 138, the standard analysis in an infringement case compares the plaintiff's and defendant's marks based on their sound, meaning, and appearance. The relative importance of the three factors depends on, for example, whether consumers typically see the product on a shelf, hear a radio ad, or otherwise come into contact with the merchandise and its trademarks.

If the trademark is not registered at all, or is only registered with a state, then probably the case belongs in state court. For a federally registered trademark (whether it's registered on the Principal or Supplemental Register), suit will usually be brought in federal court. The general rule is that the suit should be brought in the district where the alleged infringer is incorporated, licensed, or does business, or else in the district where the infringement occurred.

The federal court system is divided into Districts, with between one and four District Courts in each state. Appeals from District Courts go to the Circuit Courts of Appeals; there are eleven geographically divided circuits covering the states, with a District of Columbia Circuit covering the District of Columbia as a geographic area, and a Federal Circuit that hears special types of federal cases such as patent cases.

An injunction—a court order forbidding something, or directing that something be done—is the most common remedy in trademark cases. An injunction can be granted to prevent infringement that hasn't occurred yet, but is threatened, or to prevent an infringer from resuming its past course of conduct. The injunction can require the defendant to place "corrective ads" apologizing for misleading consumers and setting the record straight.

A Temporary Restraining Order (TRO) is a very short-term injunction that can be granted at the beginning of a case to preserve the status quo. A preliminary injunction can be granted after a case has been brought, but there hasn't been time yet to have a full trial. A permanent injunction is issued after the trial, if the facts justify it.

The importance of injunctions is that they are court orders. Therefore, if the defendant fails to live up to the terms of the injunction, it is in contempt of court, and can be punished by fines—possibly even by prison sentences for the person(s) considered responsible for the contempt.

There are two kinds of fines imposed for contempt of court. The first one is supposed to make sure that compliance will occur in the future. The fine is paid to the court, and the amount is supposed to balance the *risk* of future harm if the injunction is not obeyed against the *likelihood* that the fine will make the defendant behave. The second type of fine, which is paid to the plaintiff, punishes contempt that occurred in the past. The size of the fine is supposed to represent whatever money the plaintiff lost as a result of the defendant's past contempt, or the profits the defendant earned by its contemptuous conduct.

Attorney's fee awards are allowed in trademark cases, but only in exceptional circumstances, such as intentional infringement or when a plaintiff brings a groundless case or brings the case with the intention of stifling competition—or when either side acts unreasonably in connection with the litigation.

Trade Dress Infringement

The whole appearance and image of a product and its packaging is known as its *trade dress*. (See Chapter 5 for more discussion). Infringing on someone else's trade dress is a form of unfair competition, and is also recognized as a separate tort.

The usual remedy for trade dress infringement, like the remedy for trademark infringement, is an injunction against further misappropriation and exploitation of the trade dress. (Some examples of trade dress are registered as trademarks, so ordinary trademark remedies would apply.) However, if the defendant makes a believable claim that it will change its trade dress immediately to avoid confusion, the court may decide that an injunction is not necessary. Attorney's fee awards are available, but only in exceptional circumstances.

In many instances, the trade dress infringement plaintiff has both state claims of unfair competition and federal Lanham Act claims. A legal concept called *supplemental jurisdiction* allows federal courts to hear the state-law claims as long as they are combined with a substantial related claim under the Lanham Act or another federal intellectual property statute such as the copyright or patent laws.

Remedies Against Counterfeiting

A distinction has to be made between trademark infringement and counterfeiting. An infringing trademark is confusingly similar to a trademark that was registered earlier. However, infringing trademarks can be adopted by legitimate manufacturers and used on their own merchandise, sometimes in good faith.

A counterfeit trademark, however, has no purpose other than confusing customers and making them believe that the manufacturer's own (probably inferior) merchandise was manufactured by another company. Therefore, much more dramatic legal remedies are available against counterfeit merchandise than against simple trademark infringement.

TIPS & TECHNIQUES

Liability Insurance

The section of standard business liability insurance policies that covers advertising injury often excludes trademark infringement (i.e., the policy doesn't cover the business when it is charged with infringing someone else's trademark in its advertisements). But charges of trade *dress* infringement are probably covered under the policy.

The law is drafted to define a counterfeit as an imitation that is identical or substantially indistinguishable from the original. (The provision about substantial identity was added to prevent counterfeiters from getting off the hook by making undetectably tiny changes in the false trademark.)

Under Lanham Act §34(d)(1)(A) as amended by the Anticounterfeiting Consumer Protection Act of 1996 (Public Law 104-153), federal courts have the power to order seizure of counterfeit trademarks, the goods that carry the counterfeit mark, means of making the mark, and records documenting the use of a counterfeit mark. (The defendant's assets can also be frozen until the trial is over.) But in order to get these drastic remedies, the applicant has to prove the following:

- No other adequate remedy exists to protect the applicant's legitimate interests in the trademark that was counterfeited—that is, if the defendant is likely to obey an ordinary court order to maintain the status quo, then seizure will be denied.

- The allegedly counterfeit items can be found at the location given in the application for seizure.

- The applicant hasn't publicized its request to the court that a seizure be made.

- The applicant will probably be able to prove its case against the defendant once the case comes to trial.

- There is a real risk that the defendant will hide or destroy counterfeit merchandise, making it harder or impossible for the plaintiff to prove its case.

- The plaintiff's business will suffer immediate and irreparable injury if the seizure order is not granted.

- The plaintiff will be harmed more by denial of the seizure request than the defendant will be harmed by the seizure. If the plaintiff wins the case, the court might make the defendant recall the infringing goods from buyers, or at least notify customers that they purchased counterfeit goods. More drastically, the court could order that the infringing goods be destroyed.

Once the U.S. Customs Service is notified by a trademark holder that counterfeit goods are being brought into the United States, it will seize any counterfeit merchandise that it detects. However, if Customs finds merchandise that has a trademark that is confusingly similar to a U.S. trademark, but is not counterfeit, the merchandise can legally be imported into the United States as long as the trademark is removed.

In 1984, the Trademark Counterfeiting Act amended the Lanham Act to allow penalties of three times the plaintiff's loss, or three times the defendant's profits (whichever is larger) for intentional trafficking in merchandise known to be counterfeit. However, if there are extenuating circumstances, the court can reduce the award (for instance, if the defendant is a small-scale operator who used the money to support a family).

The Anticounterfeiting Consumer Protection Act of 1995 added another option, called *statutory damages*. At any time up until the case is finally resolved, the plaintiff can choose to get damages as set out by the statute (instead of having to prove the actual amount of damages it suffered). The statutory damages can be as high as $100,000 per coun-

TIPS & TECHNIQUES

Fee Awards

Reasonable attorneys' fees are mandatory in a §32(1)(a) case if the defendant knew it was dealing in counterfeit goods. Furthermore, a reasonable fee for the plaintiff's investigator, acting under the supervision of an attorney, can be included in the attorney's fee award.

terfeit mark or type of goods or services offered, distributed, or sold by the defendant.

Attorneys' fee awards are always made in counterfeiting cases where the defendant intentionally dealt in fake merchandise.

Trademark Defenses

An old joke says that one ancient Greek was angry at another one for returning a borrowed vase with a crack in it. The accused sputtered out, in quick succession, that he didn't borrow the vase, it was cracked when the other guy lent it to him, and it was perfectly OK when he gave it back.

That sums up the basic approach to legal defenses against claims of trademark infringement. A company that is accused of trademark infringement can defend itself by showing that its conduct had legal justification; that trademarks that are alleged to be confusingly similar actually could not cause confusion; that the plaintiff didn't have a valid trademark in the first place; that the plaintiff forfeited trademark rights through carelessness or misconduct; or that there are technical defects in the plaintiff's legal case that prevent the court from providing relief.

There are several possible legal defenses in trademark cases:

- *Fair use,* as defined by Lanham Act §33(b)(4) to mean good-faith use of a trademark in a purely descriptive, nontrademark sense: calling a light jacket with many pockets a safari jacket, for instance, even if someone has registered SAFARI as a trademark for clothing.

- *Abandonment*—The holder of the trademark has abandoned it (failure to use the trademark that extends over a significant amount of time, in conjunction with intent not to resume use of the trademark in the future).

- *Naked licensing*—The licensees have been allowed to use the trademark without policing their quality performance.

- *Laches*—There is no statute of limitations in federal law for trademark infringement. That is, there is no specific date on which a claim will be considered too old and stale to pursue. However, if a plaintiff knew or should have known that infringement occurred, excess delay (known as *laches*) in doing something about it can mean that damages will not be available, although the plaintiff still might be able to get an injunction. (Time that the plaintiff is involved in good-faith negotiations aimed at eliminating infringement is not considered a delay.)

- *Unclean hands*—Plaintiffs who have been guilty of false advertising, improprieties in the trademark application, antitrust violations, or other wrongdoing might be denied relief from the courts because of their own improper activities.

- *Fraud by the party that obtained the trademark*—This is grounds for a cancellation proceeding before the TTAB, and can also be raised as a defense in an infringement case. In fact, under 15 U.S. Code §1120, someone who is harmed by a fraudulent trademark registration can sue in federal court and get damages from the registrant.

Because of First Amendment considerations, parodies are entitled to a strong defense in copyright infringement cases. Trademarks, however, have less to do with expressing ideas and more to do with commercial communications. So calling something a parody is not a complete defense in a trademark infringement case. It's just one factor to be considered in determining whether consumers are likely to be confused. But if they are aware that something is a parody, they will not be confused about its source, and won't think that the parodist is claiming affiliation with the original manufacturer.

How Big a Problem Are Parodies?

In 1998, the District Court for the Central District of California ruled that a song making fun of Barbie dolls was a noncommercial fair use of the BARBIE trademark. The records were sold, and not given away, but the intention was to parody a cultural phenomenon, not to make money by selling competing fashion dolls and doll clothing.

In another case, the court refused to make the company that sold "Dom Popignon" popcorn in a champagne bottle pay Dom Perignon's attorneys' fees. The court's rationale was that although the popcorn copied the appearance of the vintage champagne bottle, it was supposed to be an amusing parody, not a serious attempt to suggest that the vineyard also sold popcorn. Attorneys' fees are awarded only in "exceptional" cases, and here the bottle design that was copied was at least arguably functional and therefore perhaps not protectable. Furthermore, the defendant was a small company that had not made many sales; it had not engaged in large-scale profiteering.

Remedies Under the UDTPA

Under the Uniform Deceptive Trade Practices Act (UDTPA; see Chapter 7) an injunction can be granted to any person or corporation likely to be damaged by a deceptive trade practice. It isn't necessary to prove monetary damages or losses already incurred to get an injunction. The plaintiff doesn't have to prove that the defendant's conduct was willful. However, relief under the UDTPA for copying trademarks or trade dress is limited to preventing confusion or mistake as to the real source of the goods.

In a UDTPA case, court costs will be awarded to whichever side wins, unless the court directs otherwise. The court also has discretion to make the losing side pay the winner's attorneys' fees—a losing defendant might have to pay attorneys' fees if it willfully engaged in practices that it knew were deceptive. If the defendant wins, the plaintiff might have to pay the defendant's attorneys' fees if the plaintiff brought a suit that it knew was not legally justified.

UDRP: ICANN'S Domain Name Resolution Policy

In the early days of the Internet, ICANN, the Internet Corporation for Assigned Names and Numbers, was the only body anywhere in the world that was allowed to assign URLs. Today, registration of domain names has been opened up to competition, and there are dozens of domain name registrars, but ICANN is still a kind of respected elder statesman in the Web world.

ICANN has developed a Uniform Domain Name Dispute Resolution Policy, or UDRP, for coping with questions that the Anticybersquatting Consumer Protection Act (ACPA) does not reach. The ACPA covers only bad-faith attempts to exploit someone else's commercial goodwill.

There are circumstances under which more than one business can legitimately use the same, or similar, trademarks: if the goods and services are completely distinct, for example, or if the businesses are purely interstate and operate in different states. But there is no way for two registrants to use identical URLs (although www.blurch.com, www.e-blurch .com, www.blurchdrugs.com, and www.blurch.net are *not* considered the same URL, even though they are certainly similar enough to induce real-world confusion).

Therefore, there will be many cases in which domain name disputes will arise, even if no one attempts to profit from cybersquatting. The UDRP, which became effective on December 1, 1999, is designed to offer a convenient, quick, inexpensive method of using arbitration to resolve problems without going to court. The information in this section comes from the UDRP and the fine details provided by the procedural rules.

The text of the UDRP can be found online in many places, including http://www.icann.org/udrp/udrp-policy-24oct99.htm. The procedural rules governing resolutions, the Rules for Uniform Domain Name Dispute Resolution Policy, are available at http://www.icann.org/udrp/udrp-rules-24oct99.htm.

Under this policy, a trademark holder who claims that someone else has registered a .com, .net, or .org domain name that interferes with the trademark can go to any dispute resolution provider approved by ICANN. However, the UDRP can only be used where the trademark holder claims that the registration was made in bad faith and without legitimate rights to the name.

The UDRP can be used by the holder of a state-registered or even a common-law trademark—not just a federally registered trademark. For the trademark holder to win the case, all that is necessary is to prove that the domain name is "confusingly similar" to the trademark, not that it is identical.

As of September 2001, ICANN authorized four dispute resolution providers:

- The World Intellectual Property Organization, or WIPO (Geneva) (WIPO is also studying adoption of Local Dispute Resolution Policies—LDRPs)
- National Arbitration Forum
- CPR Institute for Dispute Resolution
- eResolution (formerly known as DeC)

Whenever a .com, .net, or .org domain is registered by any accepted domain name registrars, the agreement between the registrar and the registrant of the domain name will "incorporate the UDRP by reference."

TIPS & TECHNIQUES

UDRP History

The current list of registrars can always be checked at http://www.icann.org/registrars/accredited-list.html. Section 6 of the UDRP says that ICANN doesn't participate in the process in any other way beyond issuing the rules; the dispute resolution providers have complete responsibility. If you want to see how past cases have been decided, the decisions in UDRP cases are stored on the Harvard Law School search engine: http://eon.law.harvard.edu/ search_udrp.html (no www).

This is a legal term that means that all of the provisions in one document are adopted as part of another document that refers to the first one.

The application to register a domain name (or a request for maintenance or renewal of a domain name) acts as a pledge that the statements in the Registration Agreement are complete and accurate. The registrant also states that, as far as it knows, the registration wouldn't infringe on anyone's rights, that the domain name is not being registered for improper purposes, and that the registrant will not knowingly use the domain name to violate any law or regulation. It is up to the registrant (and not, for instance, the registrar) to find out whether the registration violates any rights.

A domain name registrar will cancel, transfer, or otherwise change the registration of a domain name in three situations:

- Voluntary action by the registrant or its authorized agent, as expressed in written or electronic instructions to the registrar

- A court or arbitration panel that has legal power over the dispute orders the change

- A UDRP Administrative Panel has ordered the registrar to act.

ICANN waits 10 days after learning about a panel decision to implement the decision. That 10-day period is provided to give the respondent the chance to file a lawsuit (and inform ICANN that the suit is pending). ICANN suspends its action until it finds out that the suit has settled or been decided. If ICANN doesn't get this notification within the 10-day time frame, it cancels or transfers the registration.

Section 4 of UDRP covers Mandatory Administrative Proceedings—in other words, the circumstances under which one of the approved providers will settle the dispute. Administrative proceedings have to be held whenever a complainant tells a provider (which, in this context, means a provider of dispute resolution services) that someone is interfering with the complainant's trademark. However, there is only one remedy available under the UDRP: having the respondent's domain name canceled or transferred to the complainant. UDRP panels aren't allowed to award money damages at all, much less punitive damages.

Unless the panel or the dispute resolution provider is guilty of some kind of deliberate wrongdoing, they are not liable to anybody for anything that they do or fail to do in connection with the administrative proceeding.

The Petitioner's Case

There are three things that the petitioner has to prove to win a UDRP case:

- A domain name has been registered that is identical or confusingly similar to a trademark or service mark in which the complainant has rights.
- The registrant has no rights or legitimate interests in the domain name.
- Registration, and use of the domain name, involves bad faith.

Therefore, neither the UDRP nor the ACPA will be available if both parties are acting in good faith, and each has some reason to believe that it has a legitimate right to the domain name. In that case, if they can't negotiate a mutually acceptable settlement, they will have to go to court using trademark infringement or unfair competition theories.

The first step in a UDRP proceeding is to file a complaint.

To start a proceeding, the petitioner sends a complaint (in both hard copy and electronic form) to any dispute resolution provider approved by ICANN. The complaint is a simple document that explains the elements of the case:

- The petitioner's request that the complaint be submitted for decision in accordance with the Policy and Rules.

- The complainant's name and contact information.

- Whether the complainant wants a three-person panel instead of just one panelist to conduct the proceeding. A complainant who wants a three-person panel has to choose three people from an approved provider's list of panelists.

- The respondent's name; contact information so the provider can notify the respondent about the complaint.

- The domain name(s) involved in the dispute—a complaint can cover more than one domain name registered by the same respondent.

- Registrar of the domain(s).

- The trademarks or service marks infringed by the registration of the contested domain(s); the goods and services with which each mark is used or that the complainant intends to use in the future.

- The domain name's identity with or confusing similarity to the trademark; how the domain name has been registered and used in bad faith; and why the respondent does not have legitimate rights to use the domain name.

- Any lawsuits already heard or filed about the same domain name(s).

- Copies of documents that provide evidence; a list of all the documents.

- The complainant's agreement not to sue the provider, the panelists, the registrants, or ICANN for any reason relating to the proceeding other than deliberate wrongdoing.

- The complainant certifies that the information in the complaint is accurate and complete; that the complaint is legitimate and is not filed for harassment or other wrongful purpose; and that the complaint reflects current law and the rules of cyberspace.

The provider then makes all reasonable efforts to notify the respondent (using snail mail as well as e-mail). The provider will attempt to notify everyone who is listed as a contact—which means that cybersquatters who give phony information are likely not to be notified, which serves them right.

When a provider gets a complaint, it checks the complaint to see if it complies with the UDRP Policy and Rules. If it does, and if the complainant submitted the proper filing fee, the provider sends the complaint and an explanatory cover sheet to the respondent within three days. The date when the provider forwards the complaint becomes the official *commencement date* for the proceeding.

If there's something wrong with the complaint, the provider notifies the complainant, who has five days to fix it. If the complainant doesn't correct the deficiencies, the complaint is considered withdrawn, but the complainant can start again with a new and better complaint.

The respondent has 20 days from the commencement date to submit a response to the provider, both in hard copy and electronically. The response, which has to answer the allegations in the complaint, is the respondent's chance to explain why it should be allowed to keep the disputed domain name. The respondent has an obligation to reveal any other legal proceedings that have already happened, or that were pending, relating to the domain name(s) involved in this proceeding.

This is also the respondent's chance to get a three-person panel to hear the case, if the complainant hasn't already asked for one. A respondent who asks for a three-person panel has to pay half the fee for the three-member panel; otherwise, the petitioner pays the fee. If the respondent fails to submit a response, the panel decides the dispute based on the complaint alone (unless there are exceptional circumstances that prevent the respondent from answering).

Proving the Case

A UDRP petitioner can use several factors to prove bad faith:

- The domain name was registered primarily for the purpose of selling, renting, or otherwise transferring the registration to the owner of the underlying trademark or service mark—or to a competitor of the complainant, if the respondent tried to charge more than the amount required to reimburse its own out-of-pocket costs directly related to the domain name.

- It was registered as part of a pattern of conduct of preventing trademark and servicemark owners from using their marks as domain names.

- The primary reason for the registration was to disrupt a competitor's business.

- The respondent intentionally used the domain name for profit to attract Web users to the site by confusing them about whether it was related to the petitioner's trademark.

However, the panel will find for the respondent if it finds that the respondent had rights or legitimate interests in the domain name; for instance:

- The domain name was actually the respondent's name or nickname, even if it wasn't registered as a trademark or service mark. This covers the situation in which a person registers a domain name in his own name or the name of child—and that name happens to be used commercially (e.g., as the name of a cartoon character).

- Before the respondent was notified of the dispute, it used, or at least can prove it was preparing to use, the domain name in connection with bona fide business.

- The respondent made legitimate noncommercial or fair use of the domain name (e.g., for product reviews), with no intent of gain or diverting consumers or tarnishing the domain name.

The basic rule is that the complainant will pay all the fees associated with a UDRP. But if the respondent demands a panel of three hearing officers instead of just one, then the respondent will have to pay half the fees.

The Policy says that no one is allowed to transfer a domain name's registration to another registrant (or to a different domain name registrar) while a UDRP proceeding is pending, or for 15 days after it ends. Nor can transfers be made during lawsuits or arbitration proceedings, unless the transferee agrees in writing that it will have to follow the decision of the court or arbitrator.

Hearings are informal, and don't have to follow all the strict rules of evidence that courts require. The panel has 14 days to make its decision (for three-person panels, the majority rules) and report it to the provider.

Then the provider has three calendar days to forward the decision to the complainant, respondent, domain name registrar, and ICANN. Unless the panel says that the decision should be kept private, the provider will publish the whole decision on a Web site that is available to the public. If the panel finds that a complaint was brought in bad faith, that part of the decision is always published.

UDRP or ACPA?

A business that believes its trademarks have been infringed by domain name registrations often has the right to use the UDRP—and also to sue under the ACPA (Anticybersquatting Consumer Protection Act). Each alternative has its advantages and disadvantages.

The UDRP is quick, relatively inexpensive, does not involve the complex, lengthy, and expensive process of "discovery" (investigation and document production before a lawsuit), and still allows the loser to use the court system if it is dissatisfied with the result. The UDRP rules insist on all cases being decided within 14 days of the appointment of the panel. However, the UDRP proceedings keep the status quo intact until after the proceeding is decided.

A party who needs an immediate, short-term injunction (called a Temporary Restraining Order, or TRO) to change the situation will have to bring an ACPA suit, because TROs are not available in UDRP cases.

The ACPA's advantage is that it offers greater finality. Sometimes the ability to get discovery is critical in proving a case. Furthermore, to use the UDRP, the complainant has to show both registration and use of the domain name, whereas the ACPA only requires proof of registration of the name, so the ACPA suit can nip cybersquatting in the bud.

However, the UDRP's only remedy is transfer or cancellation of the domain name registration—no monetary damages are available. Yet an ACPA suit can be lengthy and very expensive. And even if an ACPA suit is brought, if the trademark infringer or cybersquatter is located outside the United States, money damages will not be available, just the transfer or cancellation that would be available faster under the UDRP.

IN THE REAL WORLD

Weighing the Decision to Request a Three-Person Panel

According to the ICANN Web site (http://www.icann.org), by April 19, 2001, there had been 3,487 UDRP cases filed with respect to a total of 6,190 domain names. By that time, the panels had made 2,639 formal decisions. Half the cases were contested, half uncontested (i.e., the respondent didn't bother to deny the charges).

Canadian law professor Michael Geist reviewed all the UDRP proceedings between 1999 (when the system first came into operation) and July 2001. There were 3,094 decided cases. In 81 percent of those cases, the complainant (the trademark holder who brought the case) won.

Nearly all cases are heard by just one arbitrator. However, attorney Diane Cabell did her own study and found that the trademark holder won 83 percent of the cases that had just one arbitrator, but only 60 percent of cases heard by a three-person panel—a big difference!

However, these statistics have to be put into context. If there is a legitimate dispute between two parties, each of whom really thinks it is in the right, naturally both of them will participate in the proceeding. But if the respondent is a flat-out scofflaw, it will ignore the UDRP proceeding, and the arbitrator will automatically rule in favor of the petitioner.

In single-arbitrator cases, the domain name dispute resolution provider picks the arbitrator. In three-person panels, each party gets to name an arbitrator (but the arbitrator has to be a knowledgeable and neutral person—not someone with an axe to grind on behalf of the party that chose him or her!). Those two arbitrators pick the third one. Each dispute resolution provider publishes a list of its approved panelists and their qualifications. Panelists have to be independent and impartial. They have a duty to disclose to the provider any circumstances that could cast doubt on their impar-

IN THE REAL WORLD (CONTINUED)

tiality (in general or in a particular case—for instance, a personal or business relationship with a complainant or respondent).

Either party has the right to have the proceeding heard by three judges, although it does cost a little more to have a three-judge panel: between $2,500 and $4,500, instead of between $950 and $2,000 for a single-arbitrator hearing.

CHAPTER 5

Trade Dress

After reading this chapter you will be able to

- Learn how trade dress is used in marketing to convey the total image of a product
- Understand why functionality matters
- Learn how to protect trade dress rights under the federal and state systems and in other countries

Usually, when the subject of trademarks comes up, what is being discussed is the conventional trademark—a word or combination of letters, perhaps written in a distinctive typeface or combined with a logo or other design elements.

However, other kinds of trademarks can be registered. The whole subject of *trade dress* (including product design and packaging) overlaps with trademarks, as protection for this important form of marketing has gained greater recognition in the courts. Sometimes trade dress can be registered as a trademark. But even if registration is denied, or if the manufacturer does not seek registration, some protection may be available under Lanham Act §43(a), or based on unfair competition.

Trade Dress Sets the Image

The total image of a product and its marketing campaign, including the container for the product itself and the box, wrapper, or other packaging, is known as trade dress. For example, one brand of shampoo might come in a transparent, cylindrical bottle with the trademark stamped in gold. A rival brand might come in an opaque white bottle shaped like a hip flask, with the product name (but no logo) printed in black.

The basic principle of unfair competition law is that businesses just entering a market have a duty to avoid adopting trade dress that is similar enough to existing trade dress to be confusing.

Trade dress can include the configuration or shape of the product (such as slippers in the shape of bear paws; children's bubble bath in a plastic "rocket"), the product's package, the colors or designs used on the product or package, or color used in combination with other elements. For example, BUDWEISER trade dress combines red, white, and blue beer cans with the slogan "King of Beer." The "look and feel" of a computer program as experienced by the program's user can also be trade dress— and sometimes this is a better way to protect the program than copyright law.

However, what is entitled to protection as trade dress is the specific appearance of a product that is offered for sale—not just a general concept, such as greeting cards that feature die-cut photographs.

And, as another case involving photographs said, trade dress isn't a substitute for copyright. So a photographer who couldn't get copyright protection for a photograph was also unsuccessful in claiming that an allegedly similar photograph infringed on the trade dress of his photograph. The Eleventh Circuit said in 2000 that allowing trade dress claims like that would provide a new kind of monopoly that Congress never intended.

Trade dress is vital in establishing the product's image: is it supposed to be new and exciting, or the reliable product that the customer's family has used for generations? Is the product supposed to look elegant, trendy, expensive, or economical? Is the product supposed to be gentle or powerful?

Although trade dress is a key part of the product's image, not all kinds of trade dress can be protected. Exact statistics are not available, but more trade dress applications are probably rejected than are accepted (especially if the application is for product design rather than packaging). The application might be rejected for functionality (see page 129) or because the applicant hasn't shown that the trade dress is distinctive enough. And even if the Examining Attorney releases the application for publication, there might be an opposition proceeding (see page 101) or a cancellation proceeding (see page 101) after the trade dress is registered.

In thinking about trade dress, aesthetic elements that make the design of the product or its packaging more attractive have to be distinguished from the functional elements that contribute to durability, manufacturing efficiency, quality control, or cost-cutting.

It is not unfair competition to use packaging elements that are ordinary or functional, such as plastic bottles for liquids or shrink-wrap for packages. For example, packing ice cream bars in a six-pack with plastic overwrap is functional, because it keeps the product intact but the design of a foil wrapper with graphics is protectable.

When one company's trade dress is charged with infringing another company's trade dress, the test is whether the two create the same overall impression when they are viewed separately—and *not* side by side. The theory is that customers will see them at different times and might be confused by the similarity (especially if the wording on the packages is similar and uses similar type faces).

The Two Pesos Case

The Lanham Act refers to "trademarks" but doesn't mention "trade dress." However, in 1992, the Supreme Court decided a case about a Mexican restaurant that accused a rival restaurant of copying its trade dress—that is, the style of decorating the restaurant, the appearance of the menu, advertisements, brochures, and so on.

The Supreme Court's ruling was that as long as it is inherently distinctive, trade dress is entitled to trademark protection. In this reading, trade dress should be treated in the same way as a word mark or composite trademark. Secondary meaning doesn't have to be proved as long as there is inherent distinctiveness. The Supreme Court said that trade dress can be protected only if it is both distinctive and nonfunctional—whereas conventional trademarks can be protected even if they are functional.

This decision did not open up a floodgate of registrations of trade dress. The other courts, and the TTAB, didn't always give protection to product designs that could not prove secondary meaning. Their concern was that giving too much protection to product designs would create antitrust problems: Manufacturers might build monopolies by taking over all the possible forms of trade dress.

The Wal-Mart Case

In 2000, deciding a case involving the merchandising giant Wal-Mart, the Supreme Court stepped back a little and narrowed the range of trade dress protection. The Supreme Court didn't want to make it too easy to dominate an entire range of product design and crowd out competitors.

This case divides trade dress into at least two categories: product design (the appearance of the product itself) and package design (the box, bag, wrappers, and so on). The Wal-Mart case says that product designs are *never* inherently distinctive. So, unless the product design has been registered as a trademark (and some kinds of trade dress, including

What Makes
Trade Dress Distinctive?

Other courts have provided some insights into analyzing trade dress:

- Is the trade dress a common, basic shape or design? If so, it is entitled to little or no protection against copying by others.

- Is it just a refinement of a well-known, common form of ornamentation often used to dress up similar merchandise? Again, this is a factor that argues against strong protection.

- Is the trade dress unique or unusual in its field? Then protection might be available.

According to the Second Circuit (in a 1995 case), the real test of whether trade dress is inherently distinctive is the commercial activities of the owner of the trade dress. Inherently distinctive trade dress has the primary purpose of designating the source of the product (in other words, it acts like a trademark). So the more effort the owner made to use the product design as a source identifier, the more protection is likely to be granted.

designs for faucets, thermostats, and guitar heads, the polka-dot background design on cans of cleanser, and the shape of LIFESAVERS candies, have been registered), the plaintiff has to prove that the product design has acquired secondary meaning in order to win a case for trade dress infringement.

But if the PTO has registered the trade dress, that is strong evidence that the trade dress is nonfunctional. That means that, in an infringement case, the defendant has to prove that the feature is functional. The

PTO's determination means that the plaintiff doesn't have to prove nonfunctionality.

Does the Wal-Mart decision conflict with the Two Pesos decision? The Supreme Court says it doesn't, because that case involved restaurant design, which it treated as different from product design, and closer to the design of the package than to the design of the product itself.

The Supreme Court also said in its Wal-Mart decision that if it is hard to decide whether a particular design is a package design or a product design, the item should be treated as a product design. That means that proof of secondary meaning will be required, and the plaintiff will have more to prove in order to win the case.

IN THE REAL WORLD

Tabs as Trade Dress

The PTO agreed that the LEVI'S pocket tab is an item of trade dress that has secondary meaning when it is used on pants (although not on shirts), because

- The manufacturer has used tabs in different colors on its clothing for a long time (over a century, in fact).

- Many clothing items, representing a huge dollar volume, have been sold using the tabs.

- Levi's ads referred specifically to the pocket tab as a distinctive quality.

- Levi's produced a lot of evidence of secondary meaning, including a customer survey, letters from customers, and affidavits from clothing retailers.

Information in the TMEP About Trade Dress

The Lanham Act doesn't mention trade dress in so many words (see page 123 for more about trade dress), so the legal system has to develop trade dress principles by extending principles about trademarks.

The *TMEP* says that when an application is made to register the design of a product or the package or container for the product, the Attorney Examiner has to give separate consideration to two issues: functionality and distinctiveness.

If the proposed trade dress is completely arbitrary, and has no functional features at all, then the Attorney Examiner will go right to the question of whether it is distinctive or not. See *TMEP* §1202.03(a).

If the proposed trade dress is *de facto functional*—that is, if the product, its container, or a feature of either one is designed for the performance of a function, then it can be registered on the Principal Register if it is inherently distinctive, or if it acquires distinctiveness in the course of commercial use. If it is not inherently distinctive, it can be registered on the Supplemental Register.

For example, all spray bottles have to hold and distribute liquids, but they can be designed in many ways to serve this function. Some of these ways will be more attractive to consumers than others.

However, the third category is called *de jure functional*—functional as a matter of law. If the way a product or its package is configured provides a competitive advantage by being better than other available designs, or if it would cost too much for competitors to use other designs, then the mark *can't* be registered at all. (In some cases, a design patent would be available.) Once again, the interests of free competition come first, and competitors can't be locked out or forced to undergo unreasonably high costs because someone has monopolized a functional feature.

Trade Dress and Patents

The legal rules for different kinds of intellectual property don't always work well together. The trade dress for a product could involve some patented features, or some features that used to be covered by a utility or design patent that has now expired.

The problem is that utility patents cover functional features, and it is pretty clear that "functionality" is a reason *not* to protect trade dress. Remember, restricting the use of a functional feature (a valve or an aerosol spray, for instance) to one manufacturer would stifle competition by other manufacturers.

In 2001, the Supreme Court's TrafFix decision held that the fact that a feature of a product was included in a utility patent that has now expired is good evidence that that feature is functional. Once the patent expires, anyone can use that feature (it is no longer protected by patent laws). If the feature is functional, then it can't be protected as trade dress.

The PTO's traditional attitude is that a utility patent (whether it is current or expired) does not always prevent registration of a trademark or trade dress in the features covered by the patent. However, it is a tough job to prove that the features are not functional.

Remember, there are two kinds of patents (see pp. 15-16): *utility patents* (protecting practical inventions and processes) and *design patents* (protecting the way that manufactured items look).

In 1996, the federal District Court for the Southern District of New York ruled that the same item can have both a design patent and trade dress protection. The design patent covers the ornamental, non-functional features of industrial design. To qualify for a design patent, the design features have to be new, nonobvious (as compared with the design of products already on the market), and ornamental. Applicants for design patents do not have to prove that the design is inherently distinctive. Once the design patent expires, then competitors can copy the item—but if it is protected as trade dress, they have to do so in a way that prevents customers from being confused.

In 1997, though, the Attorney Examiner refused to grant an application to register a design of stylized fluting on a metal beverage can as trade dress that had already gotten a design patent. The TTAB agreed with the examiner that the fluting was functional and could not be protected as trade dress. According to the TTAB, a design patent is important evidence of nonfunctionality, but it is not conclusive proof.

Functionality

The issue of functionality can also come up when the trade dress does not have any features that ever were or could have been patented. An element in the overall trade dress is functional if that element is essential for the product to serve its purpose (i.e., ice cream packages have to prevent the product from melting) or if it affects either the cost or quality of the product itself. Shampoo has to come in some kind of container, probably a bottle, but making the bottle pink or making the top gold-colored metal instead of white plastic is nonfunctional trade dress.

A 1987 Second Circuit case is helpful in thinking about functional versus design issues in trade dress. The case says that there's a whole spectrum. At one end, there's the unprotectable "functional design" that assembles purely functional features in a unique way. At the other end is a distinctive but arbitrary arrangement of mostly ornamental features. This is entitled to protection, because competitors can create their own arrangements to try to appeal to customers. That way, everyone benefits from energetic competition.

Less protection is available when the supposedly distinctive features actually serve the purpose of the product (including keeping manufacturing costs down). The defendant's efforts to distinguish the two products

TIPS & TECHNIQUES

Protective Tactics
for Trade Dress

To protect trade dress, manufacturers should consider the following:

- Design ads to feature the trade dress as a whole (including boxes and overwrap), not just the product by itself.

- Include phrases about the trade dress in the ads: "Look for the green box with the red stars," for example.

- However, trade dress owners who take the position that their trade dress is nonfunctional (and therefore entitled to protection) should *not* run ads that say something like, "Our unique Valv-o-sprayer does the job in half the time," because that would suggest that the manufacturer takes the position that this is a valuable functional feature.

- Trade dress owners should develop evidence of design alternatives, which can be submitted in case an alleged infringer claims that the trade dress is "aesthetically functional" and therefore should not be protected.

- A Third Circuit case from 2000 rules that protection of trade dress can extend to separate items within a product line (e.g., a complete line of power tools, household cleansers, or hair care products). But the manufacturer must provide a consistent overall look that gives consumers a single, ongoing commercial impression. Protection will not be available if consumers would not tend to see the similarities.

- The Pantone ™ color chart is very useful in identifying the specific shades of color used in trade dress, in order to prove or disprove copying.

- Franchisors should draft their agreements to make sure that franchisees stop using the franchisor's trade dress

TIPS & TECHNIQUES (CONTINUED)

after the agreement terminates. It is very likely that consumers would be confused if, for example, every element
in a Wendy's restaurant (furniture, menu, wall and floor
design, etc.) stays the same except that the sign in front
now says Susy's.

- The International Trademark Association (INTA) has prepared a library of color slides showing trade dresses that
have been litigated. You can order the slides from INTA for
use as courtroom evidence, or just to learn more about
what worked—and didn't work—in trade dress cases.

(for instance, by applying its own trademark) also count against the
plaintiff.

According to the Second Circuit, the real test is whether the product
and its packaging, taken as a whole, is functional—it is not appropriate
to take apart the individual elements and test each one for functionality.

Some courts also follow the doctrine of *aesthetic functionality.* This
principle says that trade dress—for example, a floral china pattern—is
not protectable trade dress if the feature is attractive and appeals to customers in a way that limits the availability of alternative designs. The
implication is that if the design is aesthetically functional, then it is *not*
an infringement for competitors to copy it.

At first glance, this is a hard concept to understand—if Company
A has used its resources and talent to develop a product that customers
really like, why should Company B be allowed to imitate it instead of
doing something original on its own? It all comes down to bedrock
concepts about allowing vigorous competition instead of allowing a
monopoly (except in patented items—and even there, the monopoly is
only temporary).

Trade Dress in State Law

The Model State Trademark Bill (see page 89) doesn't define, or even mention, trade dress. But, because this law shares a lot of concepts with federal trademark law, it would probably allow registration of trade dress. However, New York—a major commercial state—has not adopted the Model State Trademark Bill. The only New York law dealing with trade dress is a criminal law that says that merchandise that infringes on trade dress is only considered counterfeit if the trade dress has been federally registered.

Trade Dress Outside the United States

A U.S. federal law, the Tariff Act, makes it illegal to engage in unfair methods of competition or unfair acts related to importing goods into the United States. Often, these acts relate to counterfeiting trademarks or unfairly imitating trade dress.

The Tariff Act allows trade dress owners to file a complaint with the International Trade Commission (ITC). The ITC has the power to investigate and issue an injunction, but it is not allowed to order the payment of damages, and it cannot have offending goods seized and destroyed the way the U.S. Customs Service can. However, if the ITC does issue an injunction, and the case ends up in the United States

TIPS & TECHNIQUES

State Registration

It can be worthwhile to register trade dress either in states that are commercial leaders or in the key states in marketing the product, before applying for federal registration of the trade dress as a trademark.

TIPS & TECHNIQUES

Foreign Laws

The International Trademark Association (INTA)'s journal, *The Trademark Reporter,* publishes an annual summary of laws and policies about trade dress outside the United States.

before the Trademark Trial and Appeal Board, the TTAB usually finds ITC decisions persuasive.

To win before the ITC, the owner of unregistered trade dress has to establish that improper importation or sale threatens to "destroy or substantially injure" a U.S. industry, prevent the establishment of an industry, or restrain or monopolize trade and commerce in the United States.

CHAPTER 6

Threats to the Trademark

After reading this chapter you will be able to

- Police trademark infringement
- Know what factors courts use in deciding whether a later trademark is "confusingly similar" to an earlier one
- Fight trademark counterfeiters
- See what special remedies are available when a "famous" trademark becomes less valuable because of dilution

Trademark Infringement

There are many instances in which the owner of a trademark believes that a trademark adopted later improperly interferes with the owner's trademark. Owners usually find out about infringing products when their licensees complain, or when the trademark owner's sales force reports on similar trademarks or counterfeit goods.

Some high-value articles, such as designer handbags or expensive jewelry, are sold with special, hard-to-counterfeit technologically advanced labels (with holograms, for example) or authentication cards that link the individual product to the authorized dealer. Trademark owners can hire private investigators to track down counterfeits, or can engage in sting operations by claiming that they want to buy or manufacture counterfeit merchandise.

If, after taking advice from an experienced intellectual property lawyer, the owner still thinks that the trademark has been interfered with, the next step is to send a "cease and desist" letter putting the potential defendant on notice that the potential plaintiff thinks there is a dispute to resolve. Then the parties try to work out an amicable settlement. If that doesn't work, the owner's recourse is trademark litigation, in either state or federal court.

Trademark Confusion

Trademark confusion can arise when marks sound similar, have design similarities, have similar meanings (for instance, FLEUR and BLOSSOM), or are used on similar goods. When courts have to decide an infringement case, they look at factors such as similarities between products, the defendant's intent, and the strength or weakness of the plaintiff's trademark. It makes it easier for the plaintiff to win by proving actual confusion, but trademark law only requires proof of the likelihood of confusion.

In a basic confusion case, the risk is that someone will buy the defendant's products, believing that the products were actually made by the plaintiff. But there are also "reverse confusion" cases, where the defendant engages in heavy advertising and promotion—and the upshot is that when consumers see the plaintiff's product, they might think that it was actually manufactured by the defendant.

To win an infringement-by-confusion case, the plaintiff has to prove three bottom-line issues:

1. The plaintiff has protectable rights in a trademark
2. The defendant uses a confusingly similar mark
3. The consuming public is likely to be confused, mistaken, or deceived about the true source of products, or that the defendant and its products are associated, affiliated, connected, approved, or otherwise involved with the plaintiff.

Factors Used to Decide Infringement Issues

Depending on whether it is a federal or state case, and the interpretation that the particular court gives to trademark law, the five basic factors used in every trademark infringement case are:

- *Similarity of the overall impression conveyed by the two marks* (in looks, sound, and meaning)—but bear in mind that even identical marks can legitimately be used if there is no overlap in the goods and services with which they are connected.

- *Similarities in goods and services*—this includes whether the plaintiff and defendant use the same marketing channels (including marketing channels for both goods and services).

- *Strength of the plaintiff's mark*—remember, descriptive marks are not as strong as arbitrary or suggestive ones. A strong mark will be protected even against noncompeting goods. But a weak mark will be protected only against a mark used on similar goods and services.

- *Evidence of actual confusion experienced by consumers.*

- *The defendant's intent in adopting the mark*—did it really believe that it was entitled to the mark? Was it careless in doing a trademark search? Did it have bad legal advice? Or did the defendant deliberately try to trade on the goodwill developed by the plaintiff?

In addition to these five, there are other factors that may be taken into account in a particular case:

- Were the goods sold in the same place?

- How much care is the consumer likely to use? (more so in the case of an expensive or potentially dangerous purchase, less so for a casual or impulse purchase)

- What are the suggestions and connotations of the two marks?

- If the two marks are used in different geographic markets, to what extent might consumers mix up the two marks?

- What is the likelihood that the trademark owner will expand its product line to cover products of the type on which the allegedly infringing trademark is used?

If it is not really clear that the two marks are similar enough to create confusion, the court will go beyond examining the trademarks themselves and consider the whole context of trade dress in which the marks appear. The trade dress (the shape, color, design, and patterns of containers and packages) becomes the background against which trademarks are displayed. However, only elements of trade dress that show some creativity will count, not common functional elements like clear plastic packaging or styrofoam trays for meat products.

When the whole presentation of the two items is confusingly similar, the plaintiff can charge both trademark infringement and unfair competition by copying trade dress.

If the plaintiff can prove that the owner of the second trademark (the *junior user;* the owner of the first mark to be registered is the *senior user*) intended to mislead consumers, then the court will presume that confusion was likely. If the marks are very similar, then the likelihood of confusion will also be presumed—as it will be if the defendant continued using the disputed mark even after the plaintiff made its claims. Even the junior user's failure to do a thorough trademark search (and therefore find out about the senior user) can be treated as intent to copy the plaintiff's trademark.

Describing a product as "Our version of" a trademarked product, using the trademark, is permissible as long as it is clear that the product does not come from, and is not endorsed by, the owner of the trademark. As long as the packaging is not a possibly misleading imitation, it would not be trademark infringement to describe a lipstick as "PRETTY PATTY's LIPGLIMMERS—our version of CHANEL Rouge à Levres."

Comparing Similar Trademarks

This chart shows the results of many infringement cases. It also shows that it is hard to draw lines or make hard and fast rules, because one judge's perception that two marks are similar might not be shared by another judge in a different case.

Confusingly similar on phonetic grounds:

ARROW	AIR-O	
AVEDA	AVITA	
BELLOWS	FELLOWS	
CYGON	PHYGON	
DRAMAMINE	BONAMINE	
LISTERINE	LISTOGEN	LISTERSEPTINE
SMIRNOFF	SARNOFF	

NOT confusingly similar on phonetic grounds:

COCA-COLA	COCO LOCO or POLAR COLA
GLIDE	EASY SLIDE
HOUR AFTER HOUR	SHOWER TO SHOWER
REAC	REACH
SURF	SURGE

Confusingly similar because of similar meaning:

ARISE	AWAKE (breakfast drinks)
BEAUTY-REST	BEAUTY SLEEP
BEER NUTS	BREW NUTS
BLUE NUN	BLUE ANGEL
CHICKEN OF THE SEA (canned tuna)	TUNA O'THE FARM (canned chicken)
LONDON FOG	SMOG (raincoats)
GASTOWN	GAS CITY (gas)
MANPOWER	WOMENPOWER (temp agencies)
MISTER CLEAN	MISTER STAIN
SPICE ISLANDS	SPICE VALLEY (tea)

It is not trademark infringement to sell genuine branded merchandise in its original state, without altering it—although it might be a breach of a contract with the manufacturer or distributor. It is false advertising for someone who is not an authorized dealer to claim to be one.

However, as long as the consumer who thinks he or she is getting a genuine CASABLANCA ceiling fan, or JOHN DEERE tractor really does get one, there is no trademark infringement. There might be infringement and/or dilution, however, if the seller altered the condition of the merchandise while retaining the trademark, or if "seconds" or damaged merchandise were sold as first quality.

It is also permissible to make a statement (as long as it is accurate, of course) that parts are "compatible with" or "replace" trademarked parts. For example, "FRED AND ED'S CARTRIDGE SHOP #307 makes 3,500 fresh, clear copies in your HEWLETT-PACKARD LASER JET 1200se copier for only $29.95" would not infringe on Hewlett-Packard's trademark, because it is clear that the cartridge is made by Fred and Ed and not by Hewlett-Packard.

Trademark Counterfeiting

In an infringement case, the defendant may at least be able to make a reasonable argument that it believed its own trademark was valid and did not impair the plaintiff's rights. But trademark counterfeiting is a different and more serious matter. Not only is trademark counterfeiting always deceptive, it can actually be dangerous (if the counterfeit merchandise consists of drugs or low-quality mechanical parts that cause malfunctions or fires, for example).

Trademark counterfeiting is considered very serious because even if the buyer is not confused (she knows that GUCCI bags are not sold by street vendors for $25), other people may be confused when they see what they think is designer or other trademarked merchandise.

In 1984, the Lanham Act was amended by the enactment of the Trademark Counterfeiting Act, which also adds penalties to the federal criminal code. This act applies only to counterfeiting of trademarks that are registered on the federal Principal Register, and only to situations in which the counterfeit trademark is used on the same goods and services as the original. In other words, it applies to counterfeit LOUIS VUITTON handbags and luggage, but would not apply if an unauthorized party tried to market LOUIS VUITTON gourmet chocolates.

A successful plaintiff who sues a counterfeiter and wins can probably get treble damages and attorneys' fees. Federal prosecutors can also seek criminal penalties against those who intentionally deal in materials that are known to be counterfeit.

The court can make what is called an *ex parte* seizure order if it seems likely that the defendant would conceal or move the merchandise. *Ex parte* means that the order is made based on the plaintiff's application—the defendant doesn't get a chance to argue against the order, and, in fact, is only notified of the seizure when it occurs. The seizure order can't be appealed, on the theory that it isn't final yet because the goods might be returned if it is determined that they are not counterfeit. The court can also order the seizure of vehicles, equipment, and even storage facilities involved in counterfeiting.

If the court case results in a determination that the goods are coun-terfeit, then they will probably be destroyed. Before 1996, the Customs Service had the option of delivering seized goods to a federal agency or charity that would use them. However, current law says that the seized goods must be destroyed unless the trademark owner allows something else to be done—and the court determines that the coun-terfeit goods do not threaten the health or safety of consumers.

In addition to civil suits by trademark owners against counterfeit-ers, and criminal penalties, the U.S. Customs Service has the discretion to impose civil fines on anyone who has any kind of involvement in the importation of counterfeit merchandise. For a first offense, the civil penalty is the manufacturer's suggested retail price on the genuine goods. This amount is doubled for second or repeat offenses.

Infringement Cases in the Courts

Although only federal courts can hear patent or copyright cases, both state and federal courts are authorized to handle trademark cases. The general rule is that suits can be brought in federal court only if the plaintiff and defendant come from different states (this is called *diversity jurisdiction*), but trademark cases can automatically be heard in federal court because of the special nature of trademarks.

In other words, "federal question original jurisdiction" exists over trademark cases, so they can be heard in the federal court system. But there can be some severe problems in getting infringers from outside the United States to respond to subpoenas from the United States—and some activities that occur outside this country might not be subject to U.S. law anyway.

Trademark cases are also exempt from the general rule that federal courts can only handle cases where more than $75,000 is at stake—

trademark cases can go to federal court, no matter how high or low the "amount in controversy" is.

The most common remedy in trademark cases is an injunction ordering the junior user to stop using the trademark. The Lanham Act does theoretically make it possible to get an award of money damages (e.g., ordering the defendant to pay the plaintiff $50,000 to compensate the plaintiff for sales lost because of infringement), but courts seldom award them. The Lanham Act allows the loser to be ordered to pay the winner's attorneys' fees, but only in exceptional cases.

Dilution

In 1995, the Federal Trademark Dilution Act (FTDA) was passed to amend the Lanham Act and extend its reach. See 15 U.S. Code §1125(c), which provides a special range of remedies (including injunctions, damages, and destruction of infringing goods) for trademarks that can be classified as "famous" and that are used by a third party (not, for instance, a licensee) in a way that dilutes the mark's "distinctive quality."

Dilution means using a famous mark, without the owner's consent, on unrelated merchandise. For example, someone who tried to sell NIKE personal computers would be guilty of dilution, even if consumers don't really think that the athletic shoe manufacturer has entered the computer market.

The effect of dilution is weakening the famous mark's ability to identify and distinguish the trademark owner's goods and services from those of others.

To win a trademark dilution case, it is not even necessary to prove that consumers were confused by the dilutive use. In fact, the defendant doesn't even have to have been in competition with the plaintiff for the plaintiff to win the dilution case.

TIPS & TECHNIQUES

Too Late!

Once a trademark has been registered long enough to become incontestable (i.e., five years), it is no longer possible to bring a dilution claim against that trademark. Therefore, owners of famous marks have to keep track of new marks being registered and must police possible cases of dilution.

For the statute to apply, the dilutive use has to begin after the mark becomes famous. So the FTDA doesn't apply if, for instance, the mark was registered in March 2001, the dilutive use began in July 2001, and the mark didn't become famous until 2003.

Attorney Examiners do not consider possible dilution when they decide whether to grant an application for trademark registration. However, since the Trademark Amendments of 1999, the owner of a mark does have the right to bring an opposition or cancellation proceeding before the TTAB (see page 99) on the grounds that its famous mark is being diluted.

When the FTDA was passed, half the states already had their own antidilution laws. Most of those laws merely allowed injunctions, not money damages. The Model State Trademark Bill, for instance, allows an injunction to be granted when there is likelihood of injury to business reputation or dilution of the distinctive quality of a state-registered mark, or a common-law mark or a trade name that is valid under common law concepts—even if the plaintiff and defendant are not competitors. Nor is it necessary to allege that the dilution causes confusion as to the source of goods or services.

Under the FTDA, state actions are preempted if the mark is federally registered. *Preemption* means that only the federal legal system, not the state system, is allowed to tackle the question. It is hard to imagine a famous mark that is *not* federally registered.

There is no single, simple definition of *famous mark*. There are federal and state trademark registers, of course, but there is no listing or directory of famous marks, so it is impossible to search in advance to see if a mark falls into this category.

However, courts use many tests to assess whether a mark is famous. This eight-factor test is typical:

- If the mark has been federally registered
- The extent and duration of the plaintiff's use of mark
- The extent and duration of advertising for the mark
- If it has been used nationwide; geographic scope of use if it has not been
- The extent to which the mark is inherently distinctive, or has acquired distinctiveness in use
- The degree of recognition that consumers show for the trademark
- In which channels of trade the product bearing the mark is distributed
- What the defendant did in connection with the allegedly famous mark

The Federal Trademark Dilution Act forbids two kinds of dilution. The first one, *blurring,* causes the connection in consumers' minds between the trademark and the plaintiff's goods (or the service mark and plaintiff's services) to get weaker. The other, *tarnishment,* occurs when the defendant detracts from the goodwill and reputation of the trademark by associating it with inferior products—or, worse, with something that is unwholesome or unsavory (e.g., illegal gambling, pornography, drugs).

However, the statute specifically allows some kinds of use of the famous mark. For example, comparative advertising is permitted ("SNURKLE Peanut Butter has 20% less saturated fat than FAMOUS BRAND"). So is noncommercial use of the trademark such as reviews, news reporting, and commentary. ("After being washed 10 times, LOCAL BRAND T-shirts had brighter colors than FAMOUS BRAND.")

In most cases, if the plaintiff wins a case under the FTDA, the only remedy available will be for the court to order the defendant to stop the activities that resulted in dilution. However, if the plaintiff can prove that the defendant willfully attempted to trade on the trademark owner's reputation, or that the dilution was willful rather than the byproduct of a campaign that had no wrongful intent, then the defendant might be ordered to pay money damages and/or the plaintiffs' attorneys' fees.

In a really outrageous case, the defendant might have to pay treble damages (i.e., three times the actual damages the plaintiff suffered because of the dilution; the extra damages are imposed to punish wrongdoing).

In 1999, the Second Circuit came up with a 10-factor test to check whether "dilution by blurring" had occurred (i.e., whether the defendant's mark, although it does not cast a bad light on the plaintiff's mark, still tends to make the public less certain about the source of the goods that carry the famous mark):

- The extent to which the plaintiff's mark is distinctive

- The degree of similarity between the two marks

- Whether the products on which the two marks are used are similar or related—and the likelihood that the plaintiff might "bridge the gap" by using the mark on the same kind of goods as the defendant does

- The relationships among distinctiveness, similarity of trademark, and similarity of goods—a dilution case might still be valid if one of these factors is comparatively weak, as long as the others are strong

- Overlap between the markets for the plaintiff's and defendant's product
- How sophisticated the consumers are
- Whether actual confusion has occurred
- Whether the mark is merely descriptive, or is a stronger arbitrary or fanciful mark
- The balance between the amount of harm that the defendant would suffer if it were found guilty of dilution, and whether the plaintiff enforced its rights promptly or delayed
- Whether the plaintiff was vigilant in policing its marks against infringement and dilution.

MSTB Dilution Law

Even before there was a federal law forbidding trademark dilution, many of the states had their own antidilution laws. The Model State Trademark Bill (MSTB) also awards rights to the owner of a mark that is famous within the state. As long as it is fair to do so, and on whatever terms the court finds reasonable, the owner of the famous mark can get an injunction against anyone else using the famous mark in a way that dilutes the mark's distinctive quality.

The court can also order money damages, surrender of profits improperly earned by the defendant, or destruction of infringing merchandise—but only if the plaintiff can prove that the defendant "willfully intended to trade on the owner's reputation or to cause dilution of the famous mark." The court has discretion to award up to three times the profits and damages and/or reasonable legal fees incurred by the prevailing party.

Courts and the FTDA

How do courts apply the FTDA? Well, in a 1996 case from the Southern District of New York, Clinique Labs, Inc. tried to get a preliminary injunction against BASIQUE, which Clinique described as "cheap knock-offs" of the CLINIQUE cosmetics and treatment product line. But the court refused to grant the injunction, saying that Clinique was not tarnished. The knock-off products were not shoddy or unwholesome, and Clinique was not associated with obscenity, sex, or illegal activities.

The FTDA refers to trademarks and service marks, and doesn't specifically mention famous trade dress. However, in 1997 the Fifth Circuit extended the FTDA's reach by allowing a dilution claim to be placed involving the shape of the MIXMASTER kitchen appliance, because the inherently distinctive shape is nonfunctional.

In 1989, the Second Circuit ruled that the trademark LEXIS (for computerized legal research services) was not diluted by LEXUS (for automobiles). Even though the trademarks sound the same, both of them are marketed to sophisticated audiences, who can be expected to understand that the two businesses are completely different.

A Fifth Circuit case from 2000 says that *Polo* magazine infringed Ralph Lauren's POLO trademark when the magazine expanded from simply covering the sport of polo to a broader interest in equestrian sports and lifestyles. But Lauren's dilution claim failed, because actual harm is required for a successful dilution claim, and it was not shown in this instance. There was also a First Amendment question (the right to commercial free speech when titles are being chosen for publications). So, although the federal District Court granted a permanent injunction against the magazine, the Fifth Circuit vacated the injunction and ordered the lower court to re-hear the case and come up with a more appropriate remedy.

The MSTB sets out eight factors for courts to use in determining whether a mark is distinctive and famous:

- How much distinctiveness the mark has inherently—or has acquired—in the state
- How long and broadly the mark has been used in connection with the goods and services with which it is now used
- Extent and duration of advertising and marketing using the mark within the state
- The size of the trading area within which the mark is used
- The marketing channels for the goods or services
- The degree of recognition within the state for both the allegedly diluted mark and the allegedly dilutive mark
- Whether the same or similar marks have been used by third parties who are not involved in the litigation
- Whether the allegedly famous mark is registered in the state or federally registered with the PTO

CHAPTER 7

Other Issues in Trademark Law

After reading this chapter you will be able to

- Decide whether you own any properties suitable for licensing
- Think about what issues to include in the licensing agreement
- Control the quality of licensed merchandise
- Protect know-how and trade secrets
- Make sure that your ads satisfy state and federal standards for accuracy and correctness

Licensing

Traditional trademark law concepts did not allow for the possibility of licensing. The only function of trademarks that was recognized was identifying the source of goods or services. Therefore, the theory was, if more than one source was involved, the public would be confused about the identity of the products they bought.

However, trademark law has finally caught up with business realities. Not everyone who owns a trademark that has commercial potential is also a manufacturer. For example, a celebrity, a band, or a sports team has valuable goodwill and public recognition that can make trademarked merchandise (clothing, cosmetics, collectible items) successful in the marketplace. A movie or television studio has many properties and characters that can be successfully used to merchandise goods. A fashion designer can allow manufacturers of cosmetics, apparel, and household goods to produce merchandise using the designer's name.

Trademark licenses cover only uses of the trademark that would be infringing if there were no contract. Therefore, wholesalers, retailers, dealers, and distributors of trademarked merchandises do not need licenses (because they are already allowed to sell the merchandise with the trademark attached)—but manufacturers other than the trademark owner need a license to make and sell merchandise using the trademark.

Even consumer goods manufacturers who have a strong brand may be able to gain additional revenue from the popularity of the brand by allowing their names, trademarks, and logos to be used on licensed merchandise. Two manufacturers who have done this successfully are the

IN THE REAL WORLD

Categories of
Licensed Properties

There are four general categories of licensed properties:

- Popularity properties (based, for instance, on a TV show, band, or cartoon)

- Status properties (Calvin Klein, Gucci, Yves St. Laurent)

- Personification properties (embodying a desirable lifestyle, such as Polo or Martha Stewart)

- Distinctive ornamentation properties (the Hermes H, Louis Vuitton's pattern of interlocked LVs, Nike swoosh)

Transactions that involve the names, pictures, or images of celebrities also raise questions under the right of publicity: see page 203 for discussion of these issues.

makers of WINNEBAGO camping equipment and the broad range of collectible items using the COCA-COLA logo or the company's vintage advertisements.

Trademark law now recognizes and regulates the possibility of licensing to extend goodwill. Licensing is now a multibillion-dollar business under which trademark owners, manufacturers, and distributors enter into contracts that control the licensing relationship. In exchange for use of the trademark, the owner gets a royalty, usually calculated based on net sales of the licensed product.

Licensing usually involves names, titles, symbols (for instance, the Nike "swoosh" design), photographs or images of celebrities, or combinations of these elements.

Initially, exclusive licenses were most common, so that only one company had the right to manufacture and sell licensed products. The more modern trend is to negotiate nonexclusive licenses, where more than one licensee has rights to develop and sell trademark merchandise. (To prevent the market from being flooded—and to keep the licensor's quality-control job manageable—usually the number of licenses within a product category will be limited.) There's a difference between a sole license, which grants rights to only one outside licensee but allows the trademark owner to keep manufacturing trademarked merchandise, and an exclusive license, where the licensee is the only one allowed to make the particular category of merchandise covered by the license.

In most cases, the licensed products will be mass-market, low-price impulse items. One key to a successful licensing program is choosing products that appeal to the target audience: lunch boxes showing characters from a child-oriented property would probably be more successful than leather checkbook covers, for instance—and certainly more successful than automobile accessories.

Should the Product Be Licensed?

There are many factors that determine whether a property is a good candidate for licensing, based on its potential to be used on popular products that will provide adequate returns for both the licensor and the licensee. Depending on the nature of the property and the products, the strategy might call either for wide distribution of mass-market, inexpensive merchandise, or a more selective distribution of higher-priced products such as designer- or lifestyle-oriented products.

The factors in the decision may include:

- To what extent has existing promotion by the trademark owner or other licensee made the property visible and prominent to consumers?

- Does the property appeal to a group of consumers that can easily be targeted—such as the fans of a sports team or band?

- Are many versions of the property available and archived (e.g., Norman Rockwell magazine covers that can be turned into calendars, coasters, or similar merchandise)?

- Is there at least one recognizable character (e.g., Fonzie from *Happy Days* or Buffy from *Buffy the Vampire Slayer*) associated with the property? If so, it will be easier to create a marketing program. Separate trademarks and licenses may be available for the property as a whole and for individual characters.

- Is the property associated with a special event (e.g., the World Series) or an anniversary that can be used to create a marketing campaign?

- Does the property appeal to a particular lifestyle image?

- Can retail sales of licensed merchandise be supplemented with premiums and promotions to enhance the strength of the brand in the public eye?

- Can the property be adapted to more than one industry?

The typical trademark license is for specific products, for a limited time, and it covers only a limited, specified geographic area. Exhibit 7.1 details classes where licenses are common. However, the potential licensor should get advice from antitrust attorneys. Unless there is an economic justification for restricting the geographic territory of the license to only part of the United States, there may be antitrust law violations. Under antitrust law, a manufacturer's attempts to control where and how a licensee sells or distributes licensed products can give rise to questions.

Licensing agreements often require the licensee to inform the licensor if the licensee becomes aware of potential infringements of the trademark. The agreement is typically drafted to give the licensor the power to determine whether infringement has occurred, and whether to sue the infringer. If the licensor does decide to bring suit, the licensee then has a contractual duty to cooperate with the licensor (for instance, by giving evidence or turning over records), but the licensor is responsible for financing the suit.

Gray-Market Goods

Gray-market goods, also known as *parallel imports,* raise some tough problems in licensing law. As an example, assume that a designer handbag wholesales for $400 to U.S. distributors, but only $200 to distributors outside the United States. An unscrupulous distributor can buy the

TIPS & TECHNIQUES

Monitor Art Quality

The property owner should monitor closely and require approval of all artwork used in the campaign for the licensed merchandise, to make sure that the underlying trademark is not diluted by vulgar or low-quality merchandise or marketing materials.

EXHIBIT 7.1

Classes Where Licenses Are Common

According to trademark experts, most licenses are concentrated among several of the classes in the International Classification System. Other classes offer limited scope for licensing. (These are summaries of the classes, not their official names.)

The categories marked with an asterisk are the most likely to involve licensing deals:

2	paints
***3**	cosmetics and cleaning preparations
4	lubricants and fuels
6	metal goods
8	hand tools
9	electrical and scientific apparatus
11	environmental control apparatus
12	vehicles
***14**	jewelry
15	music boxes
***16**	paper goods and printed matter
***18**	leather goods
19	building materials
20	furniture
***21**	housewares and glass
22	cordage and fibers

EXHIBIT 7.1 (CONTINUED)

23 yarn and thread

*24 fabrics and linens

*25 clothing

26 fancy goods

27 floor coverings

*28 toys and sporting goods

*30 food

*33 wine and spirits

34 smokers' articles

38 communication

*41 education and entertainment

Until January 1, 2002, there were 42 classes, with Class 42 covering all kinds of miscellaneous services. However, WIPO adopted new classes, splitting up Class 42 into new categories. Some of these categories seem suitable for franchising, so they may join the classes in which licensing is already common (and which should be searched prior to adopting a new trademark or licensing an existing trademark):

*42 scientific and technical R & D and services; computer and software development; legal services

*43 services related to food, drink, and lodging (e.g., travel agents—but *not* tourist agencies or rest homes)

*44 agricultural, medical, veterinary, or beauty care services

*45 personal and social services, including security services

bags for $200 each, promising to sell them in Belgium and Portugal, but then turn around and sell them in the United States—earning a higher profit than the legitimate U.S. distributor and attracting U.S. customers by undercutting the price of the bag.

Gray-market goods are legitimately manufactured, and the U.S. trademarks are attached legitimately by the manufacturer. Therefore, they are not the same as counterfeit goods, which use or imitate a trademark unlawfully without consent—and the laws that allow for seizure of counterfeit goods (see page 143) don't apply because the trademarks are genuine.

It has been estimated that in 1998, manufacturers lost as much as $10 billion a year because of gray marketing. Originally, gray marketing tended to involve only high-ticket items because the profit margins were high enough to make it worth the trouble and expense of importing the goods from the countries where they were supposed to be sold to the United States.

Now, however, the Internet makes it easier and less expensive to undercut the U.S. market, because a would-be gray marketer can go online and get instant information about merchandise available throughout the world—and can sell the merchandise on its own Web site without having to open a store.

The goodwill of the trademark (e.g., ROLEX watches, GUCCI handbags, top-of-the-line sporting equipment) impels purchases, especially if potential buyers do a Web search for the trademark—and especially if they use software that classifies merchants by the price they charge for the same merchandise, or if the gray marketer has made a deal with a Web portal such as Yahoo to buy a "keyword" such as ROLEX.

However, the licensing agreement covering these goods calls for them to be sold outside the United States, so importing them into the United States and selling them in competition with the goods that are

TIPS & TECHNIQUES

Copyright Misuse?

Gray marketers often copy the manufacturer's advertisements, logos, and other copyrighted materials and put them on the gray marketer's Web sites—so there may be a copyright infringement case on this basis, even though the underlying gray-market sale is legal.

supposed to be sold in the United States violates the agreement. In most cases, the gray-market goods are slightly different from the goods intended for the U.S. market—and sell for lower prices, creating an incentive to import them and attract bargain-hunters.

In 1988, the Supreme Court decided the case of *K-Mart Corp. v. Cartier,* permitting the items to be imported because, although the license agreement is not observed, the goods themselves are genuine and consumers are therefore not at risk of being deceived. A legal principle called the first-sale doctrine basically says that anyone who purchases an item is allowed to use it in any lawful way, including re-selling it to someone else. This is true even if the original seller doesn't want the goods to be re-sold at that price, or in that market, or in that form.

However, that doctrine applies to goods that are *identical* in both the U.S. and non-U.S. markets. A gray-market importer is guilty of trademark infringement whenever the gray-market goods are significantly different from the goods sold within the United States, even if they aren't inferior.

Under a 1993 case decided by the D.C. Circuit, the holder of a U.S. trademark is entitled to seek relief under Lanham Act §42 against the importation and/or sale of gray goods that are materially different from the goods sold in the United States under the same trademark.

IN THE REAL WORLD

Recording a Trademark for Customs Purposes

To record a trademark for §42 purposes, a status copy of the trademark registration, five copies of the registration, and a fee of $190 per class within which the trademark is registered, should be sent to the U.S. Customs Service, Intellectual Property Rights Branch, 1300 Pennsylvania Avenue NW, Washington, DC 20229. The fee should be paid by check or money order payable to the U.S. Customs Service.

The U.S. Customs Service adopted regulations to enforce the ruling of this case. Gray goods can be seized by Customs if they are different from the U.S. goods carrying the same trademark. To dissolve the seizure, the importer has to put a label on the goods that says that the merchandise has been imported without the manufacturer's authorization and is physically and materially different from the authorized merchandise sold in the United States.

As an example, importation of items into the United States after the manufacturer has discontinued them in the U.S. market would infringe the trademark, and any difference that consumers would likely take into account in making purchasing decisions would be considered material, and therefore could make importation of the gray goods an infringement on the U.S. trademark.

Preparing for a Licensing Transaction

There are many books and periodicals that provide information about the licensing industry, and can provide contact information for businesses in search of partners. Periodicals in this marketplace include *The Licensing Journal, The Licensing Book, The Licensing Report,*

Licensing International, and *The Licensing Letter.* There are also numerous general and specialized directories, such as *The Thomas Register, MacRae's Blue Book, International Licensing Directory, Toy Manufacturers Association Directory of Toys,* and *Trade Names Dictionary.*

Both the potential licensor and licensee should review the scheduled licensing program to make sure that it does not violate trademarks held by others. The process of trademark clearance is similar to the initial trademark search that should be undertaken before adopting a trademark (see page 49). This is an essential preliminary step because the more successful and profitable the marketing program, the more likely it is to attract attention—possibly in the form of lawsuits from other trademark owners claiming infringement.

Defining Sales for Royalty Purposes

The typical licensing agreement calls for payments of royalties (usually 3–15 percent of net sales) from the licensee to the licensor. An important negotiating issue is whether part of the payment will be refundable

TIPS & TECHNIQUES

Scope of the Search

The search will probably yield more useful results if the company commissioning the search tells the search firm what types of merchandise will be involved, and lets the search firm decide what classes should be searched, rather than specifying the classes.

Some search firms offer what is known as a *merchandising class search,* that covers all of the classes usually involved in licensing for approximately four times the cost of a one-class search. It is a good idea to order a search that covers state and common-law trademarks, rather than one limited to federally registered trademarks.

because of subsequent recalculations. A powerful licensor might even be able to collect an advance against the anticipated future income from the license.

Not every licensing agreement uses the same definitions, but *net sales* usually means gross sales minus quantity discounts and returns actually credited. Licensing agreements usually do *not* call for deductions relating to the licensee's expenses (e.g., discounts for cash, other discounts, commissions, amounts that are uncollectable, taxes, fees, or assessments).

Like any other contract negotiation, the balance of power will determine whether the terms favor the licensor or the licensee. For example, any license agreement will have to explain the licensee's obligations to make reports and payments to the licensor. The more powerful the licensor, the more likely it is that interest will be charged on late payments, and the greater the discretion the licensor will have to audit the licensee's books.

Licensing agreements should anticipate potential problems and determine how they will be handled. Significant issues include the following:

- *The start and end dates for the license*—Will the licensee be required to start sales no later than a particular date? Or will there be a *hold-back period* (for instance, until a movie opens or an anticipated best seller is published) to increase interest in the merchandise and the underlying licensed property? Will the licensee have a certain amount of time after the end of the license during which it can dispose of its remaining inventory?

- *The extent of the territory*—How does this affect cyberspace as well as bricks-and-mortar stores?

- *Royalty computations*—Will there be one royalty rate for U.S. and another for foreign sales?

- *Conditions under which the licensor will be justified in terminating the license*—Will it apply to sales that fall below a specified minimum? Will termination be justified if quality control standards are not met?

- *How returns and discounts will be handled*—How will they affect royalty payments? Will refunds to the licensee be available?

- *Safety*—Who will be liable, and to what extent, if licensed products are unsafe for users?

In order to protect trade-secret confidentiality, it is common for licensing agreements to include confidentiality provisions. Potential licensees who investigate the licensor's product line and operations agree that this does not give them the right to use or publicize the licensor's trade secrets. If a licensing relationship does develop, the license agreement should stipulate that all confidential materials should be returned at the end of the license period, and that the ex-licensee will not be entitled to continuing use of the trade secrets.

From the licensee's point of view, the significant issues include:

- Whether the licensee is permitted to sublicense to others. Sublicenses may not extend beyond the term of the original license.

- Whether the license is exclusive. A nonexclusive license that theoretically permits sublicensing is not necessarily very valuable, because potential sublicensees might get a better deal by securing another nonexclusive license from the original licensor.

- If the terms of the license extend to all the products the licensee wishes to offer.

- For properties with numerous options, the license must clarify exactly which options are involved—for example, all of the characters in an animated film, or only some of them?

- Whether the license calls for a one-time flat fee or ongoing royalties—and how the royalties are computed.

Quality-Control Measures

One of the most important features of a trademark license agreement is the quality-control provision. A trademark is supposed to be a guarantee to consumers of uniform quality of goods, so if the licensee sells inferior goods, the trademark is not only objectively less valuable, but may become legally vulnerable on the grounds of *abandonment*.

IN THE REAL WORLD

Quality Control

- Minimum acceptable quality-control provision: the licensee must agree to produce products of quality at least as good as that already manufactured by the licensee under other circumstances.

- A better quality-control program covers advertising and promotion as well as manufacturing itself, and gives the licensor the right to review and approve marketing materials before they are put into use, as well as approving final product designs and the first production line sample of the product before it is placed on the market. (The designer may also have the right of pre-sale review and approval.)

- The licensor should retain the right to re-inspect and review samples on a periodic basis.

- The licensor should demand that the licensee place the appropriate copyright and trademark notices on the merchandise, tags, labels, sales documentation, and so on.

- The licensee should agree that it will not use a trademark as a generic term in any of its advertising or marketing materials

- The quality-control program should require destruction or re-working of defective goods, instead of permitting their sale (even their sale as "seconds").

Therefore, it is absolutely mandatory that the licensing agreement include language setting out the quality-control program.

Just putting the language into the agreement isn't enough—the licensor has to be able to produce evidence of active policing and enforcement.

Even after a particular item has been approved by the licensor, the licensee should be required to get the licensor's advance written approval before changing it. Otherwise, unscrupulous licensees could submit an acceptable sample, but then switch to producing inferior goods in quantity.

It's also important for the license to include an "exploitation clause," mandating that the licensee meet a schedule for introducing the product (typically, this will be done at a trade show) and making the first shipment to paying customers.

If the license covers territory both inside and outside the U.S., usually the dates for foreign introduction and shipment will be set later. Another aspect of the exploitation clause is the licensee's ongoing obligation to continue to distribute licensed merchandise within the territory. The license can be terminated if the licensee fails to do so.

Franchising Considerations

In effect, a franchise is a sophisticated program of trademark licensing. Customers who go to a franchised operation expect that quality and service will be uniform throughout the franchise system, and products will be at least roughly comparable. A conscientious franchisor will want to make sure that franchisees maintain at least acceptable minimum standards—otherwise, the goodwill of the entire franchise operation will suffer and its trademark will become far less valuable.

On the other hand, excessive interference in franchisees' operations can create unfair competition and antitrust problems. *Tying* is an antitrust

TIPS & TECHNIQUES

Cover Future Technologies

As developments from home video to e-commerce show, technology continues to advance. Long-term licensing agreements should therefore allocate rights in technologies that are now in the process of development, as well as those that will be developed in the future.

violation that requires customers to purchase merchandise they do not want as a condition of getting what they do want. In the franchise context, this could mean forcing franchisees to buy supplies and materials directly from the franchisor (usually at higher prices than competitors would charge).

Sometimes tying of this kind is acceptable, on the grounds that it supports the franchisor's legitimate objective of maintaining quality standards throughout the whole franchise operation. This is especially true if the products involved use secret formulas or trade secrets, because exactly comparable products are not available on the open market. But requiring franchisees to buy something as standard as white paper napkins or plastic spoons from the franchisor would probably be vulnerable to a legal challenge.

A licensing program that restricts licensees to distinct territories and limits their freedom to compete with one another could be considered a contract, combination, or conspiracy in restraint of trade that violates antitrust laws.

Licensing and the Internet

Some licenses have a very long duration, so many licenses are now in effect that predate 1996 (the year in which Internet access became broadly diffused among non–technologically sophisticated consumers).

These licenses should be reviewed. In all probability, they will not mention Internet sales, although there may be implied coverage (for instance, if the license spells out the licensor's and licensee's respective rights in technology developed after the agreement was signed).

One way to handle the problem is to negotiate a new rider dealing with Internet issues. If the licensee already has global rights, then there's no problem; but if the licensee's geographic territory is limited, then the global reach of the Internet could be a problem. An easy solution is for the licensee to agree to accept online orders only if they come from within the specified territory, and to put a notice on the Web site that orders cannot be accepted outside the territory.

When it comes to matters like the licensee's ability to sell competing brands on the Web, a site should probably be treated like a bricks-and-mortar store. If there are antitrust or unfair competition problems with forbidding sales of competing products, that is probably just as true for online sales.

IN THE REAL WORLD

When to Review Changes

As already noted, it is a good idea for the licensor to require approval of the licensee's marketing materials, and a Web site definitely falls into this category. But it would probably be a waste of resources to review every trivial change on the licensee's Web site, because it is the nature of Web sites to be updated frequently. The agreement should probably put the burden on the licensee to notify the licensor before the site is changed in a way that has a significant impact on the marketing of the licensed merchandise, and for the licensor to do some routine monitoring for compliance—but not for the licensor to review every change to the site.

Sub-Licenses

A sublicense is an agreement between a licensee and other people that duplicates the relationship between the original trademark owner and the licensee.

The holder of a nonexclusive license, even if it has the right to issue sublicenses, might find that potential sublicensees can get a better deal by obtaining another nonexclusive license from the original trademark holder than by entering into a sublicense.

Even if the license is exclusive, the agreement may forbid or limit sublicenses. The legal principle is that a sublicense cannot extend beyond the term of the original license, so sublicenses entered into late in the cycle might be too short to attract potential sublicensees.

Winding Up

Some issues arise after the scheduled termination of the licensing agreement, because it is likely that the licensee will still have some unsold merchandise. It will also have access to intellectual property, including trade secrets and know-how.

One approach is for the agreement to schedule a meeting a certain number of months before the expiration date. The purpose of the meeting is to negotiate post-termination issues. The problem, though, is that the meeting is likely to be inconclusive.

Another possibility is to treat payment of the licensing fees as the equivalent of a permanent, paid-up license to use the trade secrets and know-how (and perhaps even the trademarks) indefinitely after the expiration date, on the theory that the license fees already paid represent payment in full.

Yet another approach, one that powerful licensors are likely to favor, is to call for royalty payments to continue (although possibly at a reduced rate) after the end of the formal term of the agreement, to account for the licensee's continuing use of the know-how.

Patent Licensing

As already discussed, it is common for businesses to own several types of intellectual property. Companies that own patents face additional questions when it comes to licensing those patents.

Patents get very strong protection, so not only is it unlawful to infringe on a patent, the patent holder may be able to get legal remedies based on the following:

- Sale of unpatentable components of a patented product
- Sale of materials and apparatus that can be used to carry out a patented industrial process
- Supplying unpatented components of a patented product with the intent that the patent product be manufactured outside the United States without the consent of the patent holder
- Importing, selling, even using a product made by a patented process without the consent of the patent holder

On the other hand, patent holders who misuse their patents forfeit legal protection. The patent is unenforceable until the misuse has stopped and all of its effects have ended. A misused patent is unenforceable against infringers, even against infringers who were not harmed by patent misuse.

A patent is misused if the overall effect of licenses of the patent is to restrain competition unlawfully in the relevant market. The basic, underlying question is whether, on balance, the effect of the licensing agreement is to favor or suppress competition.

It is a misuse of a patent to force a licensee to agree not to sell products that compete with the products sold under the license. This is true whether or not the agreement will stand up to scrutiny under antitrust law.

Package licensing (of patents or any form of intellectual property) is also forbidden. Although it is perfectly acceptable to license a group of patents or trademarks together, it is not allowed to require licensees to undertake the whole group of licenses, or one or more less desirable licenses, as a condition of getting access to the desired license(s).

A patent owner has the legal right to refuse to license the patent at all, or to refuse to license it to a particular party. However, it is not legally acceptable for a patent owner to enter into agreements with other businesses that call for not using the patent, or that involve refusal to license the patent.

Trade Secrets

In modern business, intellectual property provides some of the company's most significant and valuable assets. Within that category, trade secrets can be among the most valuable types of business intellectual property.

According to a traditional formula used by tort lawyers, a *trade secret* is any formula, pattern, device, or collection of information that is used in business and that provides an advantage over those businesses

TIPS & TECHNIQUES

Patent & Trademark

Patents have an expiration date; trademarks do not (unless the holder forgets to keep the registration current). So a patent is a *wasting asset,* whereas a trademark can actually become more valuable over time as it becomes more familiar and accepted by consumers. Therefore, an agreement that covers not only patents but trademarks may continue to have economic value even after the patents expire, because the licensee will want to maintain access to the goodwill developed by the trademark.

that don't know the secret. For example, a chemical formula, manufacturing process, or customer list could be a trade secret. Negative information ("You can't produce Chemical X by using Process Y") can also have commercial value and therefore can become a trade secret. Most trade secrets relate to production, but some relate to marketing (e.g., data about customer preferences in different parts of the United States).

The law treats trade secrets very differently from other types of intellectual property. Getting a patent requires making full disclosure of the specifications for the invention. Getting a trademark requires making the proposed trademark available for publication and possible objection by the public. Although it is not necessary for works to be published to qualify for copyright protection, most copyrighted works are published eventually. But a trade secret, as the name suggests, has to be kept secret, and publication will remove protection.

Another difference is that the federal government grants patents and trademarks (and state governments can also register trademarks) based on examination. Copyrights are granted more or less automatically. There are no government agencies involved in supervising or registering trade secrets.

This also means that, although a patent can be granted to only one inventor, it is perfectly possible for the same trade secret to be used simultaneously by many companies, all of whom have developed it independently or gotten licensing rights to it.

Our legal system reserves important roles for both the federal and state courts. That means that it is often important to decide whether state courts can tackle a particular issue, or whether it is federally preempted—that is, only the federal system is allowed to make decisions.

In 1974, the Supreme Court ruled that federal patent law does not preempt state trade secret law, so trade secret cases can still be brought in state courts. (In contrast, all patent cases have to go through the federal system—state legislatures are not allowed to make patent laws, and state courts are not allowed to hear patent cases, although they may sometimes handle contract cases or other cases that have only a limited contact with patents.)

The Supreme Court's rationale was that inventors should have the option of choosing trade secret status for their inventions, especially if it is not clear if the inventions are patentable. The already hard-working Patent Office should not be burdened with a lot of useless or borderline applications.

In some cases, the company's intellectual property lawyers will indicate that some of the company's technology could be patented. In that case, it becomes necessary to decide whether to seek a patent (which provides exclusive rights, but only for a limited period of time) or treat the technology as a trade secret (which can continue indefinitely, but does not protect the company against independent discovery of the same technology). However, most trade secrets, although they are commercially valuable, are not patentable: because they do not involve enough of a development over the general state of knowledge to be truly original, for example.

The owner of a trade secret has the right to control its use—for example, if a licensee fails to abide by the terms of the license, or if outsiders use industrial espionage or other improper means to learn the secret, the trade secret owner has the right to sue the wrongdoer.

Many factors can be used to determine whether a particular item or collection of information should be protected as a trade secret:

- The extent to which the so-called trade secret information is known outside the industry.

- How broadly it is known by the company's employees and by other people in the same industry. Knowledge by employees is important because most trade secret lawsuits involve information allegedly misappropriated by disgruntled employees or ex-employees.

- The value of the information to the business—and to its competitors. For example, if the business is the only one that has been able to solve something that is acknowledged as a tricky problem for the industry.

- The degree of effort and/or money expended to develop the trade secret.

- Whether it would be hard or easy for someone else to duplicate the information.

- The measures taken to guard secrecy. This is perhaps the most important factor.

There is no hard and fast line between trade secrets and know-how (facilities or procedures developed by a business that can improve efficiency or cut costs, and therefore provide a commercial advantage). Any or all of these might qualify for trade secret protection—as long, of course, as the company prevents dissemination:

- Databases used for design or testing protocols

- Safety procedures for handling hazardous materials

- Sources for raw materials

- Participation in joint purchasing arrangements

- Training methods and manuals

- Quality assurance procedures

- Pay planning formulas

Many courts take the position that a plain list of customers is not a trade secret, because anyone could accumulate the same information just by observing delivery trucks, or contacting businesses listed in the Yellow Pages. However, a more detailed list, containing information about customer characteristics and preferences, would be more likely to be treated as a protectable trade secret.

There is no requirement that trade secrets have enough novelty to support a patent application. However, if the secret really is a *novel invention,* then someone who wrongfully appropriates it will have a legal obligation to turn over the profits earned through the misappropriation, and will be enjoined against continuing to use the information that was obtained wrongfully. If, on the other hand, the trade secret is something that any good mechanic could have developed, then probably the plaintiff will only be able to recover whatever profits it lost because of the misappropriation, and an injunction might be denied because the defendant conceivably could have developed the trade secret independently.

Furthermore, if the plaintiff continues to pursue its case once it is clear that the plaintiff was lax in protecting its trade secrets, the plaintiff might be ordered to pay the defendant's attorney's fees because of this abuse of the legal process.

Uniform Trade Secrets Act

The Uniform Trade Secrets Act was finalized by a group of state commissioners in 1979. It got the approval of the American Bar Association in 1980, and was adopted by many states. Amendments were approved in 1985. The reason why Uniform Acts are drafted, and are often eagerly adopted by states, is to create a single uniform standard instead of varying state laws that can be confusing and set up barriers to trade between states.

The UTSA definition of a trade secret is "information, including a formula, pattern, compilation, program, device, method, technique, or process" that meets two criteria. First, the secret has at least potential independent economic value just because it is not generally known to other parties that could use it profitably. Second, the owner of the trade secret has to make reasonable efforts to *keep* it secret.

Under the UTSA, a party can become liable for improper acquisition, use, or disclosure of a trade secret. But there is no liability without improper actions. For instance, merely copying an item that is not patented is legal. Competitors are also allowed to invent the same thing independently; to reverse engineer a product (take it apart to see how it works); to license the trade secret from its owner; or to read published literature or observe the item in public use or display.

The introduction to the UTSA points out that patents can be invalidated. That means that someone who applies for a patent might be in the awkward position of disclosing how to make the invention (because this is part of the patent process). After the patent is invalidated, though, the invention will be public knowledge. If, on the other hand, the inventor had kept the process a trade secret, there would be no duty to disclose, and the technology could be kept a secret.

The UTSA doesn't require continuous use in business as a condition of trade secret status. Therefore, a company can bring suit under the UTSA if its trade secrets were taken before the owner had a chance to use the secrets commercially.

IN THE REAL WORLD

Licensing After Patent Expiration

In 1979, the Supreme Court decided that federal patent law does not prevent making licensing deals under which the licensee agrees to keep making royalty payments after a patent expires—because the payments can be treated as paying for trade secrets about the product that were not disclosed by the patent.

The UTSA defines *misappropriation* (proof of which can justify an injunction or other relief) to include four elements:

- There is a trade secret.

- The defendant learns the trade secret because of a relationship between the parties (e.g., the defendant is an employee or another company that licenses the trade secret).

- The defendant is aware that the plaintiff considers the information to be valuable property that must not be used outside the relationship.

- The owner of the trade secret has been harmed, or is at risk of future harm, because the trade secret has been disclosed without permission, or there is a risk that this will happen.

If these elements are proved, the court will either find that there was an implied contract that the defendant broke (this is usually the result when the plaintiff wins a case against an ex-employee) or that there was a confidential relationship, and the defendant breached its duties under this relationship.

According to the UTSA, *disclosure* in the trade secret context doesn't necessarily mean that the general public can gain access to the information. All it means is that those who could gain economic advantage from the information can get it. Using this interpretation, information

IN THE REAL WORLD

Damages Limited

If more than one party is entitled to treat the same process or information as a trade secret, and misappropriation occurs, only the actual victim of the misappropriation is entitled to damages—not everyone who has a legitimate right to use the secret.

in trade journals, reference books, and other publications is considered readily available.

Also, if it is easy to figure out how the finished product is made just by analyzing it, it is hard to claim trade secret protection. However, if Company #2 does a lot of research and hard work to *reverse-engineer* Company #1's product, Company #2 can treat the results of the work as its own trade secret.

Section 2 of the UTSA says that the owner of a trade secret can get the court to issue an injunction against the misappropriator, to stop further misappropriation. Usually, the injunction ends when the information stops being a trade secret. However, the injunction can continue for a reasonable period of time afterward, to make sure that the misappropriator doesn't get commercial advantage from its wrongdoing. Another possibility is that the misappropriator will be allowed to keep using the trade secret—but will have to pay a reasonable royalty for the privilege, up until the time when the information would have become generally known anyway, losing its trade secret status.

Damages (the money the trade-secret owner lost because of the misappropriation; money unfairly earned by the misappropriator) can be ordered instead of or in addition to an injunction. The court can also order punitive damages of up to twice the actual damages in cases of willful and malicious misappropriation.

When it is impossible to figure out the damages any other way, the court can order the misappropriator to pay the equivalent of a reasonable royalty for the use of the trade secret—as long as there is usable evidence of what would be a reasonable royalty! But damages will not be granted for the period of time that an injunction was in force—the UTSA's position is that this would provide "double-dip" benefits for the plaintiff.

Under UTSA §4, either side can be required to pay the other side's attorneys' fees if the other side prevails. That is, the defendant may have to pay the plaintiff's fees based on bad-faith misappropriation, or for unfair conduct during litigation. But unfair litigation conduct can also be a reason to make a losing plaintiff pay the winning defendant's attorneys' fees.

Section 5 of the UTSA makes sure that courts will maintain the secrecy of trade secrets that are being litigated. For instance, the court can issue protective orders and seal records to make sure that the trade secrets are not released to the public.

UTSA cases have to be brought either within three years of the time the owner of the trade secret actually finds out about the misappropriation, or when it should have been discovered if the owner had been careful about investigating (§6).

Restatement of Unfair Competition

A group of legal scholars, in the *Restatement of Unfair Competition,* came up with some slightly different definitions. According to this authority, a trade secret is any information that can be used in the operation of a business, as long at it is valuable and secret enough to provide an economic advantage (or at least the potential for one).

A party can become liable under the *Restatement* when it acquires, by improper means, materials that it knows or should have known to be trade secrets, whether the material is used in the appropriator's business or is disclosed to others.

The *Restatement* calls for injunctions against further use of improperly acquired trade secrets, and allows damages to be imposed, based on factors such as these:

- The degree of certainty to which the plaintiff has established its losses and the defendant's gains
- The type and amount of misappropriation

- Whether an injunction would be enough of a remedy to put the plaintiff back in the position it would have been in if the misappropriation had not occurred

- The defendant's knowledge about the trade-secret status of the material; its intent in taking and using it; if the defendant had any reason to believe that it could use the material legitimately

- Whether the plaintiff was guilty of any kind of carelessness or improper conduct

Protecting Trade Secrets

There are two issues in deciding whether a trade secret has been wrongfully acquired. The first is whether the defendant clearly did something wrong (hiring industrial spies, for example) or behaved reasonably (analyzing products already on the market). The second issue is whether the plaintiff recognized that certain material constituted trade secrets and tried to protect confidentiality.

A company that does not make reasonable efforts to maintain confidentiality won't be allowed to sue others for stealing its trade secrets. The legal system acknowledges that an ordinary commercial business can't be expected to satisfy the same security standards as a military base. So the question becomes what is a reasonable protection program.

There are elements of a sound program that indicates that the company is aware of its responsibilities to defend its trade secrets:

- There is ongoing review of the company's security needs.

- Physical security—documents and back-ups are locked up in a fire-safe location; visitors sign in; access to areas where trade secrets are written down or used in production is controlled; employee ID badges and security cameras are used.

- Computer security—passwords are required for access to confidential material; confidential material is not placed on company Web sites. Allowing employees to put trade secret material on their laptop computers, or keep backup copies at home, could create problems, but does not absolutely disqualify the material from trade-secret protection.

- Label confidential and trade-secret material so there can be no claims that the material was publicly available information.

- Production security—limit the number of people who are familiar with the whole process; divide the process into a number of steps; label secret ingredients something like "Component #2," and express the amount of secret ingredients as something like "10 mg Component #2" instead of giving the actual names and ratio of the ingredients. In some cases, it makes sense to divide production into steps, with a different department handling each—once again, to limit the number of people who have all the information.

- Make employees sign pledges to maintain trade secret confidentiality, and remind them regularly of this obligation.

- Have employees get clearance before publishing technical articles or making presentations at seminars and conferences, to make sure that they do not inadvertently disclose trade secrets.

- Have employees surrender all copies of trade-secret documents when they leave the company; make it a condition of getting severance pay that they remove trade secret information from their home computers and continue to maintain confidentiality in the future.

- Trade secrets should not be included in the company's data sheets—even if distribution of the data sheets is supposed to be limited to qualified customers.

- If trade secrets have to be released to a third party (such as a licensee or a company that might merge or acquire the company), a confidentiality agreement should be signed before the information is released.

False Advertising

One of the underpinnings of the legal rules about trademarks and unfair competition is that marks are used commercially to provide consumers with accurate information about the source of merchandise they might want to buy. Trademark infringement and unfair copying of merchandise or trade dress interfere with this objective. So does false advertising, because consumers get inaccurate disparaging information about competitors' goods, inaccurate praise of the advertisers' goods, or both. This interferes with their ability to make sound buying decisions.

The Federal Trade Commission Act

A federal law, the Federal Trade Commission Act, establishes the Federal Trade Commission (FTC) as an enforcement agency, and also defines various business practices as unfair and illegal.

IN THE REAL WORLD

Power of Peer Pressure

Although lawsuits and threats of administrative enforcement are important in keeping businesses from inappropriate business conduct and in punishing inappropriate conduct after it occurs, sometimes peer pressure is at least as effective. Guidance from peers can also be very helpful in establishing business policy and practices.

The Council of Better Business Bureaus (BBB) publishes a pamphlet, *Do's and Don'ts in Advertising Copy,* covering concepts of false versus appropriate advertising. The BBB's National Advertising Division (NAD) monitors national ads and provides a forum for challenges to the accuracy of national ads. The BBB also maintains a National Advertising Review Board (NARB) for advertisers who disagree with NAD pronouncements about their advertising.

The central expressions of this policy are found in §5 of the FTC Act (15 U.S. Code §1117(a)). This section forbids unfair methods of competition in or affecting interstate commerce, as well as unfair or deceptive acts or practice in or affecting commerce.

It is clear that false advertising of food, drugs, devices, and cosmetics is an unfair trade practice—because that's what §12 of the FTC Act says. Under §15, false advertising means an advertisement (but not labels, which are excluded from coverage under this section) that is misleading in a material respect. *Materiality* is a complex legal concept that means something like "significance" or "importance." Furthermore, under the materiality test, an advertiser can be penalized not only for saying something that is false, but for suggestions that create a false impression, and for failure to provide all of the facts needed for consumers to get an accurate picture.

The FTC can get involved only with respect to business actions in or affecting commerce. The FTC's job is to act in the public interest, not to protect the interests of individual competitors or consumers. The FTC Act gives powers only to the government agency. It does not provide what is called a "private right of action." In other words, individuals and businesses are not allowed to bring suits to enforce the FTC Act.

The Act gives the FTC the power to investigate, seek consent orders (where the challenged company agrees to modify its business practices), adjudicate violations, get cease and desist orders (ordering the company to change its business practices), civil penalties, restitution for consumers, and orders that the challenged company publish corrective advertisements to give more accurate information to consumers.

The FTC has published rules requiring that advertisers have a reasonable basis for making claims before the claims are made to consumers. Under these rules, there is a three-part test for deception:

- The advertiser made a misrepresentation or omission that is likely to mislead consumers.

- The consumers were acting reasonably under the circumstances.

- The misrepresentation or omission is material.

In deciding whether it would be appropriate to order corrective advertising, the FTC considers factors such as these:

- The amount of exposure consumers had to the claim

- The persuasiveness of the advertising

- How the advertiser's inaccurate claims were presented

- The nature of the audience (less sophistication means more protection)

- Whether consumers are likely to retain misconceptions about the goods even after the ad campaign ends.

The FTC Act also gives the FTC the power to impose civil penalties of up to $10,000 for every violation of one of the agency's final orders. The agency can bring a civil suit for penalties of up to $10,000 for every knowing or willful violation of the FTC trade regulation rules.

TIPS & TECHNIQUES

Advertising Rules

Part 16 of the Code of Federal Regulations (CFR), a paperback encyclopedia of the regulations issued by various federal agencies, includes guides that the FTC has published to explain what constitutes legitimate versus abusive use of terms such as "new" and "free" in advertisements. The FTC rules also cover topics such as comparative price advertising ("Only $100! Elsewhere $200!"), other kinds of comparative advertising, and testimonials from satisfied customers.

The same penalty can be applied for every knowing or willful violation of a cease-and-desist letter that the agency issued about unfair or deceptive acts and practices.

In addition to the federal law, all the states have laws known as *Little FTC Acts* to control unfair and deceptive business practices.

Lanham Act §43(a)

Section 43(a) of the Lanham Act not only protects unregistered trademarks against infringement, it provides a cause of action (type of lawsuit) for false advertising. Section 43(a) was originally adopted in 1946, but until the Trademark Law Revision Act of 1988 was passed, it did not explicitly cover false advertising. (See page 9 for more about §43(a).)

Unlike the FTC Act, which only provides for government enforcement, §43(a) allows private suits by businesses. Consumers do not have standing to sue under this section (i.e., they are not permitted to bring lawsuits of this type). The appropriate plaintiffs are competitors of the company alleged to have engaged in false advertising, or other parties who have a significant commercial interest.

Under the current version of §43(a), a business is liable to anyone who believes he, she, or it is likely to suffer economic damage:

- In connection with any goods or services or any container for goods that the defendant uses "in commerce" (which pretty much means interstate commerce, defined broadly to include all kinds of business).

- The case involves any word, term, name, symbol, device, or combination or any false designation of origin, false or misleading description of fact, or false or misleading representation of fact.

- This false or misleading representation is likely to deceive or cause confusion about the defendant's affiliation, connection, or association, or to deceive or cause confusion as to whether the defendant's goods originate with someone else, or are sponsored or approved by someone else.

OR

- The false or misleading representation constitutes commercial advertising or promotion that misrepresents the nature, characteristics, qualities, or geographic origin of the goods sold by *any* business. This provision was added to the federal law in order to penalize *product disparagement* (i.e., false statements about a competitor's products or services).

When the false claims made in the advertising are clear and not ambiguous, then the court can decide what the advertising message is just by viewing the ads. Evidence about public perceptions is not necessary. But if the claims are ambiguous, the case will probably require "extrinsic" evidence (material outside the ad), such as consumer surveys.

Once the advertising claim and express or implied message have been determined, the court has to determine if the message is "false." Section 43(a) covers affirmatively misleading statements, partially correct statements, and failure to disclose material fact. Section 43(a) extends to false representations in brochures and promotional material, such as packaging.

There's an important exception. "Puffery"—nonspecific positive statements about a product ("You'll love BLURCH's delicious, home-style taste") isn't covered by §43(a), because it is accepted as a harmless, legitimate part of the process of attracting customers. However, if BLURCH did not contain any butter—or if the competing products used vegetable shortening—a statement that "BLURCH uses only pure, fresh creamery butter...our competitors use rendered camel fat" would violate §43(a).

Section 43(a) penalizes only false or misleading descriptions or representations of *fact*. Therefore, opinions in advertisements do not violate this section. An *opinion* is a belief, conclusion, or prediction that can-

IN THE REAL WORLD

The Skil Test

Probably the most common test that courts use in Lanham Act §43(a) deceptive advertising cases is the five-factor Skil test (named after a 1974 case decided by the federal District Court for the Northern District of Illinois). Using this analysis, deceptive advertising has occurred if

- The defendant made false statements about a product (including its own products in a comparative ad)—whether the statement was inappropriately disparaging to the competing product, or inappropriately positive about its own products.

- The statements actually deceived or tended to deceive a substantial segment of the audience.

- This deception was material (i.e., likely to influence purchasing decisions).

- The goods that were falsely advertised entered into interstate commerce (if they stayed within one state, §43(a) doesn't apply).

- Either the plaintiff actually was injured or was likely to be injured by the defendant's actions—whether in the form of lost sales that went to the defendant instead of the plaintiff, or customers' opinion of the plaintiff's products became less favorable.

not be substantiated by objective proof: for example, "Our new fall line includes the freshest fashions and covers all the new trends!" An advertiser's argument or subjective assertion, addressed to consumers, who can then make up their own minds about its persuasiveness, is a pure opinion that is protected by the First Amendment.

It is clear that the First Amendment not only protects the freedom of speech of individuals; it also protects "commercial speech" on behalf of businesses. However, businesses do not have an absolute right to say anything and expect to be protected.

Commercial speech is protected only to the extent that it deals with a lawful activity and is not misleading. However, government is only allowed to regulate speech if the regulation directly advances a substantial governmental interest (such as protecting public safety). Even then, the regulation isn't allowed to be any broader than the minimum needed to carry out the public interest.

Remedies in §43(a) Cases

In §43(a) cases, like most cases in the trademark/unfair competition area, the major type of relief is the injunction. In this context, the injunction would forbid the defendant to engage in any further false advertising or disparagement of the plaintiff's products. The defendant might also be ordered to publish corrective advertising.

However, the burden is always on the plaintiff to prove both the false and misleading nature of the advertising, and the extent to which the plaintiff was injured by it.

To get an award of money damages instead of just an injunction, the plaintiff has to prove that consumers were deceived by relying on the advertisement. The plaintiff also has to prove that it lost sales for that reason, or otherwise that its business was actually (and not just potentially) harmed.

TIPS & TECHNIQUES

No Defense

If the plaintiff can prove that the ad in question was false and misleading, it is *not* a defense that the defendant acted in good faith, or that it was mistaken about the facts presented.

CHAPTER 8

Unfair Competition

 After reading this chapter you will be able to

- Understand what businesses can—and cannot—say about each other
- Use covenants not to compete to make sure that ex-employees don't harm your business
- Use state laws to combat unfair and deceptive trade practices
- Know how the rights of privacy and publicity work together

In our legal system, a crime is something that is considered an offense against the public as a whole, and therefore is prosecuted by the state. A tort is something that is considered an offense against one or more private parties, and therefore can become the subject of a lawsuit by the parties who allege that they suffered some kind of damage because of the wrongdoing of the tortfeasor.

Business torts, also known as *torts of unfair competition,* are a broad range of categories under which a business can become liable. The theory behind allowing business tort suits is that the legal system is supposed to protect legitimate business relationships and honest business, by enforcing rules of fair play.

In most cases, laws are passed against business torts based on the tortfeasor's intent to block healthy business competition. However, in some instances—especially where trademarks are involved—the legal system focuses on the property to be protected, so there may be a viable tort case even if the infringement on protected property happened innocently and does not involve bad faith.

Some of the legal categories into which unfair competition cases can fall include

- Interference with contracts.

- Interference with employment relationships.

- Unfair trade practices: Intentional torts like defamation and trade libel. The 1988 revisions to federal trademark law made it possible to sue for trade disparagement or trade libel in the form of false or misleading representations or descriptions of fact. A company can get sued if its claims that its products are superior tend to deceive consumers.

- Infringement of trademarks, copyrights, patents, and other forms of intellectual property.

- Improprieties in the relationship between franchisor and franchisee—especially in connection with termination of the franchise.

State Unfair Competition Laws

Most of the states have passed at least one statute regulating commercial behavior. Usually, these laws are broadly drafted—extending to, for instance, "any unlawful, unfair, or fraudulent business act or practice," as well as unfair, deceptive, untrue, or misleading advertising.

The purpose of these laws is to maintain a healthy climate of vigorous but law-abiding competition. Therefore, the laws protect trade secrets; make it possible to enter into and enforce noncompete agreements with former employees; protect lawful contracts against unfair interference by outsiders; and protect one company's products against illegitimate disparagement by competitors that is intended to cause economic harm.

Covenants Not to Compete

As long as a person continues to be employed by a company, he or she owes a duty of loyalty to that company. However, when someone resigns, is laid off, or is fired, in many cases that person will seek employment elsewhere or will start a new business that competes with the former employer. That puts the first employer at risk of having its intellectual property given to the new employer.

Therefore, it is common for written employment contracts to contain *covenants not to compete*—or even for employers to use a separate form for this purpose when a person who does not have a written employment contract ceases being an employee. For instance, the covenant not to compete could be part of the outplacement process or part of the negotiations for a severance package.

In a covenant not to compete, the individual agrees to avoid direct or indirect competition with the employer. But the legal system will not tolerate depriving an individual of the right to earn a living, so usually the covenant will be subject to restrictions (such as lasting for a certain number of years or months; covering only a certain geographic area; and being limited to activities that could actually threaten economic harm to the ex-employer). Whether the covenant will be legally enforceable depends on whether the ex-employee got enough economic value (*consideration*) in return for signing it and whether the agreement is reasonable.

In order to be reasonable, limitations on when and where the ex-employee can work must not harm the public interest. The limitations must not be greater than what is required to protect the employer's legitimate economic interests, and they must not impose undue hardship on the ex-employee.

The restrictions should also be linked to the employer's use of trade secrets, intellectual property, and other forms of protectable information. So the geographic restriction should not be broader than the territory in which the employer actually uses the information. By the same token, the length of time during which the ex-employee is bound by the covenant not to compete should not be longer than the time that the ex-employer would be able to use the information to compete in business. After all, customer lists become obsolete; fashions change; newer and better manufacturing processes are developed—no matter what the ex-employee does.

A person who has not entered into a valid covenant not to compete has the legal right to take a job, or start a business, that competes with the former employer, or to recruit employees of the former employer to work in the new business.

Furthermore, the legal system allows both employees and entrepreneurs to use general knowledge, skills, and experience they acquired in one job in other business settings. However, the legal system does not allow an ex-employee to use or disclose to others confidential information or trade secrets that belong to the former employer.

In this context, *confidential business information* means any item of data or knowledge that is not generally known in the industry, that is not a trade secret, but still provides a competitive advantage to those who have it. Current employees (and former employees who have agreed not to) are not permitted to disclose information that they knew or should have known was confidential.

Depending on the court and the circumstances, a covenant not to compete that is too extensive will be subject to either a "void per se" rule (i.e., no part of the agreement can be enforced if it contains any unreasonable provisions) or a blue pencil rule. Under the *blue pencil rule* or the *rule of reasonableness,* the court "edits" the agreement to make it reasonable, or throws out the unreasonable provisions but enforces the rest.

If the ex-employer sues the ex-employee for violating a covenant not to compete, in order to win and get money damages, the ex-employer has to show that it lost net profits as a direct result of the ex-employee's violation of the agreement. Furthermore, it is usually necessary to show that the amount of lost profits can be determined with a reasonable degree of certainty. Courts won't make an award of damages based on mere speculation.

Commercial Defamation and Trade Libel

The legal system protects the reputations of businesses, not just individuals, against disparaging comments that are made without justification, under circumstances that would not provide a privilege that protects making a statement.

The torts of defamation (trade libel, product disparagement, and injurious falsehood) involve a false communication that damages the reputation for quality of the plaintiff's goods or services. A statement made to one person is slander; a broadly published defamatory statement is libel. Defamation that occurs using an electronic medium such as e-mail or a Web site will probably be treated as libel, not slander.

Several elements have to be present for the subject of the statement to have a legal claim of commercial defamation or related tort:

- There must be a communication with a third party, not just internal communications within either the plaintiff corporation or the corporate defendant.

- A false, derogatory statement must have been made.

195

- The statement must involve the reputation of the plaintiff company or its products.

- The third party that receives the communication has to understand that it is defamatory, and that it involves the plaintiff's products. For example, Company A's ad that says, "Be sure that when you buy industrial chemicals, you only buy high-quality, tested chemicals," is not defamatory to Company B—but it would be if it said, "Buy quality-controlled chemicals, not Company B's shoddy, low-quality products."

The legal system recognizes a difference between a suit for trade libel (which protects a business's interest in being able to sell its products) and a defamation action (which protects the plaintiff's interest in its good reputation in the business community). Trade libel unfairly attacks the quality of the plaintiff company's goods or services. Commercial defamation says that the plaintiff company itself is lacking in integrity or honesty. Although the two concepts are somewhat different, the same conduct by the defendant could involve both trade libel and defamation.

A suit for trade libel is usually brought against a competitor, but other possible defendants are customers, employees, and third parties.

Privileges

Our entire legal system depends on finding the right balance between competing interests, each of which has some value and some claim to be defended. Therefore, even though some negative statements about a business are defamatory and can give rise to lawsuits and damages, the legal system recognizes *privileges* in some kinds of negative statements. That is, the negative statements have justification or value, and therefore do not create legal liability.

Statements of opinion (for instance, product reviews) and fair comment on matters of public interest (such as the environmental consequences of using certain products or concerns about health risks of drugs) are privileged.

The *Restatement (2nd) of Torts* (a legal commentary compiled by influential experts) says that a business has a conditional privilege to compare its goods to the goods of a competitor. In other words, the privilege does exist, but it is not absolute, and it will be taken away in cases of misuse, such as making specific, unfavorable, false statements about competing companies' products.

If the case is brought as a commercial defamation case, then the legal system presumes that the defendant acted with malice; the defendant has to prove that it didn't. On the other hand, in a trade libel case, it is up to the plaintiff to prove that malice was present. But if the defendant should reasonably have foreseen that a statement would be considered disparaging, then the defendant is deemed to have intended to disparage the plaintiff.

Misappropriation

Misappropriation involves taking away or making inappropriate use of business intellectual property—even if there is no deceit used, and even if consumers are not subjected to the risk of confusion. *Idea theft* is a typical reason for a misappropriation suit. This is sometimes phrased as *reaping where you have not sown* by making unauthorized use of a competitor's work, skill, or expenditures. In a classic case, for instance, one news syndication service was enjoined against pirating a rival syndicate's news releases.

Misappropriation can also be used in cases where there is no real trademark involved. For example, the management of a rock band may want to sue unauthorized vendors of T-shirts and other memorabilia involving the band. This is not really a trademark issue, because the fans at the concert don't really believe (or care one way or the other) that the band sponsored the items of merchandise. However, the band and its management have the legal right to control merchandising, and violating this right is misappropriation.

Section §43(a) of the Lanham Act extends beyond simple infringement of trademarks. It is broad enough to cover false designations of origin and false or misleading descriptions or representations of fact such as false advertising and promotion.

UDAP Laws

All of the states have passed laws against Unfair and Deceptive Acts and Practices (UDAP). These UDAP statutes have been nicknamed *Little FTC Acts,* because they are similar to the federal Fair Trade Commission Act, which also bans improper business conduct. A UDAP law proscribes infringement-related conduct, such as causing confusion as to the source or sponsorship of goods or services, or passing off goods as someone else's.

Many states have adopted or been influenced by the 1964 and 1966 versions of the Uniform Deceptive Trade Practices Act (UDTPA). Uniform Acts are written by teams of state commissioners, then released to

TIPS & TECHNIQUES

UDAP Damages

Drafting the complaint in a business tort case to include a cause of action under the state's UDAP law (as long as the cause of action can be asserted in good faith) can make it easier for a plaintiff who wins the case to recover double or treble damages or get an attorneys' fee award.

help state legislatures decide how to word the statutes in their own states. The 1966 version of the UDTPA says that historically, one business could sue another business for *passing off* or *palming off* if the first company lost sales because the second company claimed that its own products came from the first company.

Another possibility is *reverse palming off*—taking off trademarks and selling the plaintiff's product under the defendant's name. This violates §43(a) of the Lanham Act because it falsely designates the origin of the product.

The purpose of the UDTPA is to allow people and businesses to sue if they are at risk of economic harm because of someone else's false or deceptive advertising or misleading identification of business or merchandise. The UDTPA works in conjunction with state laws for trademark registration.

But it can be easier to get an injunction under the UDTPA than under trademark laws. That's because the UDTPA does not require the plaintiff to prove that the defendant was actually a business competitor, or that the defendant intended to deceive the public.

UDTPA §2 lists the types of conduct (including, but not limited to, trademark infringement) that can be penalized as deceptive trade practices:

- Passing off goods and services as coming from someone else. Originally, this meant unauthorized use of trade identification. Today, it also includes covert substitution of a different brand of goods for the one requested: for instance, when someone orders a COKE in a restaurant and instead is served a different brand of cola soft drink. Passing off doesn't necessarily involve trademarks. The essential feature of the tort is selling one manufacturer's goods on the basis that they come from a different manufacturer. To win the case, the plaintiff has to prove intent to deceive the public. However, the plaintiff does *not* have to prove that the plaintiff and defendant were business competitors. Nor does the plaintiff have to prove that any actual consumers were confused or misunderstood the source of the goods—only that confusion was likely to result.

- Causing a likelihood of confusion or of misunderstanding as to source, sponsorship, approval, or certification of goods or services.

- Doing the same thing with respect to affiliation or certification (e.g., by calling a store that has no connection with the Boy Scouts an OFFICIAL BOY SCOUT STORE).

- Deceptive geographic representations or designations.

- Claiming that goods have sponsorship, approval, characteristics, ingredients, uses, benefits, or qualities that they lack. This category includes false representation that a person is the representative, successor, associate, or affiliate of another.

- Misrepresenting the grade, standard, or quality of merchandise; selling used or reconditioned merchandise as new.

- Using false or misleading representations of fact to disparage someone else's goods.

- Advertising anything that the advertiser does not intend to sell as advertised (bait and switch) or without having enough stock to supply the reasonably expected demand. A defense is available if the advertiser discloses that quantities are limited— for example, in a clearance or odd lot sale.

- Making false or misleading statements of fact about the existence of, amounts, or reasons for price reductions. This covers both fictional "retailer's listed price" quoted so huge discounts can be claimed, and also perpetual Going Out of Business Sales.

- Finally, the UDTPA bans any other conduct that has a similar effect of creating a likelihood of confusion or misunderstanding.

Interference with Contractual Relations

The enforceability of contracts is a bedrock on which the business system rests. That's why the legal system includes remedies when one party deliberately and without legal justification interferes with another party's contracts. (It's legally impossible for a party to interfere with its *own* contracts; improper behavior is just plain breach of contract.) Interference with contractual relations has also been defined as impairing the plaintiff's right to carry out its lawful business.

For example, if a raw material is in short supply, a company with a lot of cash might induce Supplier Co. to break its contract with Honest Co. and deliver the material to Rich Co. instead.

There are five elements involved in a case of interference with contractual relations:

- A legal contract exists (not just an "understanding" or a "handshake deal").

- The defendant knows about the contract.

- The defendant intended to interfere; carelessness isn't enough to make a case.

- The interference directly caused economic harm to the plaintiff.

- The plaintiff had no reasonable way of avoiding the harm (in the supply case suggested above, if the plaintiff could have bought the supplies it needed somewhere else at a reasonable price, it wasn't really damaged by the interference with its contract).

A winning plaintiff can get an injunction against further interference with the contract. Other remedies can include compensatory damages (to make up for what the plaintiff lost), punitive damages (to punish outrageously wrong conduct by the defendant) and restitution of benefits that the plaintiff should have gotten under the contract.

In some cases, intentional interference with contracts may also violate federal and/or state antitrust laws. One advantage of antitrust suits is that treble damages are available. That is, when all the factors are proved, the defendant might have to pay not just the damages it caused to the plaintiff, but three times that much.

Antitrust questions are involved if interference with contract has anticompetitive effects; if it restrains trade or promotes monopoly; if it substantially lessens competition; or if it involves illegal price maintenance.

Interference with Employment Relationships

There is a related tort of interfering with employment relationships. Of course, employees have a right to quit, and new employers have the right to hire them—but the question is whether employees were hired for the wrong reasons (to gain access to a competitor's trade secrets instead of to use the employee's own talents).

There are two situations in which written employment contracts are common: union contracts, and contracts negotiated with top managers. Other employees may also have written contracts. It's common for laid-off or terminated employees to have to sign contracts in order to receive severance benefits. In any of these cases, the contract may impose limitations on their ability to go to work for a competitor.

Employees who do not have any kind of employment contract are called *at-will* employees, because their job lasts only as long as the employers want it to (i.e., they work "at the will of the employer"). It's harder to prove that a competitor has interfered with an at-will work relationship than a contractual one.

Acts that might give rise to a claim of interference with employment relationships:

- Threats, intimidation, coercion

- Causing employees to breach their fiduciary duty to be faithful to the employer

- Causing employees to divulge corporate secrets, contrary to their duty of confidentiality

- Raiding a competitor's staff if the intention is to deplete its work force rather than hiring workers that the new employer needs

Rights of Privacy and Publicity

The right of privacy and the right of publicity fit together and work together. The right of privacy protects each person's right to be left alone. Therefore, it can violate the right of privacy to make a public disclosure of private facts that do not have the status of news of public interest. (The First Amendment protects speech—including visual "speech"—about matters of public interest.)

Greater protection is given to ordinary citizens than to public figures (politicians and celebrities, for instance) who have put themselves into the public eye.

IN THE REAL WORLD

More on Privacy Rights

There are many federal statutes that describe privacy rights in various contexts. Although they are outside the scope of this book, anyone who collects or uses information about credit ratings has to comply with the Fair Credit Reporting Act. Anyone who is regularly engaged in collecting debts from consumers has to follow the Fair Debt Collection Practices Act. The Gramm-Leach-Bliley Act protects privacy of financial data, and the Health Insurance Portability and Accessibility Act, despite its name, is broad enough to cover individuals' privacy rights with respect to data about their health status and health care.

Privacy rights are also violated by using someone's name or likeness for commercial profit, without that person's consent. Here, too, exceptions are made for news reports. So focusing a news camera on Jennifer Lopez when she attends a benefit is allowed, but reproducing that picture and selling it as part of a calendar would only be allowed if she agreed. Reporting on her presence at a public event is one thing; using a telephoto lens to snoop inside her house would be forbidden as a violation of the right of privacy.

Not only do people have a right to be left alone, and to keep their image private, they also have the right to decide how their name and image will be used for publicity as long as they are alive. This is known as the *right of publicity.*

The basic legal principle is that celebrities have an investment in themselves as a "brand," and have a right to control the way their fame is used commercially. A celebrity will usually win a case if his or her nickname or stage name is used without permission, in a way that suggests that the celebrity endorses a product when this is actually not the case.

Some celebrity names and likenesses are used as trademarks, so the same person may make trademark and right-of-publicity claims in the same case.

TIPS & TECHNIQUES

Survival of Rights

State laws take different positions on what happens to the right of publicity after someone dies. In some states, the right dies along with the person, and anyone can then use the name and image. Other states say that the right continues, except that now it belongs to the heirs. Another group of states takes a middle position: if the person used the right of publicity for economic benefit while he or she was alive, the heirs take over that right. Otherwise, anyone can publicize the dead person's name and image.

However, a license to take advantage of publicity rights can be broader than a trademark license. For one thing, it can cover all rights, whereas trademark licenses are limited to particular kinds of merchandise. For another thing, the right of publicity can be assigned in the abstract, but a trademark license has to involve specific goodwill in items that are already available for sale. Quality control restrictions—one of the most important features of a trademark license—are not necessary in a right-of-publicity license. However, it does make sense to forbid using the celebrity's name and likeness in any way that casts an unfavorable light on him or her.

In 1970, the Ninth Circuit ruled that a "sound-alike" imitation of a celebrity in a commercial could not be used as the premise for a lawsuit (because no one claimed that the other singer performing a song associated with Nancy Sinatra actually was Nancy Sinatra).

However, the Ninth Circuit changed its mind in 1988, in a case involving Bette Midler. This time, the court decided that a well-known popular singer, whose voice was imitated to sell a product, had the right to sue for misappropriation. A 1991 case upheld $375,000 compensatory damages plus $2 million in punitive damages for singer Tom Waits, whose voice was imitated in a Frito-Lay commercial. In this analysis, a distinctive voice—the particular qualities or characteristics that allow a listener to identify the singer—is entitled to protection. However, to preserve both artistic freedom and free competition, styles of singing are not protected.

If a complete appropriation is made of a celebrity's persona, goodwill, and popularity, then the right of publicity is violated. Using "look-alike" performers is analyzed as a trademark issue instead of a privacy issue, because the real legal risk is that theater goers, record buyers, and other consumers would be deceived about who is actually performing.

Appendices

SAMPLE CONFIDENTIALITY CLAUSES

(for use in employment contracts, or contracts with consultants)
EMPLOYMENT CONTRACT (or contract with consultant)

"Confidential information" means information developed by or disclosed by the employee OR consultant, with respect to the employer company's products, processes, services, inventions, research and development, and/or marketing, whether or not the information could result in a patentable process or product, as long as the information is not generally known in the relevant industry or industry segment, defined as:_____.

One factor in computing the employee's compensation OR the fee to be paid to the consultant is that the employee OR consultant agrees that, for a period of _____ months/years after termination of employment OR the end of the consulting agreement, he or she will not accept employment or consulting assignments with a major competitor of the employer, defined as follows: _____.

Furthermore, for a period of time lasting _____ months/ years after termination of employment OR the end of the consulting agreement, he or she will not accept employment or consulting assignments dealing with products that conflict with the products on which the employee OR consultant will work for the employer. Conflicting products are defined as: _____.

The employee OR consultant agrees that the scope of employment OR consulting includes work dealing with the following products and/or processes: _____. To the extent that any trade secrets or patentable products or processes are developed during the term of this agreement, they will have the status of works for hire. Therefore, the company will have the right to patent these inventions (if patentable) and in any case to use them in perpetuity with no obligation to make royalty payments to the employee OR consultant. The employee OR consultant agrees not to make any assignments of intellectual property rights to any party that conflict with this provision.

The employee OR consultant agrees that at no time will he or she disclose to any party, any information that he or she knows or should have known to be trade secrets or know-how belonging to the company. The company will have the right to review in advance all technical publications and conference presentations and to require deletion of any trade secrets or know-how appearing in them.

On termination of employment OR the consulting arrangement, the employee OR consultant agrees to return all hard copy, disk copies, and backups of corporate documents containing trade secrets or know-how. He or she also agrees to delete all such materials from his or her home and laptop computers, and to give back disk copies and backups of such materials made for home office use.

DECLARATION OF FACT TO PTO
(To be used on documents filed with the PTO)

I further declare that all statements made herein of my own knowledge are true and that all statements made on information and belief are believed to be true; and that these statements are made with the knowledge that willful false statements and the like so made are punishable by fine or imprisonment, or both, under section 1001 of Title 18 of the United States Code, and that such willful false statements may jeopardize the validity of the application and/or document or any registration resulting therefrom.

PETITION FOR CANCELLATION
IN THE UNITED STATES PATENT AND TRADEMARK OFFICE BEFORE THE TRADEMARK TRIAL AND APPEAL BOARD

Petitioner WUNDERLAND CORP.	PETITION FOR CANCELLATION
v.	Cancellation No. _____*
Registrant-Respondent	Registration No. 999-999-999-999
HOOPLA INC.	Date of Issue: October 3, 1999

Petitioner Wunderland Corp., a Euphoria corporation located at and doing business at 1234 Alice Avenue, Red Queen, Euphoria, petitions to cancel Registration No. 999-999-999-999 on the grounds that it believes it has been/will be damaged by that registration. Therefore, Petitioner requests that the TTAB cancel this registration, which is invalid for the reasons described in this petition.

Respondent Hoopla Inc., a Grace corporation, filed an application for the mark FNUURKLE, which was registered on the Principal Register on October 3, 1999. It was registered in Class 49, for wizard's robes and magic wands. Hoopla Inc. claimed first use on April 2, 1999.

Petitioner claims the following grounds for this petition:

☐ 1. Ownership of Registered Mark

Petitioner owns U.S. Trademark Registration No. 777-777-777-777 for the mark FNERK-EL, which was registered on the Principal Register on May 2, 1998, based on an application filed on January 23, 1998, asserting use in Class 49 (crystal balls, potions, and sorcery supplies). The application therefore precedes not only the date that Respondent filed its application, but the date Respondent claims for first use of the FNUURKLE mark.

Petitioner's registration in the mark FNERK-EL continues to be valid and provides prima facie evidence (but not conclusive evidence in that mark FNERK-EL is not yet incontestable) of Wunderland's exclusive right to use the FNERK-EL mark in commerce for crystal balls, potions, and sorcery supplies.

Given the relationship between the products specified in the registrations and the similarity between the two registered marks, the Petitioner alleges that the Respondent's registered mark is similar enough to the Petitioner's registered mark as to be a likely source of confusion, mistake, or deception.

OR

☐ 2. Prior Adoption and Use of Similar Mark

Petitioner has made continuous use of the mark FNERK-EL in connection with the sale of crystal balls, potions, and sorcery supplies since October 2, 1997, and has never at any time abandoned use of the trademark. Petitioner has developed significant goodwill in this trademark in the relevant community of consumers, in part through investment of advertising and promotion. The Respondent's mark is so similar, and the goods sold in connection with both trademarks are so closely related, that the Respondent's trademark is likely to cause confusion, mistake, or deception.

OR

☐ 3. Cancellation Under §2(e)

When it is applied to the goods in connection with which it has been registered, the Respondent's trademark is invalid under Lanham Act §2(e) and therefore should be canceled because it is:

☐ merely descriptive (geographically)

☐ deceptively misdescriptive (geographically)

Because "fnerkle" and its cognates are common terms of art used in sorcery, such terms are descriptive, and Petitioner should be allowed to use fnerkle or a related term as a descriptive term for the merchandise. If the TTAB refuses to cancel Respondent's registration, and if Respondent is permitted to assert exclusive rights in this term, Petitioner will suffer business harm because it will be impaired in its ability to use the descriptive term fnerkle. Nor does the trademark asserted by the Respondent serve to identify its goods in the marketplace. Therefore, the trademark registration should be canceled.

OR

□ 4. Cancellation Under §2(a)

Ever since its first use on October 2, 1997, Petitioner has been making continuous use in commerce of its valid registered trademark FNERK-EL in connection with a full product line of sorcery and wizardry supplies. Purchasers in the relevant market associate the designation FNERK-EL with the Petitioner's products and corporate identity. Therefore, the Respondent's use of a confusingly similar mark is damaging to the Petitioner by disparaging the quality and image of its goods and falsely suggesting a connection between Respondent's goods bearing the FNUURKEL mark and Petitioner's goods trademarked FNERK-EL.

OR

□ 5. Cancellation for Generic Mark

The mark registered by the Respondent is not entitled to trademark protection because it is a generic term used in the practice of sorcery. Permitting the Respondent to continue using the generic term "fnuurkel" is harmful to the Petitioner in that it debars the Petitioner from using this generic term in the promotion and sale of its own goods. Petitioner has engaged in the manufacture and sale of materials for the practice of sorcery since October 2, 1997, and has a lawful right to use all common descriptive terms for practicing such arts, without restriction by Respondent's improper registration of a generic term as a trademark.

OR

□ 6. Abandonment

Although the Respondent secured registration of the mark by alleging use in commerce, for a period of _____ years, since _____, it has not engaged in bona fide commercial use of the mark, has not made goods avail-

213

able for sale bearing the mark, has not promoted it, and has entirely abandoned the mark. Petitioner's business, including its use of its registered mark FNERK-EL will be impaired by Respondent's revival of its use of the FNU-URKLE mark subsequent to having abandoned it.

OR

☐ 7. Fraud

Respondent's registration for the mark FNUURKLE was obtained fraud-ulently in that Respondent's application for the mark, dated June 22, 1999, and signed and verified by an authorized corporate officer, the corporation's pres-ident Jermyn B. Vermyn, states that Petitioner had executed a license under which Respondent was authorized to use the mark FNUURKLE. Respondent approached Petitioner requesting that such a license be granted, but in fact it was denied, a fact of which Jermyn B. Vermyn has personal knowledge. Thus, his verified statement was knowingly false and fraudulent, made with the culpable intention of inducing the U.S. PTO to issue a regis-tration, resulting in damage to Petitioner's business and reputation.

REQUEST FOR RELIEF

Based on the allegations contained in this Petition, Petitioner respectfully requests that, pursuant to this Petition, Registration No. 999-999-999-999 be canceled.

POWER OF ATTORNEY

Petitioner has designated the law firm of Palmer, Potter & Presley, all of whose attorneys are admitted in the state of Euphoria, to be its representative before the TTAB, with full power to engage in all lawful acts required to prosecute this petition. All communications relative to this case should be sent to the firm, at 3456 White Queen Industrial Park, Lacheln, Euphoria.

SIGNED,

Petitioner, Wunderland Corp.

By [Signature] _____.

Caroline Liddell, President★★

NOTES

★ The Petition should be filed with this left blank; the TTAB inserts the number.

★★ The Petition only has to be signed, not verified.

MUTUAL CONSENT AGREEMENT

As per negotiations ending in agreement on _____, 20 _____, the two companies (Doe and Schmo) have pending ITU applications on the same mark, VNURVOO. However, both parties agree that their intended uses can both occur without likelihood of confusion.

DOE intends to use VNURVOO in connection with financial planning services, and agrees not to use or register the mark in connection with any other services anywhere in the world. DOE specifically agrees not to use or register the mark or any confusingly similar mark in connection with whole-sale or retail sale or distribution of fishing poles, lures, and tackle (and vice versa).

Each agrees to refrain from deliberately imitating logos, trade dress, or advertising material of the other of which it is aware, and each shall have the right to submit examples of its logos, trade dress, or advertising material as it is developed, which the other agrees will constitute appropriate notice of the appearance and use of such materials.

LICENSING AGREEMENT

1. Parties: The Licensor is GlitzSparkle Entertainment Management Inc., a California corporation, whose address is 2309 Rodeo Drive West, Los Angeles, California. The Licensee is Earl's Grey T-Shirts, Inc., a New Jersey corporation, whose address is 45 Washington Way, Bloomfield, New Jersey.

2. Subject Matter: This agreement is a nonexclusive license under which the Licensee will be permitted to manufacture, distribute, sell, and market garments using the name and images of the musical group, Milky Way and the Constellations ("MW&C").

3. Representation: Under an agreement dated July 19, 2001, GlitzSparkle Entertainment is the sole person or entity in control of all merchandising rights resulting from the performances of MW&C as a musical group.

4. Composition of Group: As currently constituted MW&C consists of five performers:

Jennifer O'Meaghan ("Milky Way")

Tamara Phipps ("Cassiopeia")

DeAndrea Thompson ("Orion")

Virginia Carson-Smith ("Vega")

Elizabeth Haggerty ("Ursa Major")

However, from time to time, other performers may be substituted, performing under the names of the same or different astronomic constellations, and the identity of the group will be maintained.

5. Service Mark: GlitzSparkle Entertainment has secured a service mark, Registration No. 333-333-333-333, dated October 4, 2001, for entertainment services rendered by Milky Way and the Constellations. It is this mark which is being licensed.

6. Duration: This license runs from the date this agreement is signed, for a period of two years.

7. Renewal: Unless the license is terminated for nonperformance (see § 14 below), the license will be automatically renewed for a further two-year term unless either party gives notice not more than nine and not less than six months before expiration of the license, of its intention to cancel.

8. Territory: This license covers distribution of merchandise (as defined in §9 below) to distributors doing business in the United States, Canada, and Mexico, and Internet distribution. However, all Web sites maintained by the Licensee shall bear a legend that orders will be accepted only from the United States, Canada, and Mexico.

The Licensee hereby agrees that it will reject Internet orders that come from outside the territory.

9. Merchandise: Licensee shall be permitted to use the name MW&C, the group's logo, and the names, reproduction signatures, and images of the individual performers (whether the originals or those who join the group at a later time), in connection with the following items of wearing apparel, but no other items of any kind whatever:

- T-shirts

- Rugby shirts made of cotton interlock knit

- Baseball caps

- Pajamas and nightgowns (but not slippers)

The Licensee agrees to use the MW&C servicemark and logo on the label inside each item of merchandise, on hangtags attached to the merchandise, and in advertisements for the merchandise.

The Licensee agrees to assist in enforcement of the servicemark by promptly reporting to the Licensor whenever it becomes aware of counterfeit merchandise or of third-party infringements of the servicemark.

10. Source of Images: Licensee agrees to use only official logos and images of the group and its performers supplied by the Licensor. The images may be altered to fit the needs of the manufacturing process, but not in any manner

that will cast disrepute on the group or its members. No images that show them in a suggestive light, or wearing any outfit more revealing than their stage costumes, may be used on licensed merchandise.

11. Quality Control: The Licensee agrees to maintain standards of high quality, using only 100% virgin materials; pre-shrunk cotton knit of high quality; and high quality thread, inks, and transfers. All embroidery is to be performed in such a manner that no loose threads are visible on the right side of the merchandise.

The Licensor will provide the Licensee with detailed specifications, which may be altered from time to time. Licensee agrees to make whatever changes are necessary to conform to the altered specifications.

The Licensee agrees to submit one sample from every production run (or one from each week, if there are multiple production runs in a given week) to the Licensor, and to make prompt efforts to correct deficiencies in quality detected by the Licensor.

12. Advertising and Marketing: The Licensee agrees to use its best commercially reasonable efforts to advertise and promote the servicemarked products. However, it agrees not to place advertisements in any publication that is unsuitable for reading by the group's target audience (girls and women aged 12-23). The Licensee also agrees to submit an accurate proof or color proof of every proposed advertisement to the Licensor for approval (which is not to be unreasonably withheld) at least two weeks before the ad copy is to be submitted to the publication in which it will run.

13. Royalties: Starting on _____, 20_____, the Licensee agrees to make quarterly payments of royalties, each payment representing sales up through the date one month before the royalty payment. Each payment will be accompanied by a statement showing how the payment amount was calculated. The royalty shall be in the amount of 5% of net sales (gross sales minus returns).

The Licensee agrees to maintain accurate records of all raw materials, units manufactured, sales and returns, using Generally Accepted Accounting Practices, and to make these records available to the Licensor for its inspection at any time during normal business hours.

14. Grounds for Termination: Licensor will have the right to cancel this agreement if the Licensee fails to protect the servicemark or fails to use its best efforts to produce quality merchandise that does not detract from the value of the licensed property or the goodwill of the group. Termination will occur on 60 days' written notice from Licensor to Licensee, stating the termination date. The Licensee will have the right to dispose of its remaining stock of merchandise during the 60 days subsequent to the termination date.

JUDGMENT AND FINAL INJUNCTION
UNITED STATES DISTRICT COURT
WESTERN DISTRICT OF SIEGE

D'Aunstable Enterprises, Inc.	Civil Action No. 01-39793
Plaintiff	JUDGMENT AND
v.	FINAL INJUNCTION
Winderstorme Inc.	
Defendant	

On June 12, 2002, this Court, sitting without a jury, heard oral arguments in this case. This Court has jurisdiction over both the parties and the subject matter of this case.

D'Aunstable Enterprises, Inc. was represented by Nina Rickworth-Blair, of the firm of Henderson & Tunney. Winderstorme Inc. was represented by Jules Harbach of the firm of Black, Steadworth and Thorpe. Both attorneys submitted briefs and arguments.

THEREFORE, based on the Court's Findings of Fact and Conclusions of Law, it is hereby ORDERED, ADJUDGED AND DECREED that judgment be granted for the plaintiff.

1. Plaintiff owns the registered trademark #222-333-444-555, ("EASYEAT KITTYUM") and this trademark is valid, enforceable, and incontestable.
2. The defendant has engaged in unfair competition and has infringed the plaintiff's trademark rights in this registered mark by advertising, offering, selling, and distributing pet food products identified as "TEASYFEAST KITTYUM", using trade dress confusingly similar to that adopted by the plaintiff, causing confusion among pet owners.

3. The defendant has not asserted any counterclaims, and its arguments as to defenses against the infringement claim were not persuasive or supported by adequate evidence.

4. Use of the mark "TEASYFEAST KITTYUM" or any mark similar enough to be confusing, on the part of the defendant and/or any of its officers, agents, employees, and business associates, is hereby and permanently enjoined.

5. Pursuant to 15 USC §1118, defendant is hereby ordered to deliver, no later than _____, all packaging, labels, signs, advertisements, and wrappers using the "TEASYFEAST KITTYUM" mark to the offices of the plaintiff's law firm, at Suite 204, 1996 Merioneth Way, in order that these materials can be impounded or destroyed by the plaintiff.

6. No later than 30 days after this judgment is issued, Kate Dinsmore, President of the defendant corporation, is ordered to serve on the plaintiff and file with the Clerk of this Court a written report, made under oath, explaining the steps the defendant corporation has taken to comply with this injunction. This Court has the power to make this order under 15 USC §1116.

7. If the plaintiff applies 90 or more days from the date of this order, this Court will refer this case to a federal Magistrate Judge to set the damages that the plaintiff can recover against the defendant, and the profits unfairly received by the defendant, on account of trademark infringement and unfair competition.

8. The Clerk of this court is hereby ordered to enter judgment on behalf of the plaintiff and against the defendant in the amount of $13,416, representing the plaintiff's litigation cost and fees.

Date: July 27, 2002

_____

Hon. Roland Bostwick
U.S. District Judge

Forms

FORM A

Trademark/Service Mark Application, Principal Register, with Declaration

http://www3.uspto.gov/teas/PrintV1.22/TFORMSWIN.htm

Trademark/Service Mark Application, Principal Register, with Declaration

PrinTEAS - Version 1.22: 08/22/2000

Each field name links to the relevant section of the "HELP" instructions that will appear at the bottom of the screen. Fields containing the symbol "*" **must** be completed; all other relevant fields should be completed if the information is known. If there are multiple owners or if the goods and/or services are classified in more than one class, click on the Form Wizard. **Note:** ☐ check here if you do not want the scrolling help to be automatically shown at the bottom of the screen.

i **Important:**

For general trademark information, please telephone the Trademark Assistance Center, at 703-308-9000. For automated status information on an application that has an assigned serial number, please telephone 703-305-8747, or use http://tarr.uspto.gov.

If you need help in resolving technical glitches, you can e-mail us at PrinTEAS@uspto.gov. Please include your telephone number in your Email, so we can talk to you directly, if necessary.

Applicant Information

Please use the Wizard if there are multiple applicants.

* Name	

Entity Type: Click on the **one** appropriate circle to indicate the applicant's entity type and enter the corresponding information.

○ Individual	Country of Citizenship	
○ Corporation	State or Country of Incorporation	
○ Partnership	State or Country Where Organized	
	Name and Citizenship of all General Partners	
○ Other	Specify Entity Type	
	State or Country Where Organized	
* Address	* Street Address	
	* City	
	State	Select State ⬍ If not listed above, please select 'OTHER' and specify here:
	* Country	Select Country ⬍ If not listed above, please select 'OTHER' and specify here:
	Zip/Postal Code	
Phone Number		
Fax Number		
Internet E-Mail Address	☐ Check here to authorize the USPTO to communicate with the applicant or its representative via e-mail. NOTE: While the application may list an e-mail address for the applicant, applicant's attorney, and/or applicant's domestic representative, **only one** e-mail address may be used for correspondence, in accordance with Office policy. The applicant must keep this address current in the Office's records.	

Mark Information

Before the USPTO can register your mark, we must know exactly what it is. You can display a mark in one of two formats: (1) typed; or (2) stylized or design. When you click on one of the two circles below, and follow the relevant instructions, the program will create a separate page that displays your mark once you validate the application (using the Validate Form button at the end of this form). You must print out and submit this separate page with the application form (even if you have listed the "mark" in the body of the application). If you have a stylized mark or design, but either you do NOT have a GIF or JPG image file or your browser does not permit this function, check the box to indicate you do NOT have the image in a GIF or JPG image file (and then see the special help instructions).

WARNING: AFTER SEARCHING THE USPTO DATABASE, EVEN IF YOU THINK THE RESULTS ARE "O.K.," DO NOT ASSUME THAT YOUR MARK CAN BE REGISTERED AT THE USPTO. AFTER YOU FILE AN APPLICATION, THE USPTO MUST DO ITS OWN SEARCH AND OTHER REVIEW, AND MIGHT REFUSE TO REGISTER YOUR MARK.

Form A: 3 of 9

MARK.		
	○ **Typed Format**	Click on this circle if you wish to register a word(s), letter(s), and/or number(s) in a format that can be reproduced using a typewriter. Also, only the following common punctuation marks and symbols are acceptable in a typed drawing (any other symbol, including a <u>foreign diacritical mark</u>, requires a stylized format): . ? " - ; ( ) % $ @ + , ! ' : / & # * = [ ] Enter the mark here: NOTE: The mark **must** be entered in <u>ALL upper case letters</u>, regardless of how you actually use the mark. E.g., MONEYWISE, **not** MoneyWise.
* <u>Mark</u>	○ **Stylized** **or** **Design Format**	Click on this circle if you wish to register a stylized word(s), letter(s), number(s), and/or a design. Click on the 'Browse' button to select <u>GIF or JPG image file</u> from your local drive that shows the complete, overall mark (i.e., the stylized representation of the words, e.g., or if a design that also includes words, the image of the "composite" mark, NOT just the design element). Do NOT submit a <u>color</u> image. [Browse...] ☐ Check this box if you do NOT have the image in a GIF or JPG image file, and click <u>here</u> for further instructions. For a stylized word(s) or letter(s), or a design that also includes a word(s), enter the <u>LITERAL element</u> only of the mark here:
<u>Additional</u> <u>Statement</u>	This section is for the entry of various statements that may pertain to the mark. In no case must you enter any of these statements for the application to be accepted for filing (although you may be required to add a statement(s) to the record during the actual prosecution of the application). To select a statement, check the box and enter the specific information relevant to your mark. The following are the texts of the most commonly asserted statements: ☐ **DISCLAIMER:** "No claim is made to the exclusive right to use ⌐ apart from the mark as shown." ☐ **STIPPLING AS A FEATURE OF THE MARK:** "The stippling is a feature of the mark." ☐ **STIPPLING FOR SHADING:** "The stippling is for shading purposes only." ☐ **PRIOR REGISTRATION(S):** "Applicant claims ownership of U.S. Registration Number(s) ⌐ ." ☐ **DESCRIPTION OF THE MARK:** "The mark consists of ⌐ ." ☐ **TRANSLATION:** "The foreign wording in the mark translates into English as ⌐ ." ☐ **TRANSLITERATION:** "The non-Latin character(s) in the mark transliterate into ⌐ , and this means ⌐ in English." ☐ **§2(f), based on Use:** "The mark has become distinctive of the goods/services through the applicant's substantially exclusive and continuous use in commerce for at least the five years immediately before the date of this statement." ☐ **§2(f), based on Prior Registration(s):** "The mark has become distinctive of the goods/services as evidenced by the ownership on the Principal Register for the same mark for related goods or services of U.S. Registration No(s). ⌐ ." ☐ **§2(f), IN PART, based on Use:** " ⌐ has become distinctive of the goods/services through the applicant's substantially exclusive and continuous use in commerce for at least the five years immediately before the date of this statement." ☐ **§2(f), IN PART, based on Prior Registration(s):** " ⌐ has become distinctive of the goods/services as evidenced by the ownership on the Principal Register for the same mark for related goods or services of U.S. Registration No(s). ⌐ ." ☐ **NAME(S), PORTRAIT(S), SIGNATURE(S) OF INDIVIDUAL(S):** ○ "The name(s), portrait(s), and/or signature(s) shown in the mark identifies ⌐ , whose consent(s) to register

Form A: 4 of 9

will be submitted.

○ "The name(s), portrait(s), and/or signature(s) shown in the mark does not identify a particular living individual.

☐ USE OF THE MARK IN ANOTHER FORM: "The mark was first used anywhere in a different form other than that sought to be registered on [   ], and in commerce on [   ]."

☐ CONCURRENT USE: Enter the appropriate concurrent use information, e.g., specify the goods and the geographic area for which registration is sought.

BASIS FOR FILING AND GOODS AND/OR SERVICES INFORMATION

Applicant requests registration of the trademark/service mark identified above with the Patent and Trademark Office on the Principal Register established by the Act of July 5, 1946 (15 U.S.C. §1051 et seq.) for the following Class(es) and Goods and/or Services, and checks the basis that covers those specific Goods or Services. More than one basis may be selected, but do NOT claim both §§1(a) and 1(b) for the identical goods or services in one application.

Please use the Wizard if there is more than one class.

☐ **Section 1(a), Use in Commerce: Applicant is using or is using through a related company the mark in commerce on or in connection with the below identified goods and/or services. 15 U.S.C. § 1051(a), as amended. Applicant attaches or will submit one specimen for *each class* showing the mark as used in commerce on or in connection with any item in the class of listed goods and/or services. If filing electronically, applicant must attach a JPG or GIF specimen image file for each international class, regardless of whether the mark itself is in a typed drawing format or is in a stylized format or a design. Unlike the mark image file, a specimen image file may be in color (i.e., if color is being claimed as a feature of the mark, then the specimen image should show use of the actual color(s) claimed).**

Describe what the specimen submitted consists of:

International Class	If known, enter class number 001 - 042, A, B, or 200
* Listing of Goods and/or Services USPTO Goods/ Services Manual	
Date of First Use of Mark Anywhere	at least as early as: MM/DD/YYYY
Date of First Use of the Mark in Commerce	at least as early as: MM/DD/YYYY

☐ Section 1(b), Intent to Use: Applicant has a bona fide intention to use or use through a related company the mark in commerce on or in connection with the goods and/or services identified below (15 U.S.C. §1051(b)).

International Class	If known, enter class number 001 - 042, A, B, or 200
* Listing of Goods and/or Services USPTO Goods/ Services Manual	

227

Form A: 5 of 9

☐ **Section 44(d)**, Priority based on foreign filing: Applicant has a bona fide intention to use the mark in commerce on or in connection with the goods and/or services identified below, and asserts a claim of priority based upon a foreign application in accordance with 15 U.S.C. §1126(d).

International Class	☐ If known, enter class number 001 - 042, A, B, or 200
* **Listing of** Goods and/or Services *USPTO Goods/ Services Manual*	
Country of Foreign Filing	Select Country ⬍ If not listed above, please select 'OTHER' and specify here: ☐
Foreign Application Number	☐ NOTE:If possible, enter no more than 12 characters. Eliminate all spaces and non-alphanumeric characters.
Date of Foreign Filing	☐ MM/DD/YYYY

☐ **Section 44(e)**, Based on Foreign Registration: Applicant has a bona fide intention to use the mark in commerce on or in connection with the above identified goods and/or services, and submits or will submit a certification or certified copy of the foreign registration before the application may proceed to registration, in accordance with 15 U. S. C. 1126(e), as amended.

International Class	☐ If known, enter class number 001 - 042, A, B, or 200
* **Listing of** Goods and/or Services *USPTO Goods/ Services Manual*	
Country of Foreign Registration	Select Country ⬍ If not listed above, please select 'OTHER' and specify here: ☐
Foreign Registration Number	☐ NOTE:If possible, enter no more than 12 characters. Eliminate all spaces and non-alphanumeric characters.
Foreign Registration Date	☐ MM/DD/YYYY
Renewal Date for Foreign Registration	☐ MM/DD/YYYY
Expiration Date of Foreign Registration	☐ MM/DD/YYYY

☐ Check here if an _attorney_ is filing this application on behalf of applicant(s). Otherwise, click on _Domestic Representative_ to continue.

Form A: 6 of 9

Attorney Information		
Correspondent Attorney Name		
Individual Attorney Docket/Reference Number		
Other Appointed Attorney(s)		
Attorney Address	Street Address	
	City	
	State	Select State ⬍ If not listed above, please select 'OTHER' and specify here:
	Country	Select Country ⬍ If not listed above, please select 'OTHER' and specify here:
	Zip/Postal Code	
Firm Name		
Phone Number		
FAX Number		
Internet E-Mail Address	☐ Check here to authorize the USPTO to communicate with the applicant or its representative via e-mail. NOTE: While the application may list an e-mail address for the applicant, applicant's attorney, and/or applicant's domestic representative, **only one** e-mail address may be used for correspondence, in accordance with Office policy. The applicant must keep this address current in the Office's records.	

☐ Check here if the applicant has appointed a Domestic Representative. **A Domestic Representative is REQUIRED if the applicant's address is outside the United States.** Otherwise, click on Fee Information to continue.

Domestic Representative

The applicant **must** appoint a Domestic Representative if the applicant's address is outside the United States. The following is hereby appointed applicant's representative upon whom notice or process in the proceedings affecting the mark may be served.

Representative's Name		
Address	Street Address	
	City	
	State	Select State ⬍ If not listed above, please select 'OTHER' and specify here:
	Zip Code	
Firm Name		
Phone Number		
FAX Number		
Internet E-Mail Address	☐ Check here to authorize the USPTO to communicate with the applicant or its representative via e-mail. NOTE: While the application may list an e-mail address for the applicant, applicant's attorney, and/or applicant's domestic representative, **only one** e-mail address may be used for correspondence, in accordance with Office policy. The applicant must keep this address current in the Office's records.	

Fee Information

Number of Classes Paid

1 ⬍

Note: The total fee is computed based on the Number of Classes in which the goods and/or services associated with the mark are classified.

$ 325 = **Number of Classes Paid x $325 (per class)**

* Amount

$ ☐

Payment

☐ **Deposit Account Number**
(If checked, please enter six numbers with no space or hyphen).

The U.S. Patent and Trademark Office is hereby authorized to charge any fees or credit any overpayments to the deposit account listed above.

Name of Person
authorizing account activity

Company/Firm Name

Declaration

The undersigned, being hereby warned that willful false statements and the like so made are punishable by fine or imprisonment, or both, under 18 U.S.C. §1001, and that such willful false statements may jeopardize the validity of the application or any resulting registration, declares that he/she is properly authorized to execute this application on behalf of the applicant; he/she believes the applicant to be the owner of the trademark/service mark sought to be registered, or, if the application is being filed under 15 U.S.C. §1051(b), he/she believes applicant to be entitled to use such mark in commerce; to the best of his/her knowledge and belief no other person, firm, corporation, or association has the right to

Form A: 8 of 9

use the mark in commerce, either in the identical form thereof or in such near resemblance thereto as to be likely, when used on or in connection with the goods/services of such other person, to cause confusion, or to cause mistake, or to deceive; and that all statements made of his/her own knowledge are true; and that all statements made on information and belief are believed to be true.

Signature _____ Date Signed _____

Signatory's Name [_____]

Signatory's Position [_____]

Click on the desired action:

The "Validate Form" function allows you to run an automated check to ensure that all mandatory fields have been completed. You will receive an "error" message if you have not filled in one of the five (5) fields that are considered "minimum filing requirements" under the Trademark Law Treaty Implementation Act of 1998. For other fields that the USPTO believes are important, but not mandatory, you will receive a "warning" message if the field is left blank. This warning is a courtesy, if non-completion was merely an oversight. If you so choose, you may by-pass that "warning" message and validate the form (however, you cannot by-pass an "error" message).

| Validate Form | | Reset Form |

Note: To print the completed application AND the separate sheet showing the representation of the mark, click on the Validate Form button, and follow the steps on the Validation Screen.

* Instructions

To file a **complete** application, you must submit the following items:
- the signed and dated form (the "Scannable Form");
- a representation of the mark, preferably on a single sheet of paper (See information under the "Mark Information" section, above);
- a check or money order for $325.00 per each class of goods and services, made out to the Commissioner of Patents and Trademarks (unless using a USPTO deposit account);
- if the application is based on use in commerce, one specimen for each class of goods and services;
- if the application is based on Section 44(e), a certified copy (and English translation, if applicable) of the certificate of foreign registration.

NOTE: If your application does not include the following five (5) items, we will return your application and refund the filing fee. You would then need to correct the deficiency and re-file, resulting in a new filing date: (1) the name of the applicant; (2) a name and address for correspondence; (3) a clear representation of the mark; (4) a list of the goods or services; and (5) the filing fee for at least one class of goods or services.

You may also wish to include a self-addressed stamped postcard on which you list every item that you are submitting. This will confirm receipt of your submission.

The mailing address for standard mail is:

Form A: 9 of 9

Commissioner for Trademarks
Box-New App-Fee
2900 Crystal Drive
Arlington, Virginia 22202-3513

The mailing address for courier delivery is:

Commissioner for Trademarks
USPTO- New App-Fee
2900 Crystal Drive, Suite 3B-30
Arlington, Virginia 22202-3513

Privacy Policy Statement

The information collected on this form allows the PTO to determine whether a mark may be registered on the Principal or Supplemental register, and provides notice of an applicant's claim of ownership of the mark. Responses to the request for information are required to obtain the benefit of a registration on the Principal or Supplemental register. 15 U.S.C. §1051 et seq. and 37 C.F.R. Part 2. All information collected will be made public. Gathering and providing the information will require an estimated 12 or 18 minutes (depending if the application is based on an intent to use the mark in commerce, use of the mark in commerce, or a foreign application or registration). Please direct comments on the time needed to complete this form, and/or suggestions for reducing this burden to the Chief Information Officer, U.S. Patent and Trademark Office, U.S. Department of Commerce, Washington D.C. 20231. Please note that the PTO may not conduct or sponsor a collection of information using a form that does not display a valid OMB control number.

FORM B

Recordation Form Cover Sheet/ Trademarks Only

http://www.uspto.gov/web/forms/pto1594.pdf

Form PTO-1594	**RECORDATION FORM COVER SHEET**	U.S. DEPARTMENT OF COMMERCE
(Rev. 03/01)	**TRADEMARKS ONLY**	U.S. Patent and Trademark Office
OMB No. 0651-0027 (exp. 5/31/2002)		

Tab settings ⇨ ⇨ ⇨ ▼   ▼   ▼   ▼   ▼   ▼   ▼

To the Honorable Commissioner of Patents and Trademarks: Please record the attached original documents or copy thereof.

1. Name of conveying party(ies):	2. Name and address of receiving party(ies)
	Name:_____
	Internal Address:_____
❑ Individual(s) ❑ Association	Street Address:_____
❑ General Partnership ❑ Limited Partnership	City:_____ State:_____ Zip:_____
❑ Corporation-State	❑ Individual(s) citizenship_____
❑ Other _____	❑ Association_____
	❑ General Partnership_____
Additional name(s) of conveying party(ies) attached? ❑ Yes ❑ No	❑ Limited Partnership_____
3. Nature of conveyance:	❑ Corporation-State_____
❑ Assignment ❑ Merger	❑ Other _____
❑ Security Agreement ❑ Change of Name	If assignee is not domiciled in the United States, a domestic representative designation is attached: ❑ Yes ❑ No
❑ Other_____	(Designations must be a separate document from assignment)
Execution Date:_____	Additional name(s) & address(es) attached? ❑ Yes ❑ No

4. Application number(s) or registration number(s):	
A. Trademark Application No.(s)	B. Trademark Registration No.(s)

Additional number(s) attached ❑ Yes ❑ No

5. Name and address of party to whom correspondence concerning document should be mailed:	6. Total number of applications and registrations involved: .... ❑
Name:_____	
Internal Address:_____	7. Total fee (37 CFR 3.41)................$_____
	❑ Enclosed
	❑ Authorized to be charged to deposit account
Street Address:_____	8. Deposit account number:
	_____
City:_____ State:_____ Zip:_____	(Attach duplicate copy of this page if paying by deposit account)

DO NOT USE THIS SPACE

9. Statement and signature.
To the best of my knowledge and belief, the foregoing information is true and correct and any attached copy is a true copy of the original document.

_____	_____		Date
Name of Person Signing	Signature		

Total number of pages including cover sheet, attachments, and document: ❑

Guidelines for Completing Trademarks Cover Sheets

Cover Sheet information must be submitted with each document to be recorded. If the document to be recorded concerns both patents and trademarks, separate patent and trademark cover sheets, including any attached pages for continuing information, must accompany the document. All pages of the cover sheet should be numbered consecutively, for example, if both a patent and trademark cover sheet is used, and information is continued on one additional page for both patents and trademarks, the pages of the cover sheet would be numbered form 1 to 4.

Item1. Name of Conveying Party(ies).

Enter the full name of the party(ies) conveying the interest. If there is more than one conveying party, enter a check mark in the "Yes" box to indicate that additional information is attached. The name of the second and any subsequent conveying party(ies) should be placed on an attached page clearly identified as a continuation of the information in Item1. Enter a check mark in the "No" box, if no information is contained on an attached page.

Item 2. Name and Address of Receiving Party(ies).

Enter the name and full address of the first party receiving the interest. If there is more than one party receiving the interest, enter a check mark in the "Yes" box to indicate that additional information is attached. If the receiving party is an assignee not domiciled in the United States, a designation of domestic representative is required. Place a check mark in appropriate box to indicate whether or not a designation of domestic representative is attached. Enter a check mark in the "No" box if no information is contained on an attached page.

Item 3. Nature of Conveyance.

Place a check mark in the appropriate box describing the nature of the conveying document. If the "Other" box is checked, specify the nature of the conveyance. Enter the execution date of the document. It is preferable to use the name of the month, or an abbreviation of that name, in order that confusion over dates is minimized.

Item 4. Application Number(s) or Registration Number(s).

Indicate the application number(s) including series code and serial number, and/or registration number(s) against which the document is to be recorded. Enter a check mark in the appropriate box: "Yes" or "No" if additional numbers appear on attached pages. Be sure to identify numbers included on attached pages as the continuation of Item 4.

Item 5. Name and Address of Party to whom correspondence concerning document should be mailed.

Enter the name and full address of the party to whom correspondence is to be mailed.

Item 6. Total Applications and Trademarks Involved.

Enter the total number of applications and trademarks identified for recordation. Be sure to include all applications and registrations identified on the cover sheet and on additional pages.

Block 7. Total Fee Enclosed.

Enter the total fee enclosed or authorized to be charged. A fee is required for each application and trademark against which the document is recorded.

Item 8. Deposit account Number.

Enter the deposit account number to authorize charges. Attach a duplicate copy of cover sheet to be used for the deposit charge account transaction.

Item 9. Statement and Signature.

Enter the name of the person submitting the document. The submitter must sign and date the cover sheet, confirming that to the best of the persons knowledge and belief, the information contained on the cover sheet is correct and that any copy of the document is a true copy of the original document. Enter the total number of pages including the cover sheet, attachments, and document.

This collection of information is required by 35 USC 261 and 262 and 15 USC 1057 and 1060. The information is used by the public to submit (and by the USPTO to process) patent and trademark assignment requests. After the USPTO records the information, the records for patent and trademarks, assignments, and other associated documents can be inspected by the public. To view documents recorded under secrecy orders or documents recorded due to the interest of the federal government, a written authorization must be submitted. This collection is estimated to take 30 minutes to complete, including gathering, preparing, and submitting the form to the USPTO. Any comments on the amount of time you require to complete this form and/or suggestions for reducing this burden, should be sent to the Manager of the Assignment Division, Crystal Gateway 4, Room 310, 1213 Jefferson Davis Highway, Arlington, Va. 22202. DO NOT SEND FEES OR COMPLETED FORMS TO THIS ADDRESS. SEND TO: Commissioner of Patents and Trademarks, Box Assignments, Washington, D.C., 20231.

Forms

FORM C

United States Patent & Trademark Office
Instructions for Completing the Credit Card Payment Form

http://www.uspto.gov/web/forms/2038.pdf

United States Patent & Trademark Office
Instructions for Completing the Credit Card Payment Form

Credit Card Information

- Fill in all credit card information including the payment amount to be charged to your credit card and your signature. The United States Patent and Trademark Office (USPTO) cannot process credit card payments without an authorized signature.

- The USPTO does **not** accept debit cards or check cards that require use of a personal identification number as a method of payment.

Credit Card Billing Address

- Address information is required for credit card payment as a means of verification. Failure to complete the address information, including zip/postal code, may result in the payment not being accepted by your credit card institution.

Request and Payment Information

- Provide a description of your request based on the payment amount. For example, indicate the item as "basic filing fee" (patent) *or* "first maintenance fee" (patent maintenance fee) or "application for registration" (trademark) *or* "certified copy of a patent" (other fee).

- Indicate the nature of your request by the type of fee you wish to pay: Patent Fee, Patent Maintenance Fee, Trademark Fee or Other Fee. Complete information for each type of fee as applicable to identify the nature of your request. Indicate only one type of fee per form.

- If you are requesting and paying a fee based on a previously filed patent or trademark application, indicate the application or serial number, patent number, or registration number that is associated with your request. "Other Fee" is used to request copies of patent and trademark documents, certified copies, assignments, and other information products.

- IDON numbers are assigned by the USPTO for customers ordering patent and trademark information and products specified as "Other Fee" on the order form. If you have been assigned an IDON number from a previous customer order, include it with your request.

- For more information on USPTO fees and amounts, refer to the current fee schedule at http://www.uspto.gov. To request a copy by mail, contact the USPTO General Information Services at 800-786-9199 or 703-308-4357.

Important Information

- The USPTO will not include the Credit Card Payment Form among the patent or trademark records open for public inspection. Failure to use the Credit Card Payment Form when submitting a credit card payment may result in the release of your credit card information.

- Information on mailing addresses is available at http://www.uspto.gov (under site index-addresses, mailing). You may also contact the USPTO for additional information or to request a copy of the *Basic Facts about Patents* or *Basic Facts about Trademarks* information booklet by calling 800-786-9199 or 703-308-4357.

235

Form C: 2 of 3

United States Patent & Trademark Office
Credit Card Payment Form
Please Read Instructions before Completing this Form

Credit Card Information			

Credit Card Type:	Visa	MasterCard	American Express	Discover

Credit Card Account #:

Credit Card Expiration Date:

Name as it Appears on Credit Card:

Payment Amount: $(US Dollars):

Signature:	Date:

Refund Policy: The Office may refund a fee paid by mistake or in excess of that required. A change of purpose after the payment of a fee will not entitle a party to a refund of such fee. The Office will not refund amounts of twenty-five dollars or less unless a refund is specifically requested, and will not notify the payor of such amounts (37 CFR 1.26). Refund of a fee paid by credit card will be via credit to the credit card account.
Service Charge: There is a 50.00 service charge for processing each payment refused (including a check returned "unpaid") or charged back by a financial institution (37 CFR 1.21(m)).

Credit Card Billing Address

Street Address 1:

Street Address 2:

City:

State:	Zip/Postal Code :

Country:

Daytime Phone #:	Fax #:

Request and Payment Information

Description of Request and Payment Information:

Patent Fee	Patent Maintenance Fee	Trademark Fee	Other Fee
Application No.	Application No.	Serial No.	IDON Customer No.
Patent No.	Patent No.	Registration No.	
Attorney Docket No.		Identify or Describe Mark	

If the cardholder includes a credit card number on any form or document other than the Credit Card Payment Form, the United States Patent & Trademark Office will not be liable in the event that the credit card number becomes public knowledge.

FORM D

Trademark/Service Mark Application Form Wizard

http://www3.uspto.gov/teas/PrintV1.22/TWIZARDE.htm and
http://www3.uspto.gov/teas/PrintV1.22/TURHELP.htm

TRADEMARK/SERVICE MARK APPLICATION FORM WIZARD
PrinTEAS
Version 1.22 : 08/22/2000

Please answer all of the questions below to create an application form showing only sections relevant to you. Then press the NEXT button. For more information regarding any of the following questions or topics, either go to **HELP** or click on the underlined word. We strongly recommend that you use this WIZARD, but to skip, click on Standard Form.

PLEASE NOTE:

HELP instructions for each section of this form are available by simply clicking on the relevant words or box. While the different sections of the form may appear straightforward and easy to fill out, you are strongly advised to read the HELP instructions very carefully for EACH section PRIOR to actually completing it. Failure to follow this advice may cause you to fill out sections of the form incorrectly, jeopardizing your legal rights.

Once you submit an application, either electronically or through the mail, we will not cancel the filing or refund your fee, unless the application fails to satisfy minimum filing requirements. The fee is a processing fee, which we do not refund even if we cannot issue a registration after our substantive review.

1. What is your filing basis?

Intent to Use (Section 1(b))

⦿ Yes ○ No

Use in Commerce (Section 1(a))

○ Yes ⦿ No

Right of Priority based on Foreign Application (Section 44(d))

○ Yes ⦿ No

Foreign Registration (Section 44(e))

○ Yes ⦿ No

238

Form D: 2 of 15

2. Are your Goods and/or Services in <u>more than one class?</u>

○ Yes ● No
If the answer is Yes. enter the number of classes [⬍]

3. Are you charging the filing fee(s) to a United States Patent and Trademark Office (USPTO) <u>deposit account</u>?

○ Yes ● No

4. Does <u>joint applicants</u> own the mark?

○ Yes ● No
If the answer is Yes, enter the number of owners [⬍]

5. Is there one applicant but more than one <u>signatory</u>?

○ Yes ● No
If the answer is Yes, enter the number of signatories [⬍]

6. Is an <u>attorney</u> filing this application?

○ Yes ● No

7. Is the <u>applicant's address</u> outside the United States?

○ Yes ● No

8. Do you need to enter an <u>additional statement</u>?

○ Yes ● No

[NEXT] [CLEAR]

Privacy Policy Statement

PrinTEAS

TRADEMARK/SERVICE MARK APPLICATION HELP INSTRUCTIONS

APPLICANT INFORMATION

Name: Enter the full name of the Applicant, i.e., the name of the individual, corporation, partnership, or other entity that owns the mark. If a joint venture organized under a particular business name owns the mark, enter that name. If a trust owns the mark, enter the name of the trustee(s). If an estate owns the mark, enter the name of the executor(s). If joint or multiple applicants own the mark, enter the name of each of these applicants. **If the applicant is doing business as or trading under a different name, enter that information after the notation "DBA," e.g., John Smith DBA The Smith Company.**

Entity Type: Indicate the applicant's entity type by clicking on ONE of the four circles which appear in the boxes on the left of this section (i.e., the boxes marked "individual" "citizen," "corporation," "partnership, or "other"), and enter the corresponding information in the space to the right of the circle selected. Please note that only one entity type may be selected.

Individual: Enter the applicant's country of citizenship.

Corporation: Enter the applicant's state of incorporation (or the applicant's country of incorporation if the applicant is a foreign corporation).

Partnership: Enter the state under whose laws the partnership is organized (or the country under whose laws the partnership is organized if the partnership is a foreign partnership). Also, enter the names and citizenship of any general partners who are individuals, and/or the names and state or (foreign) country of incorporation of any general partners which are corporations, and/or the names and states or (foreign) countries of organization of any general partners which are themselves partnerships. If the applicant is a limited partnership, then only the names and citizenship or state or country of organization or incorporation of the general partners need be provided.

Other Entity Type: Enter a brief description of the applicant's entity type (e.g., joint or multiple applicants, joint venture, limited liability company, association, Indian Nation, state or local agency, trust, estate). The following sets forth the information required with respect to the most common types of "other" entities:

> **For joint or multiple applicants,** enter the name and entity type of each joint applicant. Also, enter the citizenship of those joint applicants who are individuals, and/or the state or (foreign) country of incorporation of those joint applicants which are corporations, and/or the state or (foreign) country of organization- and the names and citizenship of the partners- of those joint applicants which are partnerships.

> **For joint ventures,** enter the name and entity type of each entity participating in the joint venture. Also, enter the citizenship of those joint venture participants who are individuals, and/or the state or (foreign) country of incorporation of those joint venture participants which

are corporations, and/or the state or (foreign) country of organization- and the names and citizenship of the partners- of those joint venture participants which are partnerships.

For limited liability company or association, enter the state or (foreign) country under whose laws the entity is established.

For state or local agency, enter the name of the agency and the state and/or locale of the agency (e.g., Maryland State Lottery Agency, an agency of the State of Maryland).

For trusts, identify the trustees and the trust itself, using the following format: The Trustees of the XYZ Trust, a California trust, the trustees comprising John Doe, a U.S. citizen, and the ABC Corp., a Delaware corporation. (Please note that the trustees, and not the trust itself, must be identified as the applicants in the portion of the application designated for naming the applicant).

For estates, identify the executors and the estate itself using the following format: The Executors of the John Smith estate, a New York estate, the executors comprising Mary Smith and John Smith, U.S. citizens. (Please note that the executors, and not the estate itself, must be identified as the applicants in the portion of the application designated for naming the applicant).

Street Address: Enter the applicant's street address or the rural delivery route where the applicant is located.

City: Enter the city and/or foreign area designation.

State: If a U.S. state, enter that state by clicking on the proper entry in the pull-down box. Otherwise, select the listing "Other" in the pull-down box, and enter the information in the designated box.

Country: Enter the country by clicking on the proper entry in the pull-down box. If the country is not listed (because it is not one of our top filers), select the listing "Other" in the pull-down box, and enter the information in the designated box.

Zip Code/Postal Code: Enter the U.S. zip code or foreign country postal identification code.

Phone Number: Enter the applicant's telephone number.

Fax Number: If available, enter the applicant's fax number.

Internet/E-Mail Address: If available, enter the applicant's internet/ e-mail address.

Authorize: In accordance with the notice in the Federal Register dated June 21, 1999 [Internet Usage Policy, Fed. Reg. Vol. 64, No. 118 (June 21, 1999, pp. 33056-66)], this will grant the USPTO permission to send correspondence regarding this application to the applicant or its representative.

Policy: In accordance with Office policy, all correspondence will be sent to the applicant or its representative in the following order: 1) the applicant's attorney's e-mail address, if provided; or 2) the applicant's domestic representative's address, if no attorney has been appointed; or 3) the applicant's address, if the applicant has not also named an attorney to represent it before the Office or a domestic representative to accept service of process. If the applicant has appointed an attorney, the Office must correspond with the attorney and cannot send correspondence directly to the applicant.

MARK INFORMATION

Mark: You can display a mark in one of two formats: (1) typed; or (2) stylized or design. You may apply for only one mark in each application. You cannot present the mark in typed format and the mark in stylized or design format in one application. Each variation is considered a separate mark. Under the Typed Drawing Format, you must enter the word(s), letter(s) and/or number(s) you wish to register (e.g., THE CAT'S MEOW). Under the Stylized or Design Format, you must attach an image (which may consist solely of a pictorial element; word(s), letter(s) or number(s) in a particular stylization; or a combination thereof); and, if appropriate, enter the literal element of the mark. In a typed mark, do NOT include quotation marks around the mark unless you are actually using, or intend to use, the quotation marks as part of the mark. Also, do not include any information related to a "pseudo mark" in this field. The USPTO is responsible for the pseudo mark field in the search system, not the applicant. **NOTE**: The USPTO will automatically convert your mark into all upper case letters on the drawing page, regardless of how you enter the mark in this field (because this is the requirement for a typed format). Registration in the typed format allows use in a manner other than the "all upper case" format. E.g., a mark registered as MONEYWISE could actually be used in the manner of MoneyWise. If you prefer to register the mark so that it appears on the registration with both upper and lower case letters, you must select the "stylized" option, which will allow you to present the mark as actually used. If you wish to register a stylized or design mark, do NOT enter any information under Mark in the Typed Format section. Instead, click on the circle selecting Stylized or Design Format and attach a GIF or JPG image file to show the actual appearance of your overall mark. However, if there are literal elements in the mark, you should also enter those elements in the field underneath where the image file was attached (again, NOT under the typed mark section). If your image is such that we may not be able to determine what it is (because, e.g., the image is so highly stylized), you may use the description of the mark field (under the Additional Statement section) to describe the mark (e.g., "The mark consists of a stylized bird."). However, do NOT enter a description if the average viewer could determine the elements of the mark simply from the image of the mark. Also, do NOT enter the description within the field for LITERAL element. That field is only for use where the mark itself includes words. **NOTE**: If you do not see the Additional Statement section on the form, it is because you entered "No" on the Form Wizard for Question 8. Unfortunately, you would need to create a new form, going back to the Form Wizard and answering Question 8 "Yes."

Typed Format: This choice of mark format appears on the registration certificate as all upper case letters and/or numbers. However, this choice does not limit your use of the mark only as shown on the certificate. You may use the mark in any style or format and still receive federal protection for the word(s), letter(s), and/or number(s) that are shown in the registration certificate. E.g., a mark registered as MONEYWISE could actually be used in the manner of MoneyWise. If you prefer to register the mark so that it appears on the registration with both upper and lower case letters, you must select the "stylized" option, which will allow you to present the mark as actually used. If you wish to register a stylized or design mark, do NOT enter any information under Mark in the Typed Format section. Instead, click on the circle selecting Stylized or Design Format and attach a GIF or JPG image file to show the actual appearance of your overall mark.

ALL upper case letters: Although you must enter your mark so that it appears on the registration certificate as all upper case letters and/or numbers, this choice does not limit your use of the mark only as shown on the certificate. You may use the mark in any style or format and still receive federal protection for the word(s), letter(s), and/or number(s) that are shown in the registration certificate. E.g., a mark registered as MONEYWISE could actually be used in the manner of MoneyWise. If you prefer to register the mark so that it appears on the registration with both upper and lower case letters, you must select the "stylized" option, which will allow you to present the mark as actually used. If you wish to register a stylized or design mark, do NOT enter any information under Mark in the Typed Format section. Instead, click on the circle selecting Stylized or Design Format and attach a GIF or JPG image file to show the actual appearance of your overall mark.

Stylized or Design Format: If you are using, or intend to use, your mark with a stylized appearance or design that you want to protect, you may want to consider filing in this format; otherwise, choose the Typed Format above. Attach a GIF or JPG image file showing a black-and-white image of your mark. (Click on the 'Browse' button to select from your local drive the GIF or JPG image file-these are the only image file formats you can use.) Color images are not recommended. Although the USPTO will accept a color image, it will be converted to a black-and-white image before the application can proceed to registration. If color is an important feature of your mark, use the description of the mark field (under the Additional Statement section) to explain where the color(s) appear in the mark (e.g., "The mark consists of a bird with a blue body, a red head, and a yellow beak."). **NOTE:** If you do not see the Additional Statement section on the form, it is because you entered "No" on the Form Wizard for Question 8. Unfortunately, you would need to create a new form, going back to the Form Wizard and answering Question 8 "Yes."

Stylized or Design Format: (do NOT have the image)

Stylized or Design Format: If you are using, or intend to use, your mark with a stylized appearance or design that you want to protect, you may want to consider filing in this format; otherwise, choose the Typed Format above. If you are unable to attach a GIF or JPG image file showing a black-and-white image of your mark, then this option will allow you to print out the basic format (with the proper heading, but absent your mark). You then must "cut and paste" the black-and-white image of your mark, and attach it to the center of the page to create the complete drawing page which you will attach your black-and-white image to create the complete drawing page (click on link for additional instructions). Color images are not recommended. Although the USPTO will accept a color image, it will be converted to a black-and-white image before the application can proceed to registration. If color is an important feature of your mark that you wish to protect, use the description of the mark field (under the Additional Statement section) to explain where the color(s) appear in the mark (e.g., "The mark consists of a bird with a blue body, a red head, and a yellow beak.").

Note: If you do not see the Additional Statement section on the form, it is because you entered "No" on the Form Wizard for Question 8. Unfortunately, you would need to create a new form, going back to the Form Wizard and answering Question 8 "Yes."

No GIF or JPG image: If you wish to register your mark with a stylized appearance or design (rather than the Typed Format), but are unable to attach a GIF or JPG image file showing a black-and-white image of your mark, check this box. This option will allow you to print out the basic format (with the proper heading, but absent your mark). Therefore, you then must "**cut and paste**" a separate black-and-white image of your complete mark, and attach it to the center of the page to create the complete drawing page. Color images are not recommended. Although the USPTO will accept a color image, it will be converted to a black-and-white image before the application can proceed to registration. If color is an important feature of your mark that you wish to protect, use the description of the mark field (under the Additional Statement section) to explain where the color(s) appear in the mark (e.g., "The mark consists of a bird with a blue body, a red head, and a yellow beak.").

Note: If you do not see the Additional Statement section on the form, it is because you entered "No" on the Form Wizard for Question 8. Unfortunately, you would need to create a new form, going back to the

Form D: 7 of 15

Form Wizard and answering Question 8 "Yes."

GIF or JPG image file: 1) Mark image attachments should be submitted in bi-tonal (black and white) format. We will convert any image that is not a 1-bit image (i.e., black and white) to 1-bit; however, mark images submitted in a color format may not convert properly to black and white images. 2) Mark images should not include the trademark, service mark or registration symbols (TM, SM, ®). These symbols should only appear on specimens. 3) TEAS cannot accept animated GIF files. 4) Mark images should be submitted with as little white space around the design as possible. 5) The mark image size used on registration certificates is approximately 4" X 4". The mark image size used in the Official Gazette is approximately 2" X 2". Images are scaled to fit these sizes. 6) The image file should be scanned at a minimum of 300 DPI. However, 600 DPI will provide a clearer image.

Foreign diacritical mark: You may register a mark in typed form, if otherwise proper, even though the mark includes diacritical marks. However, because of technical limitations, the USPTO needs an "image" of this mark to capture such a mark within USPTO databases. Therefore, even though the mark will have the legal significance of a "typed" mark, you must first create a GIF or JPG "image" of this typed mark, and then click on the stylized or design format in the application form (rather than using the "typed" format in the application). Also, you should include the following statement in the record (in the "Description of the Mark" field within the "Additional Statements" section) to indicate the nature of such a mark: "The mark is presented without any claim as to special form." NOTE: If you do not see the Additional Statement section on the form, it is because you entered "No" on the Form Wizard for Question 8. Unfortunately, you would need to create a new form, going back to the Form Wizard and answering Question 8 "Yes."

Color: The GIF or JPG image file must show a bi-tonal (black-and-white) image of your mark. Color images are not recommended. Although the USPTO will accept a color image, we will convert any image that is not a 1-bit image (i.e., black-and-white) to 1-bit before the application can proceed to registration; however, mark images submitted in a color format may not convert properly to black-and-white images. If color is an important feature of your mark that you wish to protect, use the description of the mark field (under the Additional Statement section) to explain where the color(s) appear in the mark (e.g., "The mark consists of a bird with a blue body, a red head, and a yellow beak."). NOTE: If you do not see the Additional Statement section on the form, it is because you entered "No" on the Form Wizard for Question 8. Unfortunately, you would need to create a new form, going back to the Form Wizard and answering Question 8 "Yes."

Literal element: Enter the word(s) that appear within the overall composite mark (as shown in the GIF or JPG image file). E.g., if the mark consists of the design of a cat and the words THE CAT'S MEOW, you would enter in this field THE CAT'S MEOW. You would NOT enter "The design of a cat and THE CAT'S MEOW"- it is the actual image file that will show this.

Searching: Although not required, we recommend that you conduct a search in TESS (Trademark Electronic Search System) for any mark for which you may want to seek federal trademark registration in the USPTO. The purpose of the search is to help determine whether any mark has already been registered or applied for that is similar to your mark AND used on related products or for related services. The USPTO cannot provide guidance as to how you should search, beyond the HELP provided within the TESS site. However, at a minimum, please understand that a complete search is one that will uncover ALL similar marks, NOT just those that are identical.

Searching for trademark availability is NOT the same as searching to register a ".com" address. A ".com" address search may focus on exact or "dead on" hits, with no consideration given to similar names or use with related products and services. Basically, a ".com" address is either available or it is not. Also, if available, you can register a ".com" address on the same day as your search. The trademark process, on the other hand, is more complex. As part of the overall examination process, the USPTO will search its database to determine whether registration must be refused because a similar mark is already registered for related products or services. We do not offer advisory opinions on the availability of a mark prior to filing of an actual application. For the guidelines used to examine applications, see the Trademark Manual of Examining Procedures (TMEP) .

Refuse to register: Once you submit an initial application, either electronically or through the mail, the USPTO will not cancel the filing or refund your fee, unless the application fails to satisfy minimum filing requirements. Filing an application does not guarantee registration. The filing fee is a processing fee, which we do not refund even if we cannot issue a registration after our review of the application.

The USPTO may refuse to register your mark on numerous grounds. The most common are:

Likelihood of Confusion
The USPTO conducts a search for conflicting marks as part of the official examination of an application only after a trademark application is filed. In evaluating an application, the examining attorney conducts a search of USPTO records to determine whether there is a conflict between the mark in the application and a mark that is either registered or pending in the USPTO. The principal factors considered in reaching this decision are the similarity of the marks and the commercial relationship between the goods and services identified by the marks. To find a conflict, the marks do not have to be identical or the goods and services the same; instead, it is sufficient if the marks are similar and the goods and or services related. Similarity in sound, appearance, or meaning may be sufficient to support a finding of likelihood of confusion. When a conflict exists between the applicant's mark and a registered mark, the examining attorney will refuse registration of the applicant's mark on the ground of likelihood of confusion. If a conflict exists between the applicant's mark and a mark in an earlier-filed pending application, the examining attorney will notify the applicant of the potential conflict. The applicant's mark will be refused on the ground of likelihood of confusion only if the earlier-filed application becomes registered.

Merely Descriptive and Deceptively Misdescriptive
The examining attorney will refuse registration of a mark as merely descriptive if it immediately describes an ingredient, quality, characteristic, function, feature, purpose or use of the specified goods or services. A mark will be refused as deceptively misdescriptive if (1) the mark misdescribes an ingredient, quality, characteristic, function, feature, purpose or use of the specified goods or services; and (2) the misrepresentation conveyed by the mark is plausible.

Primarily Geographically Descriptive and Primarily Geographically Deceptively Misdescriptive
The examining attorney will refuse registration of a mark as primarily geographically descriptive if: (1) the primary significance of the mark is geographic; (2) purchasers would be likely to think that the goods or services originate in the geographic place identified in the mark, i.e., purchasers would make a goods/place or services/place association; and (3) the mark identifies the geographic origin of the goods or services.

A mark will be refused as primarily geographically deceptively misdescriptive if: (1) the primary significance of the mark is geographic; (2) purchasers would be likely to think that the goods or services originate in the geographic place identified in the mark, i.e., purchasers would make a goods/place or services/place association; and (3) the goods or services do not originate in the place identified in the mark.

Primarily Merely a Surname
The examining attorney will refuse registration of a mark if the primary significance to the purchasing public is a surname.

Ornamentation
In general, the examining attorney will refuse registration if the applied-for mark is merely a decorative

feature or part of the "dress" of the goods. Such matter is merely ornamentation and does not serve the trademark function of identifying and distinguishing the applicant's goods from those of others.

NOTE: For a complete list of the substantive grounds of refusal and a detailed explanation of each, see Chapter 1200, Trademark Manual of Examining Procedure (TMEP). The USPTO cannot provide preliminary legal advice as to whether we will register a particular mark; filing an application is the only way to obtain a decision on whether the USPTO will refuse registration.

Additional Statement: This section is for the entry of various statements that may pertain to the mark. In no case must you enter any of these statements for the application to be accepted for filing (although you may be required to add some of these statements to the record during the actual prosecution of the application). To select a statement, check the box and enter the specific information relevant to your mark. The following are the texts of the most commonly asserted statements:

> **DISCLAIMER:** "No claim is made to the exclusive right to use _____apart from the mark as shown." (Enter descriptive/generic wording).

> **STIPPLING AS A FEATURE OF THE MARK:** "The stippling is a feature of the mark and does not indicate color." (i.e., the mark consists, in part, of actual "dots"-- the stippling-- as a feature of the mark, rather than those "dots" being an attempt to show coloration or shading in the mark).

> **STIPPLING FOR SHADING:** "The stippling is for shading purposes only." (i.e., the "dots" -- the stippling-- that are used as part of the mark on the drawing page are only to show that the mark has lighter and darker features; the "dots" are not actually part of the mark).

> **PRIOR REGISTRATION(S):** "Applicant claims ownership of _____." (Enter registration number(s) for the same or similar marks. Do not use any commas within the number. If more than one entry, separate each with a space, with no punctuation. E.g., 1247873 1324638 1462387).

> **DESCRIPTION OF THE MARK:** "The mark consists of _____." (Enter a precise description of the mark).

> **TRANSLATION:** "The foreign wording in the mark translates into English as _____."

> **TRANSLITERATION:** "The non-Latin characters in the mark transliterate into _____, and this means _____ in English."

> **§2(f), based on Use:** "The mark has become distinctive of the goods/services through the applicant's substantially exclusive and continuous use in commerce for at least the five years immediately before the date of this statement."

> **§2(f), based on Prior Registration(s):** "The mark has become distinctive of the goods/services as evidenced by the ownership on the Principal Register for the same mark for related goods or services of U.S. Registration No(s). _____." (Enter registration number(s) for the same or similar marks. Do not use any commas within the number. If more than one entry, separate each with a space, with no punctuation. E.g., 1247873 1324638 1462387).

> **§2(f) IN PART, based on Use:** "_____ has become distinctive of the goods/services through the applicant's substantially exclusive and continuous use in commerce for at least the five years immediately before the date of this statement." (Enter the appropriate word(s)).

§2(f) N PART, based on Prior Registration(s): "_____ has become distinctive of the goods/ services as evidenced by the ownership on the Principal Register for the same mark for related goods or services of U.S. Registration No(s). _____." (In the first box, enter the appropriate word(s). In the second box, enter registration number(s) for the same or similar marks. Do not use any commas within the number. If more than one entry, separate each with a space, with no punctuation. E.g., 1247873 1324638 1462387).

NAME(S), PORTRAIT(S), SIGNATURE(S) OF INDIVIDUAL(S): Click on the first circle if the name(s), portrait(s), and/or signature(s) shown in the mark does identify a particular living individual, and enter the appropriate name(s). Click on the second circle if the mark includes a name(s), portrait(s), and/or signature(s), but this does NOT identify a particular living person.

USE OF THE MARK IN ANOTHER FORM: "The mark was first used anywhere in a different form other than that sought to be registered on _____, and in commerce on _____." (Enter both the date of first use anywhere and the date of first use in commerce, in the format MM/ DD/YYYY, e.g., 12/03/1998. Both dates may be the same, or the date in commerce may be later than the first use anywhere; however, the date of first use in commerce may not precede the date of first use anywhere).

CONCURRENT USE: Enter the appropriate concurrent use information, e.g., specify the goods and the geographic area for which registration is sought. For specific requirements, see TMEP section 1207.04.

SPECIMEN: Describe what the specimen submitted consists of, e.g., scanned or digitally photographed tags, labels, instruction manuals, containers, point of purchase displays, or the front page of a catalogue.

GOODS AND SERVICES INFORMATION

International Class: If known, enter the International Class number(s) of the goods and/or services associated with the mark, e.g., 009. For more information about acceptable classes, see the USPTO's on-line Goods and/or Services Manual, or the overall listing of all classes of goods and services.

Listing of Goods and/or Services: Enter the *specific* goods and/or services associated with the mark; e.g., "computer software for accounting purposes;" or "shirts, pants and shoes." If you are *not* specific enough (e.g., listing "Internet services"), you will *not* receive a filing date. Even if you are filing based on intent to use, you must provide a specific enough recitation so that the nature of the goods/services is sufficiently clear. While you *may* be able to amend the recitation during prosecution to clarify a broad recitation, if the initial listing is too ambiguous, you will not receive a filing date and no amendment will be permitted. Also, do **not** enter the broad class number here, such as 009 or 025 (this information belongs in the field above, namely International Class). If the goods and/or services are classified in more than one class, the goods and/or services should be listed in ascending numerical class order. For more information about acceptable language for the goods and/or services, see the USPTO's on-line Goods and/or Services Manual.

BASIS FOR FILING APPLICATION

Click on the appropriate box to indicate the basis upon which the applicant is filing the application.

Specifically, indicate whether the application is being filed pursuant to Trademark Act Section 1(a) or Section 1(b) (15 U.S.C. Section 1051(a) or 1051(b)), and/or Section 44(d)/(e) (15 U.S.C. Section 1126(d)/(e)), and enter the corresponding information. You may file under more than one basis, but you may not file an application based on both use in commerce under §1(a) and a bona fide intention to use a mark in commerce under §1(b) for the identical goods and or services (e.g., you cannot list "shirts" under Section 1(b) AND Section 1(a), but you could list "shirts" under Section 1(b) and "pants" under Section 1(a)).

Section 1(b), Intent to Use: Check this box if applicant has a bona fide intention to use the mark in commerce, rather than actual use of the mark in commerce.

Section 1(a), Use in Commerce: Check this box if applicant is actually using the mark in commerce in connection with the goods and/or services identified in the application.

Specimen: Attach one specimen showing the mark as used in commerce on or in connection with any item listed in the description of goods and/or services. This is NOT simply the same as the image of your actual mark by itself. Instead, you must show how you are actually using the mark in commerce. For example, for goods, acceptable specimens would consist of tags, labels, instruction manuals, or containers that show the mark on the goods or packaging. Invoices, announcements, order forms, bills of lading, leaflets, brochures, publicity releases and other printed advertising material generally are not acceptable specimens for goods. Examples of acceptable service mark specimens are signs, photographs, brochures or advertisements that show the mark used in the sale or advertising of the services. If the goods and/or services are classified in more than one international class, one specimen must be provided showing the mark used on or in connection with at least one item from each of these classes.

Describe what the specimen submitted consists of: Describe what the specimen submitted consists of, e.g., photograph of point of purchase display, or front page of catalogue.

Date of First Use of Mark Anywhere: Enter the date (two digits each for both the month and day, and four digits for the year) on which the applicant first used the mark in commerce anywhere. If the date consists of only a month and year, or only a year, you must enter "00" in the appropriate spaces; e.g., 00/00/1989. Please note this date may be earlier than, or the same as, the date of the first use of the mark in commerce date.

Date of First Use of Mark in Commerce: Enter the date (two digits each for both the month and day, and four digits for the year) on which the applicant first used the mark in commerce which the U.S. Congress may regulate (see "Type of Commerce"). If the date consists of only a month and year, or only a year, you must enter "00" in the appropriate spaces; e.g., 00/00/1989.

Section 44(d), Priority based on foreign filing: Check this box if applicant is filing the application within six months of filing the first foreign application to register the mark in a defined treaty country.

Country of Foreign Filing: Enter the country by clicking on the proper entry in the pull-down box. If the country is not listed (because it is not one of our top filers), select the listing "Other" in the pull-down box, and enter the information in the designated box.

Foreign Application Number: Enter the foreign application serial number, if available. If possible, enter no more than 12 characters. Eliminate all spaces and non-alphanumeric characters. For example, German application number 339 78 406.3 /39 should be entered as 33978406339. Any characters beyond the 12th will NOT be picked up in the USPTO databases nor be printed in the Official Gazette.

Form D: 12 of 15

Filing Date of Foreign Application: Enter the date (two digits each for both the month and day, and four digits for the year) on which the foreign application was filed. To receive a priority in filing date, the applicant must file the United States application within six months of filing the first foreign application in a defined treaty country.

Section 44(e), Based on Foreign Registration: Check if applicant is relying on a foreign registration currently in force. An applicant relying on §44(e) as the basis for filing and registration must file a certification or certified copy of the foreign registration before the application may proceed to registration. The foreign registration must be in force at the time the United States issues the registration based on that foreign registration. Certification must be by the issuing agency in the foreign country. If the foreign registration is not in English, the applicant must also provide a translation of the foreign registration with the certification or certified copy of the foreign registration. The translator should sign the translation, but need not swear to the translation.

Country of Foreign Registration: Enter the country of the foreign registration.

Foreign Registration Number: Enter the number of the foreign registration. If possible, enter no more than 12 characters. Eliminate all spaces and non-alphanumeric characters. For example, German registration number 339 78 406.3/39 should be entered as 33978406339. Any characters beyond the 12th will NOT be picked up in the USPTO databases nor be printed in the Official Gazet

Foreign Registration Date: Enter the date of the foreign registration.

Renewal Date for Foreign Registration: Enter the date on which the registration was renewed, if applicable.

Expiration Date of Foreign Registration: Enter the expiration date of foreign registration.

ATTORNEY INFORMATION

Correspondent Attorney Name: Enter the name of the attorney who is responsible for the filing of the application and to whom correspondence should be addressed. You may list more than one name in this field; however, correspondence will only be sent to the first listed name.

Individual Attorney Docket/Reference Number: If applicable, enter the attorney docket or reference number.

Other Appointed Attorney(s): Enter the name(s) of any other attorney(s) authorized to prosecute the application.

Street Address: Enter attorney's street address.

City: Enter the city in which the attorney is located.

State: If a U.S. state, enter that state by clicking on the proper entry in the pull-down box. Otherwise, select the listing "Other" in the pull-down box, and enter the information in the designated box.

Form D: 13 of 15

Country: Enter the country by clicking on the proper entry in the pull-down box. If the country is not listed (because it is not one of our top filers), select the listing "Other" in the pull-down box, and enter the information in the designated box.

Zip/Postal Code: Enter the U.S. zip code or foreign country postal identification code.

Firm Name: Enter the name of the law firm with which the attorney is associated. If a sole practitioner, please enter the name of the individual here (even though already provided above).

Phone Number: Enter the attorney's telephone number.

Fax Number: If available, enter the attorney's fax number.

Internet/E-Mail Address: If available, enter the attorney's internet/e-mail address.

Authorize: In accordance with the notice in the Federal Register dated June 21, 1999 [Internet Usage Policy, Fed. Reg. Vol. 64, No. 118 (June 21, 1999, pp. 33056-66)], this will grant the USPTO permission to send correspondence regarding this application to the applicant or its representative.

Policy: In accordance with Office policy, all correspondence will be sent to the applicant or its representative in the following order: 1) the applicant's attorney's e-mail address, if provided; or 2) the applicant's domestic representative's address, if no attorney has been appointed; or 3) the applicant's address, if the applicant has not also named an attorney to represent it before the Office or a domestic representative to accept service of process. If the applicant has appointed an attorney, the Office must correspond with the attorney and cannot send correspondence directly to the applicant.

DOMESTIC REPRESENTATIVE

If the applicant is not domiciled in the United States, the applicant must designate a domestic representative on whom notices or process in proceedings affecting the mark may be served.

Representatives Name: Enter the name of the domestic representative.

Street Address: Enter the street where the domestic representative is located.

City: Enter the city in which the domestic representative is located.

State: If a U.S. state, enter the state by clicking on the proper entry in the pull-down box. Otherwise, select the listing "Other" in the pull-down box, and enter the information in the designated box.

Zip Code: Enter the U.S. postal zip code for the domestic representative's address.

Phone Number: Enter the domestic representative's telephone number.

FAX Number: Enter the domestic representative's FAX number.

Internet/E-Mail Address: If available, enter the domestic representative's internet/e-mail address.

Form D: 14 of 15

Authorize: In accordance with the notice in the Federal Register dated June 21, 1999 [Internet Usage Policy, Fed. Reg. Vol. 64, No. 118 (June 21, 1999, pp. 33056-66)], this will grant the USPTO permission to send correspondence regarding this application to the applicant or its representative.

Policy: In accordance with Office policy, all correspondence will be sent to the applicant or its representative in the following order: 1) the applicant's attorney's e-mail address, if provided; or 2) the applicant's domestic representative's address, if no attorney has been appointed; or 3) the applicant's address, if the applicant has not also named an attorney to represent it before the Office or a domestic representative to accept service of process. If the applicant has appointed an attorney, the Office must correspond with the attorney and cannot send correspondence directly to the applicant.

FEE INFORMATION

Amount: Enter the fee amount to be paid. Please note that the filing fee is $325 per class of goods or services listed, and at least $325 must accompany the application in order for a filing date to be assigned.

Number of Classes: If known, enter the number of classes for which the applicant is seeking registration.

Deposit Account Number: Enter the appropriate deposit account number to which the fee should be charged. The entry should consist of six numbers, with no space or hyphen; for example, 124379, rather than 12-4379 or 12 4379.

Name of Person Authorizing Account Activity: If applicable, enter the name of the person who is authorized by the applicant to authorize the activity on the applicant's deposit account.

Company/Firm name: Enter the name of the company or firm responsible for the deposit account.

DECLARATION

Signature: The appropriate person (i.e., (1) a person with legal authority to bind the applicant; or (2) a person with firsthand knowledge of the facts and actual or implied authority to act on behalf of the applicant; or (3) an attorney who has an actual or implied written or verbal power of attorney from the applicant) must personally sign the form. If there are joint or multiple applicants, or if it is corporate policy to have two or more officers sign the application for one applicant, each must sign and provide the relevant information.

Signatory's Name: Enter the name of the person signing the application.

Signatory's Position: Enter the signatory's position, if applicable, e.g., vice-president, general partner. Or, if appropriate, enter the language "Duly authorized officer," or "Attorney."

Date Signed: Enter the date (two digits each for both the month and day, and four digits for the year) on which the application is signed. The current date is generated automatically as a default.

Form D: 15 of 15

CLICK ON THE DESIRED ACTION

Validate Form: This allows you to run an automated check to ensure that all mandatory fields have been completed. You will receive an "error" message if you have not filled in one of the fields that are considered "mandatory." For other fields that the USPTO believes are important, but not mandatory, you will receive a "warning" message if the field is left blank. This warning is a courtesy, if non-completion was merely an oversight. If you so choose, you may by-pass that "warning" message and validate the form (however, you cannot by-pass an "error" message). NOTE: A successful validation ONLY means that the required fields have an entry. WE HAVE MADE NO DETERMINATION AT THIS TIME AS TO WHETHER THE INFORMATION ENTERED IS CORRECT. This will only occur during the actual examination of the submission by the attorney or paralegal.

Once data in an application is validated, you will have the options of (1) printing the form, in whole or in part; or (2) going back and modifying the data. Clicking on the various phrases listed in the box under "Application Data" (which are available once the data has been validated via the "Validate Form" button at the bottom of the form) will generate (1) the application data in either a "Scannable Form" or in an easy to read "Input" format; and (2) the specimen image (if applicable). Any or all of these can then be printed using the print function in your browser.

Reset form: This button clears ALL information you may previously have entered in the application and allows you to start again with a "new" application.

Reset form: This button clears ALL information you may previously have entered in the application and allows you to start again with a "new" application.

FORM E

Trademark/Service Mark Allegation of Use
(Statement of Use/Amendment to Allege Use
(15 U.S.C. §1051(c) of (d)

http://www3.uspto.gov/teas/PrintV1.21/ITU/TFORMAOU.htm and
http://www3.uspto.gov/teas/PrintV1.22/PostReg/WIZARDF4S08N15.htm

Trademark/Service Mark Allegation of Use
(Statement of Use/Amendment to Allege Use)
(15 U.S.C. §1051(c) or (d))

PrinTEAS - Version 1.21: 04/20/2000

Each field name links to the relevant section of the "HELP" instructions that will appear at the bottom of the screen. Fields containing the symbol "*" **must** be completed; all other relevant fields should be completed if the information is known. If there are multiple owners, click on the Form Wizard.
Note: ☐ check here if you do not want the scrolling help to be automatically shown at the bottom of the screen.

Important:

i

For general trademark information, please telephone the Trademark Assistance Center, at 703-308-9000. For automated status information on an application that has an assigned serial number, please telephone 703-305-8747, or use http://tarr.uspto.gov.

If you need help in resolving technical glitches, you can e-mail us at PrinTEAS@uspto.gov. Please include your telephone number in your e-mail, so we can talk to you directly, if necessary.

Mark Information	
* **Mark**	
* **Serial Number**	

Form E: 2 of 7

Applicant Information		
Please use the <u>Wizard</u> if there are multiple applicants.		
* **Name**		

* **Address**	* **Street Address**	
	* **City**	
	State	Select State ⇕
		If not listed above, please select 'OTHER' and specify here:
	* **Country**	Select Country ⇕
		If not listed above, please select 'OTHER' and specify here:
	Zip/Postal Code	

Notice of Allowance
☐ Check here if you are <u>filing the Allegation of Use</u> *after* a Notice of Allowance has issued.
☐ Check here if you are filing an <u>Extension Of Time</u> Form with the Allegation of Use.

*Goods and/or Services Information
Click on ONE circle below.

○ The applicant is using the mark in commerce on or in connection with <u>all goods and/or services listed in the application or Notice of Allowance</u>.

The applicant is using the mark in commerce on or in connection with all goods and/or services listed in the application or Notice of Allowance, except the goods and/or services listed below.

○ The applicant is **NOT** using the mark in commerce on or in connection with all goods and/or services listed in the application or Notice of Allowance. In the following space, list only those goods and/or services (and/or entire class(es)) appearing in the application or Notice of Allowance for which the applicant is **NOT** using the mark in commerce and that should be <u>deleted</u>.

LEAVE THIS SPACE BLANK IF THE APPLICANT IS USING THE MARK ON OR IN CONNECTION WITH **ALL** THE GOODS AND/OR SERVICES IN THE APPLICATION OR NOTICE OF ALLOWANCE.

Fee Information

Number of Classes

`1 ▼`

Note: The total fee is computed based on the Number of Classes in which the goods and/or services associated with the mark are classified.

$ `100` = **Number of Classes x $100 (per class)**

* Amount

$ `____`

Payment

☐ **Deposit Account Number**
(If checked, please enter six numbers with no space or hyphen).

`____`

The U.S. Patent and Trademark Office is hereby authorized to charge any fees or credit any overpayments to the deposit account listed above.

Name of Person
authorizing account activity

`____`

Company/Firm Name

`____`

Use Information
You must submit one <u>specimen</u> for each class showing the mark as used in commerce on or in connection with any item in the class of listed goods and/or services.

Describe what the specimen submitted consists of	`____`
* **Date of First Use of Mark Anywhere**	at least as early as: `____` MM/DD/YYYY
* **Date of First Use of the Mark in Commerce**	at least as early as: `____` MM/DD/YYYY

Declaration

Applicant requests registration of the above-identified trademark/service mark in the United States Patent and Trademark Office on the Principal Register established by the Act of July 5, 1946 (15 U.S.C. §1051 et seq., as amended). Applicant is the owner of the mark sought to be registered, and is using the mark in commerce on or in connection with the goods/ services identified above, as evidenced by the attached specimen(s) showing the mark as used in commerce.

The undersigned being hereby warned that willful false statements and the like are punishable by fine or imprisonment, or both, under 18 U.S.C. §1001, and that such willful false statements and the like may jeopardize the validity of this document, declares that he/she is properly authorized to execute this document on behalf of the Owner; and all statements made of his/her own knowledge are true and that all statements made on information and belief are believed to be true.

Form E: 4 of 7

Signature _____ Date Signed _____

Signatory's Name [_____]

Signatory's Position [_____]

Telephone Number [_____]

Internet/e-mail address [_____]

Click on the desired action:

The "Validate Form" function allows you to run an automated check to ensure that all mandatory fields have been completed. You will receive an "error" message if you have not filled in one of the fields that are considered mandatory. For other fields that the USPTO believes are important, but not mandatory, you will receive a "warning" message if the field is left blank. This warning is a courtesy, if non-completion was merely an oversight. If you so choose, you may by-pass that "warning" message and validate the form (however, you cannot by-pass an "error" message).

[Validate Form]   [Reset Form]

Note: To print the completed Allegation of Use, click on the Validate Form button, and follow the steps on the Validation Screen.

* Instructions

To file a complete Amendment to Allege Use, you must submit the following items:
- the signed and dated form (the "Scannable Form");
- a check or money order for $100.00 per each class of goods and services, made out to the Commissioner of Patents and Trademarks (unless using an existing USPTO deposit account);
- one specimen showing the mark as currently used in commerce for at least one product or service in each international class covered.

You may also wish to include a self-addressed stamped postcard on which you list every item that you are submitting. This will confirm receipt of your submission.

The mailing address for standard mail is:

BOX ITU
FEE
Commissioner for Trademarks
2900 Crystal Drive
Arlington, Virginia 22202-3513

The mailing address for courier delivery is:

Form E: 5 of 7

BOX ITU
FEE
Commissioner for Trademarks
2900 Crystal Drive, Suite 3B-30
Arlington, Virginia 22202-3513

Privacy Policy Statement

The information collected on this form allows an applicant to demonstrate that it has commenced use of the mark in commerce. With respect to applications filed on the basis of an intent to use the mark, responses to the request for information are required to obtain the benefit of a registration on the Principal or Supplemental register. 15 U.S.C. §1051 et seq. and 37 C.F.R. Part 2. All information collected will be made public. Gathering and providing the information will require an estimated 15 minutes. Please direct comments on the time needed to complete this form and/or suggestions for reducing this burden to the Chief Information Officer, U.S. Patent and Trademark Office, U.S. Department of Commerce, Washington D.C. 20231. Please note that the PTO may not conduct or sponsor a collection of information using a form that does not display a valid OMB control number.

Form E: 6 of 7

FORM WIZARD
Combined Declaration of Use and Incontestability Under Sections 8 & 15

PrinTEAS
Version 1.22 : 10/10/2000

You may file a Combined Declaration of Use & Incontestability under Sections 8 & 15 only if you have continuously used a mark registered on the Principal (*not* Supplemental) Register in commerce for five (5) consecutive years after the date of registration. You must file the Combined Declaration, specimen, and fee on a date that falls on or between the fifth (5th) and sixth (6th) anniversaries of the registration (or, for an extra fee of $100.00 per class, you may file within the six-month grace period following the sixth anniversary date). If you have NOT continuously used the mark in commerce for five (5) consecutive years, you must *still* file a Section 8 Declaration. You must subsequently file a Section 8 declaration, specimen, and fee on a date that falls on or between the ninth (9th) and tenth (10th) anniversaries of the registration, and each successive ten-year period thereafter (or, for an extra fee of $100.00 per class, you may file within the six-month grace period). FAILURE TO FILE THE SECTION 8 DECLARATION WILL RESULT IN CANCELLATION OF THE REGISTRATION. Note: Because the time for filing a ten-year Section 8 declaration coincides with the time for filing a Section 9 renewal application, a combined §§ 8 & 9 form exists.

To confirm that you should file now, enter a registration number and click on **Check Status** button below to learn the current status of the registration.

Enter a Registration Number: [＿＿＿] [**Check Status**]

If appropriate to file at this time, please answer all of the questions below to create an Declaration Under Section 8 form showing only sections relevant to you. Then press the NEXT button. For more information regarding any of the following questions or topics, either go to **HELP** or click on the underlined word. We strongly recommend that you use this WIZARD, but to skip, click on Standard Form.

PLEASE NOTE:

HELP instructions for each section of this form are available by simply clicking on the relevant words or box. While the different sections of the form may appear straightforward and easy to fill out, you are strongly advised to read the HELP instructions very carefully for EACH section PRIOR to actually completing it. Failure to follow this advice may cause you to fill out sections of the form incorrectly, jeopardizing your legal rights.

Once you submit a Combined Declaration of Use and Incontestability Under Sections 8 & 15, either electronically or through the mail, we will not refund your fee, because it is a processing fee for our substantive review.

Form E: 7 of 7

1. Does the Combined Sections 8 & 15 Declaration cover <u>more than one class?</u>

    ○ Yes ● No
    If the answer is Yes, enter the number of classes [⬍]

2. Are you charging the filing fee(s) to a United States Patent and Trademark Office (USPTO) <u>deposit account</u>?

    ○ Yes ● No

3. Do <u>joint applicants</u> own the mark?

    ○ Yes ● No
    If the answer is Yes, enter the number of owners [⬍]

4. Is there one applicant but more than one <u>signatory</u>?

    ○ Yes ● No
    If the answer is Yes, enter the number of signatories [⬍]

5. Is the <u>owner's address</u> outside the United States?

    ○ Yes ● No

6. Is an <u>attorney</u> filing this form?

    ○ Yes ● No

[NEXT] [CLEAR]

FORM F

Combined Declaration of Use & Incontestability under Sections 8 & 15
(15 U.S.C. §§ 105 & 1065)

http://www3.uspto.gov/teas/PrintV1.22/PostReg/TFORMS08N15.htm

**COMBINED DECLARATION OF USE & INCONTESTABILITY
UNDER SECTIONS 8 & 15**
(15 U.S.C. §§ 1058 & 1065)

PrinTEAS - Version 1.22: 10/10/2000

Each field name links to the relevant section of the "HELP" instructions that will appear at the bottom of the screen. Fields containing the symbol "*" **must** be completed; all other relevant fields should be completed if the information is known. If there are multiple owners, click on the Form Wizard.
Note: ☐ check here if you do not want the scrolling help to be automatically shown at the bottom of the screen.

Important:

i

For general trademark information, please telephone the Trademark Assistance Center, at 703-308-9000. For automated status information on an application that has an assigned registration number, please telephone 703-305-8747, or use http://tarr.uspto.gov.

If you need help in resolving technical glitches, you can e-mail us at PrinTEAS@uspto.gov. Please include your telephone number in your e-mail, so we can talk to you directly, if necessary.

Mark Information	
* **Mark**	
* **Registration Number**	NOTE: Registration Number must be 7 digits. If necessary, add a leading "0". E.g., 0936427.
* **Registration Date**	MM/DD/YYYY

Form F: 2 of 6

Owner Information			
Please use the <u>Wizard</u> if there are multiple owners.			
* **Name**			
* **Address**	* **Street Address**		
	* **City**		
	State	Select State ⬍	
		If not listed above, please select 'OTHER' and specify here:	
	* **Country**	Select Country ⬍	
		If not listed above, please select 'OTHER' and specify here:	
	Zip/Postal Code		
Internet E-Mail Address	☐ Check here to <u>authorized</u> the USPTO to communicate with the applicant at the listed e-mail address. Note: **only one** e-mail address may be used for correspondence.		

*Goods and/or Services Information Click on ONE circle below.	
◉	The owner has been using the mark for five (5) consecutive years after the date of registration, or the date of publication under Section 12(c), and is still using the mark in commerce on or in connection with all goods and/or services listed in the existing registration.
○	The owner has been using the mark for five (5) consecutive years after the date of registration, or the date of publication under Section 12(c), and is still using the mark in commerce on or in connection with all goods and/or services listed in the existing registration, except the goods and/or services listed below. If there are goods and/or services (and/or entire class(es)) appearing in the registration for which either the owner has not used the mark in commerce for five (5) consecutive years or is no longer using the mark in commerce, list those goods and/or services not covered. LEAVE THIS SPACE BLANK IF THE OWNER HAS USED THE MARK IN COMMERCE FOR FIVE (5) CONSECUTIVE YEARS AFTER THE DATE OF REGISTRATION, OR THE DATE OF PUBLICATION UNDER § 12(c), AND IS STILL USING THE MARK IN COMMERCE ON OR IN CONNECTION WITH **ALL** THE GOODS AND/OR SERVICES IN THE EXISTING REGISTRATION.

☐ Check here if the applicant has appointed a <u>Domestic Representative</u>. **A Domestic Representative is REQUIRED if the applicant's address is outside the United States.**

Form F: 3 of 6

Domestic Representative

The applicant **must** appoint a Domestic Representative if the applicant's address is outside the United States. The following is hereby appointed applicant's representative upon whom notice or process in the proceedings affecting the mark may be served.

Representative's Name		
Address	Street Address	
	City	
	State	Select State ⬍
		If not listed above, please select 'OTHER' and specify here:
	Zip Code	
Internet E-Mail Address	☐ Check here to authorize the USPTO to communicate with the applicant's representative at the listed e-mail address. Note: **only one** e-mail address may be used for correspondence.	

☐ Check here if an attorney is filing this form on behalf of applicant(s).

Attorney Information

Correspondent Attorney Name		
Individual Attorney Docket/Reference Number		
Other Appointed Attorney(s)		
Attorney Address	Street Address	
	City	
	State	Select State ⬍
		If not listed above, please select 'OTHER' and specify here:
	Country	Select Country ⬍
		If not listed above, please select 'OTHER' and specify here:
	Zip/Postal Code	
Firm Name		
Phone Number		
FAX Number		
Internet E-Mail Address	☐ Check here to authorize the USPTO to communicate with the applicant's attorney at the listed e-mail address. Note: **only one** e-mail address may be used for correspondence.	

Forms

Form F: 4 of 6

Fee Information

Combined §§ 8 & 15 Filing Fee: $300

Number of Classes   1 ⧫

Note: The filing fee is computed based on the Number of Classes in which the goods and/or services associated with the mark are classified.

Combined §§ 8 & 15 Filing Fee
(Number of Classes x $300 (per class)) = $ 300

Grace Period Fee: $100
(if filing during the six-month grace period, enter the § 8 Grace Period Fee)

Number of Classes   0 ⧫

Grace Period Fee
(Number of Classes x $100 (per class)) = $ 0

Total fee paid
(Note: The total fees paid is the sum of the Combined §§ 8 & 15 filing fee due and the grace period fee due, if applicable.)

Declaration Filing fee + Grace Period fee = $ 300

* **Amount** $

Payment

☐ **Deposit Account Number**
(If checked, please enter six numbers with no space or hyphen).

The U.S. Patent and Trademark Office is hereby authorized to charge any fees or credit any overpayments to the deposit account listed above.

Name of Person
authorizing account activity

Company/Firm Name

Use Information	
You must submit one <u>specimen</u> for each class showing the mark as used in commerce on or in connection with any item in the class of listed goods and/or services.	
Describe what the specimen submitted consists of	

263

Form F: 5 of 6

Declaration

The owner is using the mark in commerce on or in connection with the goods/services identified above, as evidenced by the attached specimen(s) showing the mark as used in commerce. The mark has been in continuous use in commerce for five consecutive years after the date of registration, or the date of publication under Section 12(c), and is still in use in commerce on or in connection with all goods and/or services as identified above. There has been no final decision adverse to the owner's claim of ownership of such mark for such goods and/or services, or to the owner's right to register the same or to keep the same on the register; and there is no proceeding involving said rights pending and not disposed of either in the Patent and Trademark Office or in the courts.

The undersigned being hereby warned that willful false statements and the like are punishable by fine or imprisonment, or both, under 18 U.S.C. §1001, and that such willful false statements and the like may jeopardize the validity of this document, declares that he/she is properly authorized to execute this document on behalf of the Owner; and all statements made of his/her own knowledge are true and that all statements made on information and belief are believed to be true.

Signature _____   Date Signed _____

Signatory's Name [_____]

Signatory's Position [_____]

Click on the desired action:

The "Validate Form" function allows you to run an automated check to ensure that all mandatory fields have been completed. You will receive an "error" message if you have not filled in one of the fields that are considered mandatory. For other fields that the USPTO believes are important, but not mandatory, you will receive a "warning" message if the field is left blank. This warning is a courtesy, if non-completion was merely an oversight. If you so choose, you may by-pass that "warning" message and validate the form (however, you cannot by-pass an "error" message).

| Validate Form | | Reset Form |

Note: To print the completed Combined Declaration of Use and Incontestability Under Sections 8 & 15, click on the Validate Form button and follow the steps on the Validation Screen.

Form F: 6 of 6

* Instructions

To file a complete Combined Declaration of Use and Incontestability under Sections 8 & 15, you must submit the following items:
- the signed and dated form (the "Scannable Form");
- a check or money order for $300.00 per each class of goods and/or services, made out to the Commissioner of Patents and Trademarks (unless using an existing USTO deposit account);
- one specimen showing the mark as currently used in commerce for at least one product or service in each international class covered.

You may also wish to include a self-addressed stamped postcard on which you list every item that you are submitting. This will confirm receipt of your submission.

The mailing address for standard mail is:

BOX PostReg
FEE
Commissioner for Trademarks
2900 Crystal Drive
Arlington, Virginia 22202-3513

The mailing address for courier delivery is:

BOX PostReg
FEE
Commissioner for Trademarks
2900 Crystal Drive, Suite 3B-30
Arlington, Virginia 22202-3513

FORM G

Suggested Format for Notice of Opposition

http://www.uspto.gov/web/forms/4-17a.pdf

Suggested Format for Notice of Opposition

(This is a suggested format for preparing a Notice of Opposition. This document is not meant to be used as a form to be filled in and returned to the Board. Rather, it is a suggested format, which shows how the Notice of Opposition should be set up. Opposers may follow this format in preparing their own Notice of Opposition but need not copy those portions of the suggested format which are not relevant.)

IN THE UNITED STATES PATENT AND TRADEMARK OFFICE
BEFORE THE TRADEMARK TRIAL AND APPEAL BOARD

In the matter of trademark application Serial No............................
For the mark..
Published in the Official Gazette on ....(Date)............................

(Name of opposer)
v.
(Name of applicant)

NOTICE OF OPPOSITION

State opposer's name, address, and entity information as follows:[1]

(Name of individual as opposer, and business trade name, if any;
Business address)

OR   (Name of partnership as opposer; Names of partners;
Business address of partnership)

OR   (Name of corporation as opposer; State or country of incorporation;
Business address of corporation)

The above-identified opposer believes that it/he/she will be damaged by registration of the mark shown in the above-identified application, and hereby opposes the same.[2]

The grounds for opposition are as follows:

[Please set forth, in separately numbered paragraphs, the allegations of opposer's standing and grounds for opposition.][3]

By _____(Signature)[4]_____   Date_____
(Identification of person signing)[5]

OMB No. 0651-0009 (Exp. 8/31/01)

Form G: 2 of 2

FOOTNOTES

(1) If opposer is an individual, state the opposer's name, business trade name, if any, and business address. If opposer is a partnership, state the name of the partnership, the names of the partners, and the business address of the partnership. If opposer is a corporation, state the name of the corporation, the state (or country, if opposer is a foreign corporation) of incorporation, and the business address of the corporation. If opposer is an association or other similar type of juristic entity, state the information required for a corporation, changing the term "corporation" throughout to an appropriate designation.

(2) The required fee must be submitted for each party joined as opposer for each class opposed, and if fewer than the total number of classes in the application are opposed, the classes opposed should be specified.

(3) Set forth a short and plain statement here showing why the opposer believes it/he/she would be damaged by the registration of the opposed mark, and state the grounds for opposing. Each numbered paragraph should be limited, as far as practicable, to a statement of a single set of circumstances. See Rules 8(a) and 10(b) of the Federal Rules of Civil Procedure.

(4) The opposition need not be verified, and may be signed by the opposer or by the opposer's attorney or other authorized representative. If an opposer signing for itself is a partnership, the signature must be made by a partner; if an opposer signing for itself is a corporation or similar juristic entity, the signature must be made by an officer of the corporation or other juristic entity who has authority to sign for the entity and whose title is given.

(5) State the capacity in which the signing individual signs, e.g., attorney for opposer, opposer (if opposer is an individual), partner of opposer (if opposer is a partnership), officer of opposer identified by title (if opposer is a corporation), etc.

REPRESENTATION INFORMATION

If the opposer is not domiciled in the United States, and is not represented by an attorney or other authorized representative located in the United States, a domestic representative must be designated.

If the opposer wishes to furnish a power of attorney, it may do so, but an attorney at law is not required to furnish a power.

Bibliography

Books

Wiley:

Schleicher, John W. *Licensing Intellectual Property: Legal, Business and Market Dynamics.* John Wiley 1996, 1999 cumulative supplement.

Other:

Battersby, Gregory J., and Charles W. Grimes. *The Law of Merchandise and Character Licensing.* West Group 2000.

Celedonia, Bailia H., chair. *Advanced Seminar on Trademark Law 2000.* Practising Law Institute 2000.

Fruchter, Lynn S., Anne Herring, and Jonathan S. Jennings, chairpersons. *Understanding Basic Trademark Law 2000* Practising Law Institute 2000.

Gilson, Jerome, and Jeffrey M. Samuels. *Trademark Protection and Practice.* Matthew Bender 1998. Includes supplement, *ACPA: A Federal Musket in the Battle Against Trademark Cyberpirates— Avast, Ye Scurvy Dogs!* by Jerome Gilson and Anne Gilson LaLonde.

Goldschieder, Robert. *Licensing Law Handbook.* West Group 2000–2001 edition.

Gundersen, Glenn A. *Trademark Searching: A Practical and Strategic Guide to the Clearance of New Marks in the United States,* 2nd ed. INTA 2000.

Kane, Siegrun D. *Trademark Law: A Practitioner's Guide,* 3rd ed. Practising Law Institute 1997, 2000 supplement.

Kirkpatrick, Richard L. *Likelihood of Confusion in Trademark Law.* Practicing Law Institute 1995, 2000 supplement.

Levin, William E. *Trade Dress Protection*. West Group 1996, 2000 supplement.

Milgrim, Roger M. *Milgrim on Trade Secrets*. Matthew Bender 1997, 2001 supplement.

Zamore, Joseph, editor in chief. *Business Torts*. Lexis Publishing 2000.

Articles

Angwin, Julia. "Are Domain Panels The Hanging Judges of Cyberspace Court?" *Wall Street Journal* (8/20/01), B1.

Chartrand, Sabra. "Solidifying Trademark Protection in a Global Market," *New York Times* (10/1/01), C4.

Viscounty, Perry J., Jeff C. Risher, and Collin G. Smyser. "Cyber Gray Market Is Manufacturers' Headache." *National Law Journal* (8/20/01), C3.

Index

271

Descriptive trademarks, 24, 25–26, 149
Design patents, 15, 16, 130
Dilution (of famous trademark), 7, 50, 101, 137, 142, 145–151, 157
Disclaimers, 58, 88
Discovery, 119
Disgorgement, 97, 149
Diversity jurisdiction (federal courts), 144
Domain name registrars, 34–37, 111–121
Domain names (Internet), 2, 33–37, 45, 50, 94–97, 111–121
Drawings (trademark applications), 46, 68, 74–76, 81, 90

E
Employment at will, 202
Examining Attorneys, 65, 67, 69, 70, 71, 77, 80, 88, 131, 146
Exclusive licenses, 155, 170

F
Fair use, 95, 108, 148
False advertising, 43, 142, 183, 184
Famous trademarks, 7, 33–34, 50, 92, 95, 137, 145–149
Fanciful trademarks, 24, 27, 149
Federal question jurisdiction, 144
Federal Trade Commission (FTC), 184, 185
Federal Trademark Dilution Act (FTDA), 145–149
Filing fees, 67, 68
First action pendency, 69
First Amendment, 42, 97, 109, 150, 188–189, 203
Foreign registration (of trademark), 90–93
Framing (Web sites), 42–47
Franchises, 132, 167–168, 192
Fraud, 109
FTC Act, 183–186

Functionality, 18, 29, 72–73, 123, 125, 127, 129, 130–133, 140

G
Generic marks, 23, 24–25, 29, 57, 72, 88, 99, 101, 166
Gray-market goods, 157, 160–162
Goodwill, 111, 153, 167

I
In personam actions, 96
In rem actions, 96–97
Incontestability, 5, 73, 82, 102, 146
Infringement, 8–9, 34, 54, 59, 99, 102–110, 125, 126, 137–142, 144–145, 157, 161, 163, 171, 192
Injunctions, 7, 103–104, 110, 134, 145, 148, 179, 180–181, 184, 189, 201
Intent to Use applications, 8, 78–79, 82–83
Inter partes proceedings, 100–102
Interference with contractual relationships, 192, 201–202
Interference with employment relationships, 192, 202–203
International Trade Commission (ITC), 134–135
Internet Corporation for Assigned Names and Numbers (ICANN), 34–35, 51, 111–121
Internet sales, 164, 168–169

J
Junior user (of trademark), 59, 140, 145

K
Know-how, 153, 170–171, 175

L
Laches, 102, 109

Index

Lanham Act, 6, 7–10, 33, 59, 66, 68,
71, 72, 79, 82, 105, 106, 107,
108, 123, 143, 145, 161, 162,
186–189, 198
Liability insurance, 105
Licensing (of trademarks), 92–93, 100,
108, 153–157, 162–171, 205
Licensing (of patents), 171–172, 177
Linking (Internet), 42–47
Little FTC Acts (state laws), 186

M

Madrid Protocol (treaty), 92
Mandatory Administrative
Proceedings, 114
Metatags, 37–40
MSTB (Model State Trademark Bill),
6, 7, 89–90, 134, 146, 149–151

N

Noncompete clauses, 191, 193
Nonexclusive licenses, 155
Nontraditional marks, 31–33, 58, 75

O

Office Action (PTO), 69
Official Gazette (PTO), 70, 74, 76
Online registration (of trademarks),
62–65
Opposition (to registration), 70, 71,
99–102
Ornamentation, 29–30, 154
Overall action pendency, 69

P

Package licensing, 172
Paris Convention, 92
Parallel imports, 160–162
Parodies, 109–110
Passing off, 43, 199
Patent and Trademark Office (PTO),
5, 8, 11, 27, 29, 44–47, 52, 53,

57, 59, 60–65, 68, 69, 70, 74, 78,
79, 81, 84, 130, 151
Patents, 15–17, 59, 81, 130–131, 132,
171–172, 173, 176, 177
Preemption, 146–147, 173
Principal Register, 5, 26, 71, 72, 82,
84, 88, 103, 129
Prior art (patents), 15, 17
Privacy, right of, 203–204
Privileges, 196–197
Product design, 126–128
Product disparagement, 187, 195
Publicity, right of, 6, 203–205
Puffery, 187

Q

Quality control, 153, 155, 157, 165,
166–167, 205

R

Registrars (domain names), 34–37
Registration of trademarks, 6, 8,
59–81, 112, 114, 123
Reverse confusion, 12, 137
Reverse engineering, 179
Reverse passing off, 43, 199
Right of privacy, 203–204
Right of publicity, 6, 203–205
Risk of confusion, 12, 110, 137, 138,
145, 146, 148, 186, 200
Royalties (licensing), 163, 164, 165,
170–171, 177, 179

S

Search firms (trademarks), 54
Searches (trademarks), 49–59, 90, 163
Secondary meaning, 23–24, 26, 27, 32,
128
Seizure orders, 106, 143–144, 160
Senior user (of trademark), 59, 140
Service marks, 21–22, 115, 117, 147,
150, 159

273